SCHOOLS ON TRIAL

SCHOOLS

An Inside Account

Abt Books

ON TRIAL

of the Boston Desegregation Case

Robert A. Dentler—Marvin B. Scott

CAMBRIDGE   MASSACHUSETTS

Library of Congress Catalog Card Number 80-69662

© Robert A. Dentler and Marvin B. Scott, 1981

Printed in the United States of America
ISBN: 0-89011-555-9

CONTENTS

LIST OF MAPS AND FIGURES

LIST OF TABLES

PREFACE

One school desegregation case to concern a big-city public school system in the North, and one that remains unimpaired by subsequent opinions, was decided by the U.S. Supreme Court in 1973 as *Keyes v. School District No. 1, Denver, Colorado.* There, for the first time, the Supreme Court considered a city public school system in which extreme racial and ethnic separation had existed for decades with no state or local law of the southern variety. The case became a landmark because the Supreme Court held that a finding of *de jure* segregation in a school system could be made by a district court *if* a connection were established between racial and ethnic separation of students (and faculty) and a pattern of school board policies that had been designed to produce that result.

We believe the Boston school desegregation case will be remembered in legal history for two major reasons. First, Judge W. Arthur Garrity, Jr.'s liability opinion in *Tallulah Morgan v. James W. Hennigan* applied and ramified the criteria and evidentiary standards of *Keyes* with a precision that made a succession of northern urban school civil action suits feasible. If *Keyes* was a landmark, the Boston case became a district court "gateway" through which northern federal case law flowed. Second, the remedy in Boston revealed, in its planning and in its implementation, a deeper, more positive concern with *educational* reform than any previous federal court case.

This book does not offer a legal or educational history of the Boston schools case. We have attempted instead to select, depict, and interpret elements of the case within the context of political, administrative, and urban social forces in ways we hope will help Boston and other northern-city residents where school desegregation will have to take place within the coming decade.

There are several reasons why we have not written a history. One is that someone else will do that better than we can do it, later on, when the coals of controversy have cooled and may be raked with more objectivity. Another is that both of us have been party to the making of the remedy, and we would be obliged to write memoirs disguised as history. Yet another is that a mere history of the Denver case would not have helped us to do a better job of planning and then supervising implementation of school desegregation in Boston, although a book that concentrated on the matters we deal with here might have helped us greatly.

We were drawn into participating in the Boston schools case on invitation from Judge Garrity, who appointed us as court experts on January 28, 1975, one week before hearings began on the permanent remedial phase of the suit. We have been active as his consultants, advisors, representatives, and sometimes as supervisors, for five and a half years. Each of us has given a total of more than two years of full-time effort during that period. Our aim as urban educators and planners has been to present in this book some parts of what we have learned in the course of this unusual experience, in the belief that the abundant literature on school desegregation, with its more than 4,000 entries since 1955, has neglected the planning and implementation features of the process.

Our approach is selective in several respects. For example, we have not tried to be comprehensive. There are aspects of the case that are barely touched upon in this book, and we barely pause to mention them. We have not tried to distance ourselves from the burden of desegregation advocacy we originally shouldered in agreeing to support and assist the court. Nor have we documented all of the generalizations we have presumed to make, trusting that the reader will take confidence from our effort to stay within the limits of our direct exposure to some (but far from all) of the facts pertinent to the case.

If our first concern is practical and is bred of the hope that we can contribute to the workmanship of participants in school desegregation in Boston and in many other cities, our second concern is strategic. Between 1973 and 1977, Boston's notorious school desegregation conflict was regarded as the type that no one in his right mind would want to have take place in his city. "Don't let this become another Boston" was the slogan that spread from New York City to Los Angeles and was used by advocates of every point of view and by the active, the apathetic, and the informed and ignorant alike. Educationally beneficial and even novel implications of the Boston desegregation plan, and the facts surrounding the overwhelmingly peaceful and successful implementation of the entire plan, fell across the city like the tree that crashed in the middle of an ancient forest but made no sound because no one was listening.

Our strategic concern is to replace that misleading slogan with an account of some of the real difficulties and real successes that took place. We believe that what has happened in Boston's public schools, as one of the oldest systems in North America, is what *will* happen in many northern cities in the not-too-distant future, and that policymakers, educators, parents, and students deserve to know what has happened and what positive role they can play in the continuing process.

We have concentrated on what seem to us to be crucial features of the Boston schools case. Recognizing that a history would give greater weight to the origins of the federal suit and to the developments in Phase I, the first year of implementation, we have focused nonetheless on Phases II, IIB, and III, and on selected features of those remedial stages, namely, design elements of the basic plan, schools as facilities and program providers, assignment of students, and magnet schools. This focus assumes that what is important in the desegregation process is who goes where to school and what is offered there. Treating these matters requires analysis of some others such as the political, administrative, and social milieu through which the framework is changed, and we have tried to recognize this context continually throughout our exposition. We have not dealt directly with some other important considerations. However, this is less a matter of preferences than of editorial choices made about what to select and to emphasize. Our hope is that a larger, more complete body of literature will soon grow up and around the Boston schools case, and will include all that we have neglected here.

As we have stated, this book is not a memoir, but its point of view and some of its evidence rest upon our direct participation in the case as agents of the court. In the jargon of research, our perspective is clinical. For this reason, we refer directly to ourselves in the book, rejecting the scholarly convention of the third person. No egomania is involved. The cast of players in this drama has numbered in the hundreds of thousands, but we were not spectators, and nothing can be gained by acting as if we were. In this way, we also hope the reader will be helped to locate our biases and errors of judgment.

Robert A. Dentler
Abt Associates, Inc.

Marvin B. Scott
Atex, Inc.

ACKNOWLEDGMENTS

Mentors, families, friends, and colleagues helped us in the writing of this book. None of them has contributed to our mistakes, of course, and none should be assumed to share our points of view.

Helen Dentler did the photo search and photo editing as well as the book jacket design and index; hence she is a member of our team. Carol Scott gave us insights that can come only from being a public schoolteacher in Boston. Judge W. Arthur Garrity, Jr., has been a source of intellectual inspiration—our mentor in understanding constitutional equity and one who encouraged us in our effort to write this book, even though he was prevented as the presiding judge from reading any of it in manuscript.

Phyllis MacDonald kept our files, typed endless memoranda, fielded countless nasty phone calls and letters, and typed part of the manuscript. Kathleen Capson set up our files and gave early editorial and research assistance. Mary Greene typed and corrected our chapters and gave us hope and cheer. Our editor, Renée Wilson, stripped away our jargon, strengthened our coherence, and with sustained consistency improved the quality of our exposition. Among those with whom we worked at the Boston School Department, we shall always appreciate Charles Leftwich, Jack Haran, Al Tutella, Arthur Gilbert, and Albert Lau.

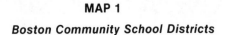

MAP 1

Boston Community School Districts

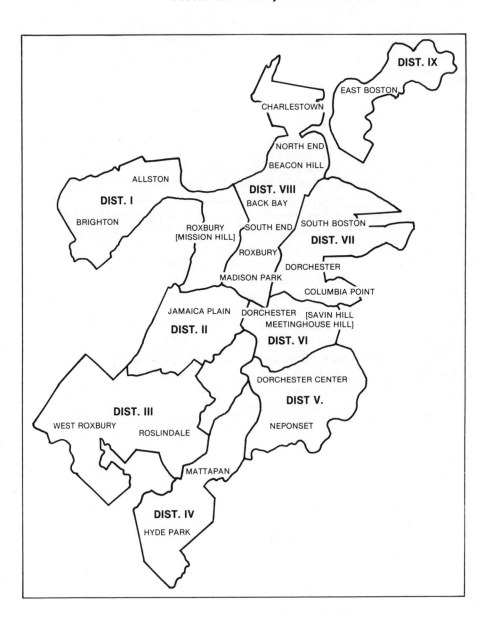

THE LIABILITY 1

WHY COURTS DESEGREGATE PUBLIC SCHOOLS

THE 14TH AMENDMENT STATES, "No State . . . Shall deny to any person within its jurisdiction the equal protection of the laws." This provision, commonly known as the equal protection clause, has become the basis for most court actions pertinent to school desegregation.

In 1896, the Supreme Court held in *Plessy v. Ferguson* that a Louisiana law requiring racial segregation of passengers in railway coaches was not racial discrimination, provided accommodations were equal in quality. This doctrine of separate but equal was applied, with few exceptions, to every service from passenger railways to public schools in federal court cases from 1896 to 1954.[1] Ever since the doctrine was overturned in *Brown v. Board of Education of Topeka*, the courts have been *undoing* what they initially did in sanctioning segregation.

As Griffin Bell noted in his testimony before the Senate Judiciary Committee in January 1976, the Warren Court "refurbished and revived" the 14th Amendment, an amendment born during the Reconstruction and put to sleep but not to death in the post-Reconstruction era. The amendment stayed awake for thirty years and then slept for nearly sixty years. It has now been awakened and has been rumbling grumpily about the house ever since.

In his book, *Government by Judiciary*,[2] legal historian Raoul Berger interprets the original drafting of the 14th Amendment. He argues that the post–Civil War Congress intended by its passage of the amendment to extend to black Americans various rudimentary civil rights, such as equal punishment for crimes and the right to own property. It did not intend, he argues, to have the 14th Amendment grant them equal access to voting booths, schools, juries, or jobs.

Berger's literal interpretation is borne out by the narrow uses to which the amendment was put in the course of its first thirty years on the books. While it stayed awake from 1866 through 1896, the amendment served not to buttress racial justice but to protect business interests. Reawakened by the Warren Court, however, it was used to require equal treatment by states as to race. In the years since 1954, *that* interpretation has ramified into every corner of American life.

Federal judges have often been cumbrous, but they have also been single-minded in their determination to order remedies wherever equal protection was found to have been deliberately denied. The awakening began with public schools. The angry, noisy confusion persists around that institution. But that awakening has been extended steadily to countless other matters with equal force.

Federal courts desegregate public schools on an inexorable schedule wherever plaintiffs gather at the bar and prove that local or state policies and practices have been designed to deny minorities equal access to public instruction. Proof is often easy to come by, for discrimination and segregation have been part of the *status quo* since the beginnings of public schooling in the United States. Only the scale of intentional discrimination is subject to reasonable argument and defense.

Every year since *Brown*, busing opponents have predicted a change in court policies or have forecast federal legislation that would put the 14th Amendment back to sleep. Take, for example, a recent Austin, Texas, case. The U.S. Supreme Court, in December 1976, remanded a decision back to the U.S. Court of Appeals for the Fifth Circuit. The basis of the remand was a decision by the Burger Court in June 1976 that the failure to take affirmative action to remedy racial disproportions in student enrollments did not establish unconstitutional segregative intent.

Boston Corporation Counsel Herbert Gleason's response to the Austin remand was typical of comments from hundreds of antidesegregation leaders around the nation. Wrote Gleason in a *Boston Globe* editorial: "The U.S. Supreme Court's startling ruling in the Austin, Texas, school desegregation

case last week forecasts a seismic change in the law of school desegregation
.... The Austin opinion certainly signals an abandonment of what many believe has been judicial overreaching—righteous to be sure, but tyrannical."[3]

In fact, the Austin decision did not even relate to the remedy phase of the issue. Instead, it dealt with finding a violation of the 14th Amendment. The Supreme Court majority simply sent a one-sentence directive to the appeals judge to reconsider his opinion. He had written a one-paragraph finding that implied that segregated neighborhoods alone, without evidence of illegal discriminatory actions by school officials, could bring sweeping busing plans to Austin.

The federal courts will continue to amend their decisions, but the large body of decisions that has evolved over a quarter century will not be reversed, suspended, or modified substantially. Federal legislation cannot change this judicial trend. An antibusing amendment to the Constitution remains as the last refuge for the antibusing movement.

Each year the federal case law evolves. In the 1977 Dayton, Ohio, case of *Brinkman v. Gilligan*, the Supreme Court toughened the evidentiary criteria for appraising the scope of the wrong done. It returned an appeals court decision, stating that the court must determine what the distribution of students by race would have been had local and state officials *not* violated the Constitution. Still, the district court's findings were left undisputed and its remedy was left intact for the forward year. The Dayton case requires unambiguous proof that school segregation was "the intended result of actions which appeared neutral on their face but were in fact invidiously discriminatory...."

The federal courts have gone the distance since 1954. There is every indication that they are prepared to go the full distance implied by the many school cases now before them. Judges now work from a foundation of a generation of cases. However, as one legal scholar has noted:

> While there has been no shortage of constitutional principles developed
> ...the ultimate end in view—securing a sound and broadly based
> education to as many children as possible—is a vision inherently beyond
> the judiciary—beyond, that is, authoritative extrapolation from general
> principles .... Education is at bottom, defined culturally.[4]

WHY THE COURT DESEGREGATED BOSTON'S SCHOOLS

On June 21, 1974, U.S. District Court Judge W. Arthur Garrity, Jr., found in *Tallulah Morgan et al., Plaintiffs, v. James W. Hennigan et al., Defendants* that the Boston School Committee had

> violated the constitutional rights of plaintiff class; that school authorities
> had knowingly carried out a systematic program of segregation affecting
> all of the city's students, teachers and school facilities and had inten-
> tionally brought about or maintained a dual school system; that the entire
> school system of Boston was unconstitutionally segregated.

3

His proofs for these findings were painstakingly presented. They withstood repeated efforts at reversal on appeal. The opinion was so well composed as to receive a bar association award the following year for its distinction as a legal document.

Organized political reaction to the opinion and to the remedies that followed, and media coverage of both, so confounded public reasoning that the body of this book is incomprehensible without a return to the wrongs identified in Judge Garrity's liability opinion. As with so many other vast, deep wrongs lodged in the social order, this one was of such long standing and required such transformative intervention as to boggle the minds of nearly everyone who did not follow the case in close detail.

From the onset of the federal civil action suit, no one associated with the Boston public schools disputed the fact that they were extremely segregated (see Table 1.1). The system included 201 schools in 1973. A total of 160 of them were segregated in the sense that their student racial compositions were

TABLE 1.1

School Utilization and Racial/Ethnic Composition
1971–72

Total List of Overcrowded Schools	White	Black	Other Minority
South Boston High	99.3	.0	.7
Patrick F. Gavin Jr. High	96.4	1.8	1.8
Wm. Barton Rogers Jr. High	96.3	3.3	.4
Roslindale High	93.3	5.1	1.6
Charlestown High	91.4	2.0	6.6
Grover Cleveland Jr. High	91.2	7.1	1.8
Hyde Park High	84.1	15.3	.7
Dorchester High	46.8	52.2	1.1
Total List of Underutilized Schools			
Boys Trade High	26.6	66.5	6.9
English High	24.8	66.7	8.5
Girls Trade High	20.0	74.9	5.1
Girls High	2.5	91.7	5.8
James P. Timilty Jr. High	1.8	95.0	3.1
Jeremiah E. Burke High	.9	89.0	10.1
Martin Luther King, Jr. Middle School	.2	94.4	5.4

SOURCE: *Morgan v. Hennigan*, Civ. A. No. 72–911G, U.S. District Court, D. Mass., June 21, 1974.

identifiably, indeed extremely, divergent from the racial composition of the student population as a whole. Of eighteen high schools, only one, Boston High School, a special occupational training site, reflected the composition of the high school student population as a whole. Eight of the eighteen were between 85 and 96 percent white, and three were between 75 and 98 percent black, within a system where about two-thirds of the enrolled high school students were white. Of 150 elementary schools in 1973, 62 were 96 to 100 percent white and 32 were 85 to 98 percent black.

Nor did anyone dispute the fact that teachers were segregated along identical lines (see Table 1.2). Eighty-one of the 201 schools had never had a black teacher. Among the 4,243 permanent teachers then in the system, 231, or 5.4 percent, were black; 161 of them were assigned to black segregated schools.

Racial and ethnic separation were so widespread as to provide one of the only obvious sources of structure common to the system. Ethnic lingual minorities such as Chinese-Americans and Hispanic-Americans were assigned to separate schools. White students who did not reside deep inside all-white enclaves were bused by the thousands past black schools and into other all-white neighborhoods.

Thirteen different grade structures existed in 1972, many of them created to ensure racial separation. Attendance zones, feeder patterns, transfer patterns, staffing decisions, repairs, material supplies, and other administrative allocative arrangements were left unstructured deliberately in order to optimize the conditions for keeping most schools white and a few black. Even overcrowding in some white schools was practiced wittingly in the service of maintaining a dual system (see Table 1.3).

TABLE 1.2

**Black Teachers Assigned to
Majority-Black Schools, 1967–72**

School Year	Black Teachers (%) in Majority-Black Schools
1967–68	67
1968–69	68
1969–70	70
1970–71	72
1971–72	74

SOURCE: *Morgan v. Hennigan, Ibid.*

NOTE: In 1972, 59 of 201 schools were majority black. There were 356 black teachers in a total teaching staff of approximately 4,500.

TABLE 1.3

**Portable Classrooms in Use
by Black Student Population, 1972-73**

Number of Schools	Black Student Population (%)	Number of Portables
6	0-5	26
4	6-15	8
1	16-30	3
2	31-50	5
0	51-70	0
2	71-100	4

SOURCE: *Morgan v. Hennigan, Ibid.*

Disputes were reserved, instead, for the question of how these and other conditions of extreme segregation came to be. After sifting, organizing, and reviewing massive documentary evidence, Judge Garrity made the following conclusions:

> On the issue whether substantial portions of the system have been intentionally segregated by the defendants, the court concludes that they have. Plaintiffs have proved that the defendants intentionally segregated schools at all levels . . . built new schools for a decade with sizes and locations designed to promote segregation; maintained patterns of overcrowding and underutilization which promoted segregation at 26 schools; and expanded the capacity of approximately 40 schools by means of portables and additions when students could have been assigned to other schools . . . . How many students were intentionally separated on a racial basis cannot be stated with any degree of precision; but the annual totals were certainly in the thousands, including graduates of nine K-8 elementary schools and four middle schools by means of feeder patterns manipulated by the same means, students making imbalancing transfers under the open enrollment policy and exceptions to the controlled transfer policy, students transported to perpetuate segregation, and students at schools identifiably black by means of assignment and transfer policies regarding faculty and staff.[5]

In other words, the Boston School Committee and its employees had for decades intentionally and deliberately operated a dual school system designed to deny equal protection under the law to black students, their parents, teachers, and other school staff (see Table 1.4). In these respects, the case was as open and shut as civil action suits become. This is not difficult to

TABLE 1.4

Racial Composition of Boston School Administration
1970–71

Position	Number of Whites	Number of Blacks
Headmaster/Principal	76	3
Assistant Headmaster/Assistant Principal	194	11
Headquarters Director or Manager	27	0
Headquarters Assistant Director or Manager	49	2
Supervisor or Consultant	29	2
Truant Officer or Attendance Supervisor	46	0
Psychologist	28	0
Home-Bound Program Teacher	42	0
Total	491	18

SOURCE: *Morgan v. Hennigan, Ibid.*

grasp. The suit was joined after seven years of conflict between the committee and the State Board of Education. The board had attempted repeatedly to implement a state law forbidding racial imbalance in public schools. These were years in which Louise Day Hicks and then other political stars shot across the Boston electoral skies, fueled by the support of thousands of citizens who rose to the call to defend the hallowed, long-standing practice of deliberate school segregation.

In the Cradle of Liberty, of course, the public does not rally to a call for racial discrimination. The call had to be couched very differently. Its first sound, therefore, was for defense of the *neighborhood* school. This had slight validity going for it: Over 60 percent of the 200 schools had been built before 1911 for neighborhood use. Residential settlements had changed drastically in locus and density since then. There could not possibly be a correspondence between where one lived and access to a school with appropriate grade levels within six blocks' walking distance. Even worse, some schools had been built for two generations on sites chosen because they were cheap or useless for other purposes, not because of neighborhood formations.

When the cry to preserve neighborhood schools went out (long before federal intervention), 30,000 out of nearly 85,000 students took cars, buses, streetcars, subways, and taxicabs each day in order to reach their out-of-neighborhood schools. A few enclaves—particularly South Boston, East Boston, and Charlestown—had vestiges of neighborhood school subsystems, and they were widely viewed as the poorest in Boston.

The second call was for freedom of parental choice. This sounded better. It resonated well with the general rhetoric of liberty, and it fit the pattern dearest to those who knew how to get their children assigned to the schools they preferred. Here lay a real, and all-white, constituency. What social and instructional advantages or conveniences some schools had to offer were well known to the parents of perhaps one-fourth of the white students. The system had been built upon a principle of extreme scarcity from its very beginnings. Those preoccupied with retaining status, therefore, and those aspiring most intensely for upward mobility for their children had learned how to play the game of preferential assignment. The right to play became touted as the right of freedom of choice, although thousands of other parents never learned how to play or were excluded from the game.

A third call was that for resistance to judicial tyranny. This call was applauded by presidents, senators, and governors throughout the nation. As the Boston citizenry turned toward lengthy preparations for the Bicentennial celebration of independence, moreover, the call became more fashionable. Within solidly Irish-American enclaves like South Boston and Charlestown, a special variation on this call developed: The federal court and its agents, including U.S. marshals, were seen through the lens of Belfast. A theory of oppression of the true Irish by Yankee elites and their pro-Anglo Irish agents began to be propagated early in 1975, and the rhetoric that had been created in the era of the Sinn Fein movement in Ireland (1905–1916) was heard.

What was difficult to grasp in the years from 1965 to 1974, the year of the liability opinion, and what proved even harder to remember in the years thereafter was the sense in which this policy of discrimination and the practice of segregation it directed were *unlawful*. Boston, the Cradle of Liberty, had its very rockers built of ethnic discrimination. Nearly every neighborhood had been formed on that principle of community action. There were not more than six naturally integrated subcommunities to be found in 1974. No part of the local social, cultural, and economic structure, public or private, stood free of commitment to the manipulation of ethnicity for the purpose of improved life chances for some. Every public agency of the city was governed by, and operated by and for, whatever ethnic group dominated in a given era.

Why should the overwhelmingly Irish-American domain of the public school system, with its thin substratum of Italian-Americans, be singled out for having embraced policies that expressed the essence of the Boston way of life? That way, what is more, had been invented and rationalized generations earlier by the very Yankees who brought public schools into being.

Nearly every informed observer and, indeed, most users of the Boston public schools had agreed in increasing numbers since 1942 that the system had egregious flaws. The school committee and its department, so the story ran, were organized around a corrupt patronage arrangement. Many of the schools were cheaply built, poorly located, dilapidated, unsafe, and unfit for school use. Teachers were poorly prepared, underpaid, indifferently managed, and subject to manipulation as the carriers of the patronage support structure. Custodians did not maintain facilities so much as specialize in the sale of tickets to banquets, buffets, and benefits for school committee members. What little influence parents had they exercised through a Home and School Association that had long since been co-opted by members of the committee. Worst of all, between 1960 and 1967, many of the schools had become grossly overcrowded, with some running on double shifts, and high school drop-out and suspension rates had been soaring for a decade. A teacher, Jonathan Kozol, recited the tragic details in a national best-seller, *Death At An Early Age*, in 1967.

Several themes comprised a widely shared critique of public education in Boston. Between 1942 and 1973, twenty panels, commissions, blue ribbon committees, and associations of specialists combed through the decay of Boston's once-proud public school system and concluded their work with gloomy pronouncements about these less than satisfactory features, together with inventories of recommendations for reform. Private elites—the financial, industrial, scientific, medical, and university communities—had not used the system for the education of their children since its modern establishment in the 1840s, anyway. The Roman Catholic Archdiocese had created a parochial school system as an alternative for its constituents by 1900. The public schools were regarded as having grave flaws but as fairly well suited to the interests of the whites who used them.

In the decade after the *Brown* decision, black influentials and white liberals began to reweave the thread of segregation which had appeared as part of the tapestry of this critique as long ago as 1849, but few commentators connected the other threads with this one. The *perceived* situation was one in which Boston seemed to be an economically depressed, declining, and aging city whose public schools shared in this period of depression and decline. That they were also unlawfully segregated seemed to be an afterthought.

The strategy was one of persistence. The Massachusetts legislature had outlawed school segregation in 1855, but this law as well as ones that followed were flouted by Boston for one hundred years.

Two events changed the perception of Boston as a depressed city. First, Boston began to revive economically. The 1960s ushered in massive federal urban development programs. Boston captured large shares of these programs relative to other cities in the nation. The city and state collaborated in the first efforts taken since the 1920s to begin to rebuild the physical plants of the public school system, in tandem with new housing, road, transportation, office, and industrial construction. English High School, planned as early as 1962 and completed in 1972, was the first new high school built for the public system in Boston since 1934. The struggle by the school committee to ensure that it would be occupied by white students became a struggle that disclosed the persistence as well as the pertinence of segregation as a strategic source of policy.

A second event of equal influence was the passage in 1965 by the state legislature of the Racial Imbalance Act. (This was the commonwealth's affirmative response to the *Brown* decision. The response was made through the votes of suburban and rural legislators, who defined racial balance in a twisted way: Any public school was racially balanced if it contained 50 percent to 100 percent white students.) State financial assistance, including that for building schools, was *linked* permanently in the Boston policy, for the first time in a century, with racial segregation. A system dependent on the state for half of its operating funds and 65 to 75 percent of all capital for construction and renovation found these resources being put in jeopardy because of racial imbalance.

By 1973, then, the salience of school segregation had begun to dawn on nearly everyone. If the public schools were going to be improved, and the first new school superintendent since 1942 announced in 1972 that they were, and if Boston were to become the phoenix of the East, then the use of *segregation* as the operating principle for allocating scarce resources seemed to become more precious than ever before. Its operational use, however, threatened to cut off the new sources of hope at their state and federal fountainheads.

Under these paradoxical conditions, Judge Garrity's finding of constitutional violations seemed to many Bostonians to be a kind of preposterous insult. More than the sacrifice of the mythical neighborhood school, more than the imagined evils of busing, more than the loss of free choice among those with influence, and more than the "Belfast neutrality" were involved. These dispositions were present, and beneath them was racism, at least for many citizens. The graffiti, the leaflets, and the street talk in several neighborhoods asserted this. The most insulting aspect was that the public schools would worsen as a result of court intervention, just when new investments and new leadership had created the impression that they would improve substantially.

The most tangible and impressive basis for this Boston renewal hope was the opening of several architecturally superb new school facilities from 1969 to 1973, with plans for more schools and other renewal capitalization coming from city hall. Another basis was the widespread impression that the physical renaissance of Boston, begun in 1961, was capable of reversing the outflow of young families that had been underway since at least 1950. Desegregation, civic leaders warned, would stem that reversal and produce a riptide of white flight.

All of these attitudes were captured in an opinion survey by Becker Research Corporation, commissioned by and then published in the *Boston Herald-American* early in 1975. In addition, content analysis of newspaper clippings for the period from July 1974 through May 1975 shows how these fears and resentments were publicized by all members of the school committee, most members of the city council, state senators and representatives, and other elected officials in the city and state.

The significance of two underlying trends—the exodus of young households and declining school enrollments—did not get adequate documentation until much later, but the effects took hold earlier. In May of 1977, the firm of Peter Hart Research Associates completed *A Survey of the Attitudes Toward the City of Boston and Its Neighborhoods*. By that time, with desegregation having begun three years earlier, what the study called "the racial and busing situation" had become a minor issue on its list of "negative aspects of living in Boston." While 35 percent of the representative sample of adult Bostonians cited the physical environment—dirty streets, noise, poor street conditions, decay—as most objectionable, and 26 percent were most plaintive about crime, vandalism, and police ineffectiveness, 13 percent viewed busing as problematical and 7 percent mentioned racial problems as a drawback to living in Boston. When subsamples in neighborhoods were asked which factors made a neighborhood "weak," school desegregation showed up at the tail end of the list of responses. Crime, poor sanitation, housing, and poor neighbors ranged in scope from 26 to 14 percent of the choices, while schools and busing captured 5 percent, alongside "noise."

In an insightful analysis of who wanted to move out of Boston and who wanted to stay, however, the Hart survey documented the cluster of family attitudes and perceptions that affect movement significantly. By 1977, schools and busing were negligible influences, but the cluster of attitudes that mattered was in all likelihood the same in 1974. Those who left before and after 1974, most of them for out-of-state locations, were households whose adults defined themselves as "non-Bostonians" for a number of compelling reasons. These included, above all, Boston's poor and declining job opportunities, expensive and poor-quality housing, poor shopping facilities, poor safety, and poor transportation facilities.

Those who defined themselves as Bostonians were over thirty-five years of age, and intensely committed to the lifeways of their immediate neighborhoods. The younger adults were newcomers to the city, many attempting to settle there following graduation from one or another of the sixty-five institutions of postsecondary education in Greater Boston, or they were the children of parents who were native to Boston who had decided they could secure better incomes and better housing in some other region of the United States.

Public education was not a trivial consideration for these young parents. For example, half of the higher-income-bracket respondents in the Hart survey stated that improved public schooling would influence them to consider staying in Boston. Better public schools would similarly affect about two-fifths of those with preschool-age children and children currently in the public schools. Of course, there was no way to estimate from the Hart survey whether some respondents interpreted the word better to mean segregated public schools, but it is noteworthy that young black and other minority parents in the poll felt as constrained to leave Boston as did their white counterparts.

The data in the Hart poll thus depict a Boston that has an aging native population committed to remaining despite the crime, poor facilities, and political chicaneries that characterize the group's perceptions of the city. The data also depict a Boston that young adults are planning to leave, as they have been leaving by the thousands each year since 1950, in search of improved life opportunities.

In 1977 city hall also commissioned a study of school enrollments and enrollment projections by the independent consulting firm of Harbridge House. That first report augments the Hart survey. It shows that the total number of births per year in Boston *declined* by more than 13 percent between 1963 and 1966, and by more than 12 percent between 1966 and 1970. From 1970 through 1973, moreover, the decline accelerated, totaling at least 15 percent. From 1974 through 1976 an additional decline of 21 percent was noted.

There is no question but that court-ordered desegregation stimulated increased withdrawals of students (see Table 1.5). Our analyses of "flight" from the public system indicate that at least 4,000 withdrew during 1974–75, and that an additional 4,000 withdrew during 1975–76, for reasons stemming, for them, from desegregation. However, the overall impact of declining birth rates on enrollment decline was greater than the combined impact of court-ordered desegregation and defective record management within the system.

TABLE 1.5
Boston Public School Enrollment
by Race, 1970–79

School Year[a]	Enrollment			
	Black	White	Other	Total
1970–71	28,822	62,014	5,680	96,516
1971–72	30,653	59,390	6,539	96,582
1972–73	31,634	56,893	7,088	95,615
1973–74	31,963	53,593	8,091	93,647
1974–75[b]	31,737	44,957	9,152	85,846
1975–76	31,092	36,244	9,125	76,461
1976–77	31,053	32,393	9,560	73,006
1977–78	30,863	29,211	10,118	70,192
1978–79	30,073	25,956	10,528	66,557
1979–80	30,083	24,017	11,520	65,620

SOURCE: Massachusetts State Board of Education.

[a]November 1 figures.

[b]First year of court-ordered desegregation.

12

Thus, we think that the inchoately expressed fear and resentment underlying widespread public reactions to school desegregation, particularly within the city's white residential majority, were shaped by the precarious prospects of viability for Boston itself. The economic base of Boston had failed to sustain its citizenry since 1930. Economic and physical redevelopment in the 1960s brought new hope but was carried out against the widening odds of large-scale and continuing population migration to high-growth regions of the nation. The population losses of the city were, from 1960 to 1970, compensated by the in-migration of an equally large college student population that proved, however, to be a transient group.

A forty-year delay in building new high schools and middle schools, combined with a policy of deliberate overcrowding in many all-white schools, masked the annually escalating enrollment declines in Boston public schools between 1968 and 1973. The high schools especially were jammed with students, while four new high schools were on the drawing board. Only in touring the 150 elementary units could an observer note the rising number of unused and underutilized classrooms. The masking was abetted by the school committee, which refused annually to undertake the closing of more than fifty unfit facilities, mainly in response to special neighborhood constituencies.

The federal liability opinion of 1974 thus unmasked but a part of the true face of the situation, at least within the public schools. Its advent coincided with the suspicion that the redevelopment hopes inspired during the 1960s were tenuous and that the reforms required were so profound as to render impossible the dream of reviving Boston on the basis of its ancient political, class, and ethnic structural foundations. The dream had been tottering under the impact of other events, anyway. Nothing about the first years of the 1970s had strengthened public hopes that a new era of improved life chances was in the making. The first experiences with the combined effects of inflation and recession were draining the hopes of Bostonians generally. Now, a federal court was going to challenge not only those fading new prospects but the prospects of maintaining insular ethnic enclaves as shelters from the forces of the larger society.

DESEGREGATION REMEDIES

When a federal court concludes that local or state school officials have engaged in illegal discriminatory actions, it must order an immediate remedy for the wrong. The discriminatory actions must be attacked "root and branch" rather than piecemeal; gradualism is unacceptable, free choice and open enrollment options are rejected, and remedies involving burdens for black but not white students are prohibited. Hence, the desegregative remedy, under Supreme Court rules, must be swift in application, comprehensive, and effective.

Still, serious difficulties have developed. One arises from federal court procedures that obligate the defendant school board, and sometimes the state board of education, to develop a remedy that meets these demanding standards. Often, boards are unwilling and incapable of accomplishing this task. In Boston, Judge Garrity had to adopt a state plan in 1974 that was defective because it was the only remedy in town. In turn, he ordered the Boston School Committee to plan an adequate remedy and gave them six months of lead time. When the day for delivery arrived, the committee voted to reject its own plan.

When judges get a desegregation plan from a local school board, it is often a poor one. If they do not get a plan, or if they reject what they get, they must find an alternative or create one themselves. Plans are hard to find and judges, as well as trial advocates on whom they rely, are, for the most part, unqualified educational planners.

Planning in public education on any matter lags years behind planning in industry and other fields, so faulty remedies have become commonplace. Only within the last decade have quality standards and expertise begun to evolve. More and more commonly, judges turn to desegregation planners for advice. There are no more than 100 such planners in the nation. Only half a dozen of our 1,300 schools and departments of education within universities have anything to do with preparing them. Where the planning is sound, inequities are remedied. Where it is faulty, the outcomes are poor or accidental.

The state plan ordered to take effect on the September 12 opening day of school in 1974, then, was not defective in any technical sense of the term. It fulfilled the requirements of the Racial Imbalance Act quite completely. These requirements, however, left untouched most of the virtually all-white schools in the system, desegregating approximately 80 of 200 schools overall. In addition, statutory limitations on how far a student could be bused were severe and had to be complied with in the state plan. As a result, the planning of congruent and well-articulated enrollment districts was rendered impossible, as all arrangements had to be aimed at selected schools and transportation plans had to dominate the shaping of districts. The result was a patchy-looking, inordinately complex plan that could not possibly meet federal court standards for the long term.

Moreover, Supreme Court standards specify that the defendant school board must prepare a remedial plan. To make desegregation a carefully planned action proposed by the Boston School Committee itself, Judge Garrity ordered the committee to implement the Massachusetts Board of Education plan in a temporary way and to prepare its own proposal for court review beginning in December 1974.

The period from June 21 through December 15, 1974, thus became a period of tension and overt, violent conflict. It was this period of defiance, protest, and even assault by antidesegregation forces that led Thomas Atkins, president of the Boston chapter of the National Association for the Advancement of Colored People, to muse that the Cradle of Liberty was "rocking a little monster called hate." The Phase I plan, prepared with the expert advice of Dr. John Finger, also an advisor in desegregation planning for the Denver and Charlotte-Mecklenberg school systems in the South, did *not* create this conflict. The plan's defects and the confusion that stemmed from hasty implementation during July and August may have exacerbated tensions in some neighborhoods, but the conflict was deliberately created and nurtured by the leaders of the antidesegregation movement. They had been organizing and rehearsing by concerted efforts to repeal and then to amend the state Racial Imbalance Act since 1966.

It was on December 16, 1974, against this backdrop of conflict, that three of the five members of the school committee voted against adoption of the permanent plan prepared by their own staff. In the chain of events that followed, the court found that it was caught in a dilemma. To force the committee to adopt its own December 16 plan would have jelled the local image of the court as a tyrannical force. To extend the finding of contempt and to punish the three in a manner commensurate with their violation of federal law would have been to offer three eager martyrs up for service to the anti-desegregation movement. But to do neither one nor both of these things would have meant that the committee could distance itself substantially from desegregation planning and, later, implementation.

In the absence of the required affirmative action by the committee, the court would have to step in to assume duties normally executed by the group. By April of 1975 the worst effects from taking the latter course were already apparent. The permanent desegregation plan was referred to thereafter as "Judge Garrity's Plan."

RECAPITULATION

Although Judge Garrity defined the wrong done to black public school-children in his liability opinion in June 1974, and although he proved conclusively that the Boston School Committee and its agents had intentionally and deliberately prevented these children from obtaining equal access to public instruction for many years, the wrong he defined using constitutional standards had been taking massive form and substance for a century. Thus, its boldly lucid identification, with the inexorability of remedies to follow, lifted a rock of granitic hardness and vastness that had lain across the entire city for generations.

Between 1870 and 1911, Boston built what was for the times a proud and even impressive system of public education. In that period, 130 buildings were erected. Elementary schools delivered a decent and fairly universal level of literacy and numeracy. Six high schools provided three distinctive levels of instruction. Two Latin schools, one of them the oldest and most renowned in North America, prepared students for entry to Harvard, Amherst, and comparable elite colleges of the time. Two others offered academic preparatory programs combined with a high-quality general or terminal program for prospective white-collar employees. Others mixed academic instruction with home economics and industrial arts. By 1922, programs of real vocational training began to evolve for boys from white working-class families. These provided qualified graduates with immediate, advanced apprenticeships in secure and wage-attractive trades.

The Great Depression shattered all semblance of educational quality for the next forty years. No new high schools were built between 1934 and 1972. Old facilities fell into extreme disrepair. By 1973, two out of three buildings had been built before 1913. Teacher salaries were gravely depressed relative to the rest of the state. Program materials were seldom replenished. Nearly all elementary schools lacked gyms, playgrounds, and libraries; they also lacked physical educators and programs or staff in art and music education. Some high school libraries contained fewer books than students; others had no libraries.

Moreover, between 1950 and 1970 more than 100,000 middle-income households, or 220,000 whites, moved out of Boston to suburbia and to the Sunbelt regions where job opportunities beckoned. The economic base of the city, its aging housing stock, and its dilapidated public facilities of all kinds improved slightly from 1962 through 1972, but the number of improvements subsided, and a pattern of grimy and grinding scarcity took shape, relieved only by the youth culture activities for the college set and the high culture of music, fine arts, museums, and scholarship built up from Yankee endowments in a previous era.

By the time the federal court intervened in 1972, Boston public schools were, as we have stated, in extreme disrepair. Corrupted by venal politicians, mismanaged by administrators appointed by those politicians, and filled with hopelessly outdated programs, the system had become one vast case study in failure. Teacher unionism had improved the wage base between 1971 and 1973, and a half dozen innovative programs had been introduced by school officials. Otherwise, the prospects seemed dim.

Above all, the schools had become a patchwork of small advantages for those with access to the school committee or city hall, and of massive disadvantagement for everyone else. Louise Day Hicks created the myth of the neighborhood school, but these existed only for the advantaged few and for those in a few white ethnic enclaves. For other students, the system offered schools with thirteen different grade structures requiring unpredictable assignment to as many as six different schools between first and twelfth grade. By 1972, 30,000 students were transported by bus and subway to non-neighborhood schools, 60 percent of them without permanent or full-time principals.

Segregation, in housing and on the beaches as well as in the schools, was a strategy of allocation. It served during each wave of Irish and then European migration to set up *ethnic niches* in the work force as well as in living spaces, schools, hospitals, and recreational facilities. To identify the strategy openly, when it had been tacit for so long, and to find it unlawful after it had become a whole city's way of life was to invite an uproar of terrifying proportions. This is what happened. Restore Our Alienated Rights (ROAR) was formed as a citizen protest group, with the tiger as its logo, and roar it did with a fury that resounded for eighteen months.

The moral is simply this: In cities where conditions are roughly similar to those of Boston, the process of revealing racial and ethnic segregation for what it is will be quite similar. This is the baseline: What can vary is planning and implementation.

POSTSCRIPTS AND COMMENTARY

The contrast between the internal calm of the court's deliberations in the Boston schools case and the external world of dispute was extraordinary to witness. On the "inside," among the attorneys and clerks, the outcomes had a predestined quality. As we noted, no one disputed the fact of systematic segregation. The public actions of the committee had, with the exception of one or two members during the years from 1963 through 1973, demonstrated the causal connection between policy decisions and the furtherance of a dual system. Thus, the only uncertainties, as far as court insiders were concerned, involved the timing and the intensity of Judge Garrity's findings of liability.

In the world outside, from 1972 through 1974, a visitor to the halls of government—Capitol Hill in Washington, the Commonwealth Statehouse, or Boston City Hall—or a visitor to college campuses and city neighborhoods alike, would have inferred that a wide range of decisions was available. It sounded as if a set of lively disputes had just begun, and as if they were to be subject to political resolution, rather than as if the issue had haunted the streets of Boston since 1963 and had come to rest, depleted of political vitality, within the confines of the federal courthouse.

In July 1974, one month after issuance of the liability opinion and the first remedial order, one of us (Dentler) was called to a dinner meeting by Mayor Kevin White, who wanted to discuss his "options." The discussion, following a hearty meal, was lively with opinions, none of them grounded in the orders of the court. The glory of Boston, as always, shone in the fiction that Bostonians were free masters of their destinies. The pity was that the time for such mastery, within the limits of the Constitution, had expired as a result of years of defiance.

We have more recently watched developments in counterpart school desegregation cases in Cleveland, Indianapolis, St. Louis, and Los Angeles. Except in the latter, where legal strategists decided to focus their efforts on state courts, we can see that the process within the courthouse and outside has a "natural historical" regularity. Civic delay persists long after judges reach their conclusions. Resistance to change toward educational equity takes a decade to reach its peak. When a remedy becomes mandatory, this cumulative force presses on, rendering first planning and then implementation impossible to accomplish with a modicum of reasonableness.

We have come to respect the magnitude of resistance to educational equity, and thus change. Racism is a vast barrier, to be sure, but it is too diffuse and multifaceted to account for the resistance to school desegregation. Our speculation is that racism is reinforced in the case of schooling by more specific cultural assumptions, some of them inherent in the very western notion of schooling.

Schools are experienced as instruments that grant advantages. Parents, taxpayers, educators, and other professionals join in celebrating the myth that, just as life chances are restricted in their distribution by the socio-economic boundaries along the pathways of persons, so schools reflect and rehearse the pageantry of restrictions of opportunity. Thus, the cultural preference at the base of the *Brown* decision—a preference for equalizing learning opportunities—sounds preposterous when separated from the language of racial justice.

For all their warts and carbuncles, the public schools of Boston were built up over a period of 200 years in response to a pervasive cultural myth that asked the city to locate and then benefit the *deserving* children in its midst. The schools that resulted were as good as the benefitting constituencies wanted them to be. Some, such as Latin (high) School, were thought by all to be excellent, while others, such as South Boston High, gave the young of that Irish-American neighborhood the social bonds and sentiments their parents shared. As one revered headmaster of Latin School liked to point out before 1974, the school "welcome[s] minority students who can read and write." His way of stating the invitation is in itself a racist slur.

The resistance is given extra strength as well, we think, because the call for equal protection by the state—in this case, the Massachusetts Board of Education—constitutes a clear threat to the sanctity of the family. The state may presume to prosecute youths for crimes. That action may extend to denial of ordinary access to public school. Conventionally, however, that is the limit. Beyond this, parental hegemony is complete and is delegated voluntarily to teachers as surrogates. The Constitution does not refer to families or children. Again, the *Brown* decision and the civil rights movement it reinforced stood outside the hidden blueprint of the culture.

We have found that as many as 20 percent of Boston's public school-children are relocated once or twice a year by their parents, moved from school to school at will, and that this practice predates desegregation by many years. Children are enrolled late, kept at home for a cumulative total of as much as a month of school days a year, and are withdrawn for a hundred diverse family reasons. Only the state and the media maintain the fiction of school stability. And now, in the case of desegregation, comes a set of enforced assignments. The hegemony of parents is under assault from every quarter in this era, and desegregative assignments represent a direct attack.

Finally, the resistance is buttressed by massive ignorance about the pedagogical conditions under which learning takes place. School desegregation remedies what educational wrong? the public asks. Who will learn more? How will this happen? Those who finished school a generation ago, with very few exceptions, imagine schooling to be what they experienced. Its *social* importance is clear, but its real bearing on learning is obscure except for the importance to the advantaged of relying upon what is already known.

Here, then, is a wrong that appears to have no commensurate remedy. The rhetoric of improving teaching and learning is arcane. In the aftermath of the era of national reforms from 1958 to 1972, an era avoided by most Bostonians, it sounded absurd, expensive, and even subversive of convention. Was this, after all, not the era when college students invaded Boston like an army of imitation Beatles?

These speculations are noted in order to suggest how *overdetermined* is the scale of resistance to school desegregation. There are wrongs in the polity that defy all thoughts of remedy. As Edward Banfield asserted in his Brahman-like overview of American cities and their "underclass," most urban problems are to be regarded as "intractable."[6] Surely, the ravages of generations of racial discrimination in urban public schools are among them. The negative answer of the Supreme Court is a nearly breathtaking denial of Banfield's premise.

NOTES

1. The legal reasoning for the doctrine of *Plessy v. Ferguson* was based largely upon an opinion written by Judge Shaw of the Supreme Judicial Court of the Commonwealth of Massachusetts in 1849. The opinion denied Sarah Roberts, a black child in Boston, access to a neighborhood public school.
2. Raoul Berger, *Government By Judiciary*, Harvard University Press, Cambridge, Mass., 1977.
3. *Boston Globe*, morning edition, December 15, 1976, op. ed. page.
4. Daniel D. Polsby, "The Desegregation of School Systems: Where the Courts are Headed," in *School Desegregation in Metropolitan Areas: Choices and Prospects*, National Institute of Education, U.S. Government Printing Office, Washington, D.C., 1977, p. 77.
5. *Morgan v. Hennigan*, Civ. A. No. 72, 911, G (33).
6. Edward Banfield, *The Unheavenly City: The Nature and Future of Our Urban Crisis*, Boston, Little, Brown & Co., 1968.

THE REMEDY 2

THE POINT OF THE REMEDY

IN CIVIL LAW, REDRESS IS DUE WHEN A PLAINTIFF is found to have been wronged. In this case, the plaintiffs are black parents of some fifty public schoolchildren enrolled in the Boston public schools. The plaintiffs, Mrs. Tallulah Morgan and others, also constituted a much larger *class* of parents and children who were unlawfully separated from access to equal educational services in a system whose policymakers and agents maintained that separation deliberately for many years.

As Edmund Burke noted in 1774, public remedies "must be quick and sharp, or they are very ineffectual." The era of the *Brown* decision (the second part of which called for "all deliberate speed," resulting in slow and sometimes vague remedies) had ended several years before 1974. In the first flush of the new era, all of the school districts of Mississippi had been desegregated within eighteen days from the issuance of a federal court remedial order.

It was in order to comply with this new imperative for promptness that Judge Garrity ordered implementation of the state board's temporary racial balance plan in the period between June 21 and September 12, 1974. The same imperative required the Boston School Committee to prepare and submit a permanent plan of its own devising by December 16, 1974.

No one in the Boston area had any reason to believe that the Boston School Committee could plan its way out of a portable classroom, let alone make plans for every school in the system. No committee member had planning credentials, although each member, by precedent, intruded deeply into direct administration of the schools.

No member of the top echelon of administrators had real system planning credentials. Indeed, no one even had consolidated authority over the system. The superintendent was in charge of curriculum and program matters, but little else. The business manager was in charge of the budget and of expenditures. He reported directly to the school committee, independent of the superintendent, as did the chief structural engineer (in charge of plant repairs), the chief custodial engineer (in charge of plant maintenance), and the secretary to the committee. In addition, the associate superintendent for personnel was detached from control by these officers and often dealt directly with city hall and with school committee members. Hence, for decades, budget had been divided from program, repairs from maintenance, and staffing from curriculum.

School headquarters boasted an Educational Planning Center, but its small, untested staff consisted of former teachers and lower-echelon administrators sequestered for the provision of technical assistance and liaison with the state on facilities. Many secretaries who had been hired through committee patronage could neither type nor file. A recently established Department of Transportation contained no transportation engineers. Its director was a former school custodian and bus driver and its assistant director arranged income tax "consultations" for school system employees on the side, including tax law consultations with school committee members. He had no qualifications in income tax accounting or the law.

The point of ordering the school committee to plan a remedy is simple enough from a legal perspective. Unless a court decides for some arguable reason to dissolve or displace a duly constituted local or state authority, it has an obligation to enable that authority to continue to govern. In order to do that, the *school committee* must, in legal theory, devise policies and practices and implement them, subject to court review and approval on matters pertaining exclusively to the identified wrong. By doing this, again in legal theory, a school board redeems itself in the course of taking affirmative action.

In legal theory, these steps are to be taken immediately, comprehensively, and effectively. That is, the remedy is to be tested by examining how well it works in application. In practice in the Boston case, the board was unfit, unwilling, and unable to grasp what a comprehensive remedy would entail, and historically slow and unresponsive.

In spite of these limitations, the theory prevailed. A chief planner was identified. He was John Coakley, a former assistant principal of a junior high school, a veteran classroom teacher, and a native son of Boston. Coakley had other qualifications: He was Irish-American, a "regular" in the ranks, and *not* a part of the committee's patronage system, and thus had a reputation for integrity. The public would come to view him as relatively independent, while the committee defined him in 1974 as politically expendable. Above all, he had a reputation for being a diligent 80-hour-a-week worker. In addition, he was intelligent and could write in standard English. Indeed, he could write plainly, quickly, and credibly. On the other hand, in 1974 Coakley favored neighborhood schools and opposed involuntary busing for desegregation.

Coakley and associates in the Educational Planning Center tried to rise to the occasion. By December 16, 1974, they had drafted a readable comprehensive plan. It had flaws, but it might have become the keystone of the remedy had the school committee not rejected it because it entailed the use of buses to transport children from their homes to a network of magnet schools.

By January 27, at the insistence of the committee, Coakley and associates had rewritten their plan in keeping with instructions to expunge busing, except on a voluntary basis, and to create a set of "resource centers" where elementary students would be bused one day each week and middle school students twice a month in order to receive interracial exposures.

THE COURT INTERVENES

Soon after the committee rejected Coakley's December 16 remedy, Judge Garrity acted to structure the remedial phase of the case in ways that would prevent further defiance and confusion and enhance chances of obtaining a second plan. For example, the range of parties in the suit was expanded to include, in addition to plaintiffs, the committee and the state board, the mayor, the Boston Teachers Union, the Boston Home and School Association, an attorney for the Boston Association of School Administrators, and El Comite, a council of Hispanic parents and educators. All were invited to submit planning proposals.

Judge Garrity then appointed us as court experts, and later formed a Panel of Masters. He charged them with taking evidence, finding facts, and recommending

> a plan meeting constitutional standards that includes systemwide desegregation of vocational and examination schools, athletic and other programs, and makes provision for bilingual education and for special programs for students with special needs . . . advanced work classes and others. The plan should include a recommended program and timetable for implementation.

The masters were Jacob Spiegel (presiding officer), a recently retired member of the State Supreme Judicial Court; Edward McCormack, Jr., former attorney general of the state; Francis Keppel, former U.S. Commissioner of Education; and Charles Willie, a professor of sociology and education at Harvard University.

We were appointed on January 28, 1975, one day after the second plan from the school committee was filed. Our appointments, like those of the masters, paralleled Judge Garrity's tactic of enlarging the circle of parties to the remedial phase. He was anticipating the consequences of school committee rejection of its own best plan on December 16. He could foresee the necessity of having to proceed in a vacuum.

The masters were appointed after we had agreed to advise Judge Garrity and after we discussed with him and outlined in writing the advisability of creating a panel competent to make findings of fact and to develop plans. We encouraged the concept of diversity in composing the panel and participated in reviewing candidates for it with the foreknowledge that we would work with the masters for a time and would subsequently return to advising Judge Garrity directly.

Unlike judges in some other cities who have been diverted from remedial action for periods of several years, Judge Garrity had moved the case with dispatch during its first two years, slowing down to ensure thoroughness only during the early months of 1974 while writing the liability opinion. His record of prompt deliberation was not to be sacrificed to the defiance of school committee members. If they did not meet his final deadline for a remedial plan by January 27, 1975, after having seven months of lead time, Judge Garrity intended to obtain a constitutionally acceptable remedy from other sources.

The masters, appointed on February 7, 1975, decided they should complete their report within the first week of April, if time were to be slotted for reasonable implementation of the plan for the opening of schools the following September. They conducted hearings from February 10 through 26, and recessed to draft their report for submission to the parties for final argument and revision on March 21.

These arrangements offered several advantages in the public interest: Judge Garrity would have final say in fashioning the remedy, but he would not preside over its development or author it himself, and the design would be a product of an expanded array of parties, since the masters could give undivided attention to fact-finding, review of plans, and plan drafting while Judge Garrity continued to meet obligations in some 1,000 other federal cases. The masters could divide the labor among themselves as well as between the lawyers and the educators. The experts were free to support and assist them, to range across the city in search of facts and planning ideas, and to provide transition between the court and the period of retirement of the masters from the case. In addition, on the recommendation of the masters and experts, Judge Garrity obtained a special law clerk to assist the team of six.

Judge Garrity's advance preparations during December and January included one strategic innovation. He charged the masters with the task of "expressing a deep educational concern," language that signalled to all of the parties his determination that the remedy should benefit learners, given the historically notorious condition of Boston's public schools. In our exploratory interviews with Judge Garrity, we had emphasized our readiness to assist in a quest for a desegregative remedy if that quest could include educational considerations. We saw no need for education experts in a narrowly defined "race case" where racial justice would be approached as if it could be separated from reforms that would make equal learning opportunities something more than equalized access to unfit facilities and miseducation. The masters expressed the same concern, one by one, as they first considered the assignment. However, it was Judge Garrity who made this concern the motivating and unifying aim of his new team.

THE PLAN AS A WHOLE

Three comprehensive and three partial proposals came before the Panel of Masters for review. There were the December 16 and January 27 plans written by John Coakley for the school committee. There was a plan submitted by the plaintiff, prepared mainly by Michael J. Stolee, a desegregation planning expert from the University of Miami retained for the task for a few weeks when attorneys for the plaintiff realized the defendant's two plans would prove unacceptable. And there were partial proposals from the mayor, the Home and School Association, and the teachers union.

The history of how these proposals were refined, combined, and augmented by the masters and experts, while noteworthy, does not illuminate the plan itself. Suffice it to say, then, that the masters published a detailed critique of each of the submissions and a draft version of their plan, based on elements from the others. This draft was in turn critiqued by the parties and by the press. New data were obtained by the experts as well, and by March 31 Judge Garrity received the final report of the masters.[1] On May 10, just a little more than a month later, Judge Garrity issued the court plan, 90 percent of which corresponded wholly with the final report of the masters.

We should note, however, that seven weeks of review and planning—the time set for completion of the report of the masters—does not begin to offset the absence of continuous planning by the school committee. This operation was a last resort, as was federal litigation itself. Absent were local sub-community reports, historical and verified data, evaluation studies from recent years, program specifics, and other sources and tools basic to modern educational planning. The parties and the seven-man team representing the court had to make do with what had accumulated in the liability phase and what could be taken as fact from their short-term inquiries.

One of the frequent results of school desegregation cases, however, has been explosion of the public fiction that school boards and departments are equipped with the facts on their own systems. The Cleveland case has been most revealing in this regard. The Cleveland public school system had built up a national reputation for efficacy during the 1960s. When the special master appointed by Federal Judge Frank J. Battisti got through the door, he found, instead of usable information, massive evidence of mismanagement, absence of planning, and little more than a bold front of pretension.[2]

No one expected the Boston system would be efficacious in the management of information. Any visitor to headquarters at 15 Beacon Street might mistake the elevators, hallways, and offices for a sort of stage set for a temporary local WPA headquarters in a period film on the Great Depression.[3] Even in Boston, however, officials and citizens alike had the false impression that agents for the committee knew how many buildings, classrooms, operating boilers, teachers, and students comprised the system. That impression was dispelled dramatically between June 1974 and April 1975.

Thus, the legal theory of well-planned development of a remedy bears no resemblance to the practices any outside group will be likely to find. Some districts west of Chicago—perhaps Minneapolis, Dallas, and Los Angeles—exhibit some of the attributes of modern public service agencies that have developed information and planning management practices characteristic of the second half of the twentieth century. But, the eastern systems we have observed tend to be mired in decay, outmoded procedures, and a kind of management system best developed by India under British colonial rule. The contrast between them and the advertised school reforms of the past twenty years is enormous.

As the U.S. Court of Appeals found several months later, the court plan met Supreme Court standards of constitutional acceptability: It was realistic and workable, it could be implemented without delay, and it converted a dual-race system into a unitary one in which racial discrimination could be eliminated "root and branch."

What all of this signifies, and what it portended for public instruction, is more complicated, however. Most of the changes introduced into the plan, from the masters' first draft through the final court plan, resulted from the correction of errors in data on the numbers and ethnic distribution of students enrolled in the public system. The masters had to work with what enrollment and facility data they could obtain in the course of four weeks. When attorneys for the school committee criticized the masters' report for faulty statistics, Judge Garrity, resuming direct control over planning, directed the committee to provide the name, sex, age, ethnicity, grade, address, and school of enrollment of every student in the system. The resulting printout of 85,001 names was then taken as authoritative and seats for that many students were replanned into the system. As the new student data were analyzed, small changes in boundaries and related adjustments had to be devised. Apart from such minor alterations and the preparation of a final legal memorandum interpreting the plan, the work of the masters and experts became the remedy, or so it was thought.

TABLE 2.1

Boston City-Wide Student Enrollments
by Racial/Ethnic Group, 1975 and 1980[a]

Grade Level	White		Black		Other Minority[b]		Total	
	1975	1980	1975	1980	1975	1980	1975	1980
K$_1$ + K$_2$	6,678	3,579	3,274	2,722	1,271	1,374	11,223	7,675
1–5	16,077	7,175	13,184	10,834	4,512	4,687	33,773	22,696
6–8	8,448	5,617	6,719	7,461	1,939	2,468	17,106	15,546
9–12	12,210	7,149	7,322	8,753	1,838	2,687	21,370	18,589
13 +	880	497	237	313	324	304	1,441	1,114
K–13 + Total	44,293	24,017	30,736	30,083	9,884	11,520	84,913	65,620
Percentage	52	37	36	46	12	17	100	100

[a]Data filed with the court by the Boston School Department on April 10, 1975, included any student enrolled anywhere in the system and attending one or more days since September 1974. (Later, we found that about 5,000 had attended for only two to five days. Still later we found that a backlog of 3,000 discharged students was included.) Data for April 12, 1980, was prepared by the Department of Implementation, Boston Public Schools.

[b]Includes Hispanic-Americans (73%), Asian-Americans (25%), and Native Americans (2%).

It was discovered later that the printout was bogus; there were not 84,913 students in the schools. More than 5,000 of the names on the list were those of students who had materialized no more than five times between September and April. Another 2,000 names were the result of students being counted more than once, under as many as three identification code numbers. Thousands more were enrolled in one school but were in fact attending another. Some students lived on as many as five different streets, according to the Alpha list, with varied spellings of the street names. Initially, the Alpha list contained only names and addresses. Our time from May through July 1975 was consumed in attempting to improve and simultaneously make use of the list (see Table 2.1).

Within three weeks of filing the allegedly complete lists (submitted with no qualifications, incidentally), the committee deleted nearly 3,000 names as dischargees. Thousands of additional discharges then began to be posted between July and October of 1975. Meanwhile, the court plan, while requiring the closing of thirty buildings, ensured provision of 84,913 seats.

DISTANCE AND STUDENT TRAVEL TIME

The Boston case was never a case about *busing*. Busing, like the neighborhood school, was an invention of antidesegregationists. Just as the myth of neighborhood schools gave its believers something "neutral" to support, so busing gave them something "neutral" to oppose. But over 30,000 out of an alleged 90,000 students had been taking buses, subways, and taxis from home to public schools in Boston for many years prior to 1974. What is more, all parties to the case, and every individual member of the school committee, agreed that transportation by buses was *necessary* if system-wide desegregation were to be achieved.

Busing was in this sense a tangential question. To oppose it meant one opposed system-wide desegregation and therefore a federal court order. Or, it meant specific opposition to coercion, that is, being *required* to attend a school that could only be reached feasibly by bus. Again, no one could pretend that assignments to public schools were not required in Boston and everywhere else in the nation, which indicated that so-called opposition to coercion was actually opposition to school desegregation.

So, the children would have to be transported, mainly by bus, because of the geography and demography of Boston. For example, we measured the greatest distance between any two schools to be thirteen miles, between the Patrick J. Kennedy Elementary in East Boston and the James Hemenway Elementary in West Roxbury. Attorneys for the plaintiffs presented the only transportation study conducted in the history of the case on February 11, 1975. It showed that it took thirty-two minutes for a bus to travel from the Kennedy School to Howe School, the latter located at the center point of the city in an all-black section of Roxbury. That run was made at 2:30 in the afternoon, in a snowstorm, through the harbor tunnel that connects East

Boston with the North End. It should, therefore, take a school bus one hour at most to move children from Kennedy to Hemenway School, the farthest point.

In contrast, in *Swann v. Charlotte-Mecklenburg Board of Education* (1971), the U.S. District Court found that the school system planned to bus 23,000 students for an average daily round trip of fifteen miles, taking about thirty-five minutes each way. Analyzing these and other student transportation studies, we recommended to the masters that they place a ceiling on their plan of not more than forty minutes each way by bus and not more than 6.5 miles one way. The time measure stemmed from the thirty-two-minute report, with eight minutes added for tolerance. The distance equalled the Kennedy-to-Howe trip, or half of the longest possible trip. Such a standard made it possible to imagine two-way busing designs for white and black students that encompassed over two-thirds of the school buildings in the system.

In our review of the literature for the masters, we found that over 40 percent of all American schoolchildren are bused to school daily, with an average distance of three miles one way. A national survey commissioned by the U.S. Office of Education in 1972 found that among public schoolchildren, busing ranked last on a list of six possible problems or difficulties associated with schooling.[4] Among white students who were to be bused to desegregated schools for the first time, busing ranked only fourth on the same list of six problems, and it declined in rank to sixth after it was experienced. All of the empirical studies reviewed indicated that busing *per se* was unimportant, while the educational values associated with what lay at the end of the ride were paramount.

We also found that in 1972, 10 percent of all Boston elementary schoolchildren were transported to school, as were 50 percent of all middle school students, and 85 percent of all high school students. Nashville, Tennessee, bused 34,000 students before desegregation, and 49,000 after. Tampa, Florida, bused 32,406 before and 52,795 afterward. It looked as if any plan for Boston would entail busing between 20,000 and 35,000 students.

After different demographic combinations were reviewed and argued, the court ordered that within any community district, the average distance from home to school not exceed 2.5 miles, and that the longest possible trip be shorter than 5 miles. Bus travel times were to average between 10 and 15 minutes each way, with the longest trip less than 25 minutes. It also adopted the standard of mandatory provision of chartered buses for elementary students assigned to schools more than 1 mile from home, for middle school students living more than 1.5 miles, and for high school students living more than 2 miles. The Massachusetts Board of Education reimbursed the city for all busing and taxi costs on trips exceeding 2 miles. This meant students could be divided fairly simply into bused and walk-in subpopulations and that 90 percent of the former group's expenses would be paid by the state. Subsequent planning showed that charter bus rides would be needed in 1975 for 24,000 students at most.

We learned quickly that busing of public schoolchildren in Boston was desirable, feasible, and necessary to achieve desegregation. The numbers to be bused would not exceed the numbers transported before the court intervened. The distances and times required were well below national averages. In the planning stage, busing became noteworthy in only one respect: Judge Garrity, after close scrutiny of our analyses and advice, decided against busing 5,000 children daily in and out of East Boston. This would have involved comparatively long trips each morning during the commuter traffic peak through narrow, always-congested tunnels. East Boston was not exempted from desegregation, but different measures were used, and nine small elementary facilities there were left essentially unaffected.

The desirability of busing was proven within the first few months of implementation. The court plan required the school department to consult with parent advisory councils in drawing up bus routes, stops, and schedules. The effect, surprisingly, was the swift generation of public pressure to add more buses. The clamor for additional transportation became intense and some of it came from the neighborhoods where the lion of ROAR had bellowed loudest. It did not come because of underprovision of buses and stops. It came because a bus ride quickly became preferable to walking—even before classes resumed in September 1975. And the clamor came irrespective of assignment to a walk-in neighborhood school or a cross-district facility.

THE PLANNING PRINCIPLES

Before Phase I, Boston schools had been essentially undistricted. This had contributed to the generation of racially identifiable schools as well as to the very uneven distribution of resources from school to school. At the request of the masters, Dentler submitted a tentative outline of criteria for gauging the effectiveness of desegregation planning proposals on February 4, 1975. The aim was to establish principles (in addition to the standards guiding constitutionality established by the Supreme Court) that would enable critical appraisal of the proposals submitted to the masters by the parties. Later, the six principles became the basis for designing the masters' plan. The following were Dentler's principles:

1. **Educational improvement.** Ways in which its implementation would improve the teaching and learning conditions characteristic of the system should be manifest in the plan. Judge Garrity had stated from the bench during a hearing on February 7 that a "desegregation plan must not simply be a reshuffling of students. There must be a deep concern for the educational dimensions of all proposals, and the necessity of considering the quality of education."

2. **Ethnic mix.** Any reader of the plan should be able to see how the redistribution of students will result in an ethnic mix within each school that reflects the system's present mix of students. Here, the concern was not with what the state law called racial balance, but with the elimination of separateness and the fixing of a standard as one reflecting overall enrollments.

3. **Educational equity.** Each local school should be affected by the plan in roughly similar ways. One school should not go unchanged, as in the Phase I plan, while others undergo one-way busing of black students only.

4. **Fiscal soundness.** Proposed change should be within realistic fiscal parameters.

5. **Clarity.** Readers of the plan should be able to infer accurately from it where pupils would be assigned; what the grade structures, feeder patterns, and districts are to be; and how the system will change. The plan should reduce, not increase, the confusion of parents, teachers, and students.*

6. **Durability.** The plan should stabilize the system for a ten-year period.

After the court plan had been implemented Mayor Kevin White devised an ingenious political strategy around the fourth principle, that of fiscal soundness. He developed a speech that argued that school desegregation was bankrupting Boston, and he carried his speech to several cities in the Northeast and Midwest. Translated, his argument was that constitutional government is fine, except where it cannot be afforded. This was his improvement on the now-stale argument that busing is bad because it is expensive. This became a center plank in his re-election campaign in 1976 and a rallying cry of mayors and school board candidates in other cities. In fact, the court plan was designed to ensure that it would not inflate program or staff costs, would use existing plants optimally, and would add only transportation and safety costs to the system, with most of the former being charged to the state. The single greatest expense generated by the court plan during 1975 and 1976 was that

*Dentler's memo noted that, "according to the U.S. Court of Appeals in *Morgan v. Kerrigan*, public clamor has long been deemed beyond the pale as justification for racial segregation. Legally sound as this is, a plan for the city could meet my criteria and fail of public acceptance. Moreover, a plan could meet none of the criteria and be widely accepted. For these reasons, the character of public concerns and expectations unique to each city must be studied in the course of appraising the effectiveness of any planning proposal . . . . The best plan will be one that meets these six criteria and exhibits a resonance to the character of the city."

of police services, and those resulted from the political mobilization of protest and racial conflict. They resulted, too, from the mayor's provision of overtime payments (double time) to all city police for any time served in guarding or patrolling the schools. Mayor White's argument had little bearing on the schools case, but it did help to solve two problems for him: It gave him someone to blame for escalating city tax rates and impending insolvency. He named Judge Garrity as the person responsible for increased taxes in the tax notices sent to every city resident in 1976. The mayor's argument also gave him a strong enough alliance with antibusing leaders to protect him from electoral defeat.

THE COMMUNITY DISTRICT

All of the planning proposals submitted to the court made use of districting. Moreover, Phase I had districted the system, at least temporarily. There was no dispute over the necessity of devising a geographical mechanism for *structuring* the system. The masters and experts simply took this central, indisputably pivotal, mechanism several steps further. They defined a community school district as a "community of the city, clearly bounded by identifiable lines on a map, within which all residents are entitled to attend the community or 'self-contained' public schools." The boundaries they used conformed closely to ward and precinct lines as they had been redistricted in 1973.

At first, the masters designed nine such districts. Later, as better data on student distribution became available, it became necessary to telescope two districts into a single one, making eight. The eight districts were arrived at inductively by measuring facilities, distances between residential locales and schools, student densities, ethnic distributions, and historic dimensions of neighborhoods within communities.

There were only two parts of the city that proved technically challenging: East Boston and Charlestown. Both are separated from the rest of Boston and accessible at some distance only through bridges and tunnels. All other areas took shape quite simply, from a planning perspective. Black, Hispanic, and Chinese settlements constituted a kind of minority backbone running down the center of the city, from the South End to Hyde Park. When all of the community district boundaries were "fused" along this backbone, the resulting districts each contained minority settlements.

Charlestown, it seemed, could be added into an adjacent district without further difficulty. East Boston, with its 95 percent white population, was a different matter. It could not be added to the most adjacent district without puffing the size of the district out of all proportion relative to other districts. Moreover, merger with other areas would have meant that at least 2,500 children would be bused twice daily, at the peak of morning traffic through the only tunnel and back again in the afternoon, and that at least 2,500 children

MAP 2

Dorchester Community School District 5,
Composition by Geocodes

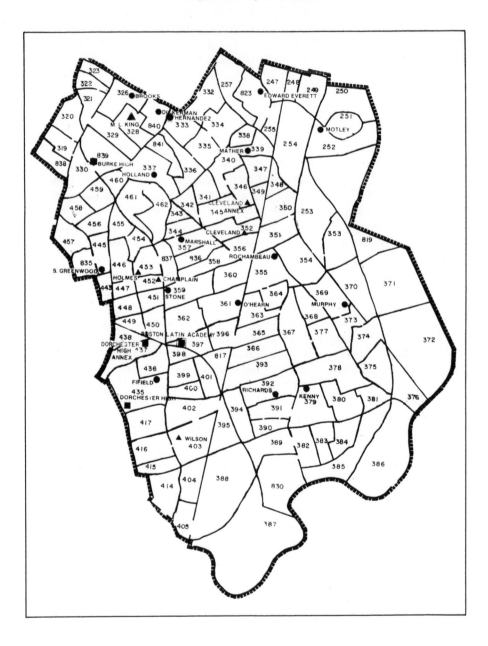

would have to make the same trip in the opposite direction. The prospect seemed unwieldy, undesirable, and constitutionally unnecessary, as Judge Garrity concluded later.

As the concept of community districts was being thought through, the idea of *variable ethnic ratios* for each of them evolved out of Dentler's concept of an interval range of ethnic composition for all of the schools in the system. The Supreme Court had never called for "racial balance." It had called for the elimination of dual systems and racial identifiability.

We concluded that these standards could be met from *within* districts, using the number of prospective black, white, and other minority students residing in the district each year as the standard by which to gauge the expected ethnic composition of all schools within the district, within ranges of plus or minus 10 percent. Later, Judge Garrity refined variance to refer to a 25 percent departure, plus or minus, from the percent of each of the three ethnic categories of prospective students, kindergarten through grade 13. Using this concept, schools in East Boston, once it was designated as a district, would continue to remain about 86 to 96 percent white, while schools in Dorchester would remain 60 to 70 percent black, reflecting residential settlements in diverse sections of Boston.

Community school districts became more meaningful the more the court team contemplated them.[5] They would enable city-wide desegregation, but on a standard that could vary as neighborhoods changed in ethnic character from year to year. No one district was wider or longer than five miles, thus delimiting mandatory busing and related expenses (see Map 2). Parents, students, and teachers could identify clearly with the schools in their districts and could see how the elementary schools would feed into middle and high schools in the same district. Expenditures could be equalized across districts. Parent participation in governance could be built into these structures. Power could be redistributed across them, away from an overcentralized headquarters bureaucracy and the patronage arrangements of the school committee.

Curriculum could also be fit to the variable needs and interests within each district, and the decentralized character of the system could enable future collaboration with surrounding inner-ring suburban districts and institutions. We also recommended restructuring the administration of the system to correspond with these features, so that every district would have a community district superintendent, a council of principals from the buildings in the district, and a community district advisory council of parents and other relevant representatives, including teachers.

ORIENTATION AND APPLICATION

Once the court team had adopted the magnet school concept from the Coakley school committee plan, as we describe in a later chapter, it began to refine it in an effort to ensure that all parents would have an equal chance to obtain placement of their children in these city-wide schools. Aware of the fact that access in the past had depended upon scarce and often distorted knowledge of programs, as well as on patronage, racial preference, and precinct, they conceived of ordering orientation and application booklets and media campaigns to explain the booklets. The approach was similar to private school and college catalog announcements, only here the team proposed that the booklets be printed in English, Greek, Italian, Chinese, Spanish, Portuguese, and French/Haitian. All programs were to be described plainly and directions were to be given on how to apply for three ranked preferences. The same booklets and forms would present the community district schools and programs.

COLLEGE-PUBLIC SCHOOL PAIRINGS

As the court team worked through the visions of city-wide magnet schools and an all-purpose booklet to guide parental preferences, they also sensed the importance of assisting the emergence of educational excellence in the programs. Dentler had led a consortium of colleges and universities in New York City into devising programs of assistance to public schools there from 1965 through 1972. He knew of efforts that had succeeded in other places such as Kansas City, Missouri. Masters Francis Keppel and Charles Willie were concerned with closing the long-standing and wide gap between Boston area higher education and the isolated public instructional system. Scott wanted to intensify the quality of practical field collaboration between the two levels. Another master, Edward McCormack, was convinced that support from colleges and universities and from business and industry would be widely and positively welcomed by Boston parents and taxpayers. The panel's presiding officer, Jacob Spiegel, urged the team to get on with accomplishing the common dream, declaring it a reasonable part of the remedy.

Business and industry had established a task force during 1974 which was proving modestly successful. Using this model, the masters summoned presidents, vice presidents, and deans from twenty colleges and universities in the Greater Boston area to the federal courthouse. Dentler developed a tentative prospectus of pairings, based on the magnet program themes of the city-wide schools and the special capabilities of each institution of higher learning. Tufts University was matched with Boston Technical High, for instance, because Tufts contained a distinguished College of Engineering and a great College of Liberal Arts faculty as well. As the idea was expanded, the masters made sure that community districts were paired with colleges and universities, too, because it was essential that no one part of the system be improved at the expense or neglect of other parts. The Metropolitan Cultural Alliance, a membership organization including 110 cultural agencies such as museums and craft enterprises, was later included in the pairing design.

When the college representatives materialized in groups at the courthouse, the masters explained their goals and asked them to commit their institutions "to support, assist, and participate in the development of educational excellence within and among the public schools of Boston." Some leaders were immediately responsive, among them the presidents of the University of Massachusetts, Boston State College, and Boston University. Others said they would consider it sympathetically. Still others were undecided about costs and the risk of becoming involved in what was already controversial. Spiegel led the discussions, which he kept brief, and then gave everyone thirty-six hours in which to reply.

Spiegel's strategy, worked out with McCormack, was crisp and decisive. There was some huffing and puffing, for his schedule was unlike the rather timeless processes through which academies reach their commitments, but Spiegel emphasized that no one was obligated; a "no, thank you," note, or no reply, would disengage any institution from the prospective pairing. Within his thirty-six hour deadline, however, as McCormack had predicted, every college and university chief officer submitted a positive pledge, albeit many of them with careful notes of qualification about costs.

The President of Northeastern University, Asa Knowles, then the head of the Association of Independent Colleges and Universities in Massachusetts, disapproved of the proposal. He gave Muriel Cohen, a leading education reporter for the *Boston Globe*, the impression that the masters were planning to have the Boston public schools run by colleges and universities, thus generating howls of protest from the school committee and mutterings of defiance from spokesmen for the Boston Teachers Union. This misleading impression was corrected publicly in quick order, however, and the pairing pledges held firm.

When Judge Garrity resumed direct charge over the case, he met twice with the college and university officers and enabled them to renegotiate specific pairings. He helped to establish a steering committee and then wrote the pairings into his May 1975 permanent plan. (See Table 2.2 for a list of 1978 pairings.)

UNIFORMITY AND CONSISTENCY

On the advice of the team, the court ensured the elimination of segregative and discriminatory arrangements of the kind generated by maintaining thirteen different grade structures. Nearly every school in the system was directed to maintain a uniform structure, with grades kindergarten through 5 in the elementary units, 6 through 8 in the middle schools, and 9 through 12 in the high schools. The plan stated that

> each high school shall be a four year, comprehensive institution which serves with equal and uniform excellence of instruction, students seeking general culminating education, those seeking vocational training or experience, and those seeking preparation for post-secondary study. Each District High school shall also serve as an Adult or Multi-purpose Community Education facility.

Approximately 6 out of 155 schools were permitted to vary from this design for specific reasons—for example, to enable continuation of an ungraded, experimentally oriented school.

Every school was directed to have a principal or headmaster, where in 1974 only four in every ten schools had permanently assigned building administrators. Administrative leadership had become corrupted, venal, and racially discriminatory over the years. With but a small handful of exceptions, administrators were recruited from within the ranks of teachers, and at least 95 percent of those holding the rank of acting assistant principal or above were Irish-Americans and Italian-Americans born and educated in Boston. Recruitment from within proceeded not from reviews of leadership potential but from such considerations as ability to muster funds for the campaign chests of committee members. Hundreds of so-called *acting* appointments lasted for many years. These increased dependency, conserved political loyalty, and reduced costs.

TABLE 2.2

College- and University-Public School Pairings, 1978

College or University	Public School (Students Helped)	Types of State-Funded Support
Boston University[a]	All District 1 (1,280)	Basic Reading and Math, Multicultural Education, Career Guidance, Bilingual Instruction, Resource Center
Curry College	Roosevelt Middle (250)	Basic Skills
Simmons College	Jamaica Plain High (886)	Occupational Education, Human Relations, Career Guidance, Special Needs
Wheelock College[a]	6 Elementaries (300)	Language Arts
Boston College	All District 3 (6,734)	Diagnostics, Special Education, Parent Training, Prescriptive Reading
Mass. State Colleges	All District 4 (475)	Special Needs, Teacher Training
Stonehill College	Hyde Park High (1,000)	Basic Reading, Student Aides, Communications, Outdoor Sports, Special Electives
Boston State College	All District 5 (4,697)	Basic Skills, Math Lab, Teacher Workshops, Student Assistance, Others

TABLE 2.2 (cont.)

Mass. College of Art[a]	Burke High (160)	Communications, Arts, Graphics
Univ. of Mass./Boston	All District 6 (5,070)	Resource Center, Diagnostics, Multicultural Arts, Tutoring
Bunker Hill Community College	Charlestown High (500)	Humanistic Education, Career Education, Instructional Aides, Cultural Enrichment
Harvard University	Roxbury High (575)	Tutoring, Special Needs, Media Program, Others
Northeastern University[a]	All District 7 (4,543)	Basic Reading, Home/School Communications
Antioch Institute for Open Education	M.L. King Middle (500)	Language Arts, Career Experience, Parent Involvement, Curriculum Development, Others
Brandeis University	English High (200)	Theater Arts, Bilingual Theater, Art for Special Needs
Emerson College	Copley Square High (500)	Communication Arts, Career Exploration, Parent Involvement
Emmanuel College	Ohrenberger Elem. (650)	Reading, Science, Values Clarification, Others
Lesley College	Hennigan Elem. (781)	Reading
Mass. College of Pharmacy	Mackey Middle (500)	Bilingual Education, Music, Fine Arts, Health Education, Animal Rescue, Others
Mass. Institute of Technology and Wentworth Institute	Umana High (640)	Parent/School Relations, Curriculum Design, Staff Development, Science Magnet, Others
Regis College	Latin Academy (450)	Tutoring, Human Relations, Communications, Others
Suffolk University[a]	Trotter Elem. (450)	Basic Skills
	Wheatley Middle (160)	Multiethnic Backgrounds Exploration (through videotaping, etc.)
Tufts University	Boston Tech. High (300)	Career Education, Reading
Univ. of Mass./Amherst	English High (750)	Alternative Programs, Curricula Upgrading
Wellesley College	Latin School (1,300)	College Preparatory, Tutoring

[a]Also works with other schools not listed.

The court plan and subsequent orders were aimed at equalizing the provision of public instruction. Segregation and the accompanying ravages of racial and ethnic discrimination depended upon the structural framework of patronage and of corrupt and indentured leadership. It was this framework that enabled the committee to execute policies that concentrated educational benefits in a few settings and withheld them from others. Thus, the court had no choice but to demolish and replace that framework. In creating a chain of administrative command, decentralizing authority through community superintendents, setting forth rules for community screening of administrators, requiring one-to-one black and white appointments, making grade structures uniform, and requiring every school to have a permanent principal, the court aimed at achieving equal protection. No mere redistribution of students and teachers would accomplish this end.

Every school was also obligated to provide staff, facilities, and materials for serving students with special needs such as physical handicaps, learning disabilities, or emotional disturbances. Each district was obligated to maintain three or more schools where special education staffs could be concentrated to serve students with severe handicaps. The plan was designed to force the schools to come rapidly into compliance with Chapter 766 of state law which guarantees full and equal educational opportunities for all special needs students.

BILINGUAL PROGRAMS

Under prompting from attorneys for El Comite, the Hispanic parents association, the court team recommended locating and maintaining bilingual programs of instruction for all students whose primary languages were Spanish, Chinese, Greek, French/Haitian, Portuguese, and Italian. Cape Verdian Portuguese instruction was added in 1976, with court approval. These programs were distributed across schools within reach of residential settlements, with some of the programs sited in city-wide magnet schools as well. One magnet school, Rafael Hernandez, was designated a Spanish bilingual and bicultural center. Its student body was established at 66 percent Hispanic and 33 percent white and black American.

The school system had been so laggard in developing programs in compliance with the state bilingual education law as to confound the way toward planning with any accuracy, however. No one could be sure whether 3,000 or 8,000 seats should be reserved, or how big the clusters of classes ought to be within any one school. Most planners were convinced that many bilingual minority students were not enrolled and were "on the streets" or kept at home. School department officials kept insisting that demand for bilingual instruction would not expand much. Court planning in this regard remained hesitant and incomplete.

PARENT PARTICIPATION

In 1974, following the Denver case in part, Judge Garrity directed the establishment of a Biracial Parents Council for every school and a Citywide Parents Advisory Committee (CPAC) to coordinate the committees. These were to be elective committees and were to monitor school desegregation, help improve internal race relations, and advise the court.

The court team recommended that these units, later redesignated Racial/ Ethnic Parent Councils (REPCs), be continued with expanded mandates. It was also recommended that the councils elect members to form Community District Advisory Councils in each of the nine districts and that a Citywide Coordinating Committee (CCC) be formed to coordinate these committees and councils and guide overall compliance with the court plan.

Judge Garrity adopted these recommendations, but he tripled the recommended size of the CCC and continued the life of the CPAC. By November of 1975, in spite of extreme resistance to the formation and election of these various parent bodies, more parents—white, black, and other ethnic groups —were more extensively involved in influencing the direction and day-to-day affairs of public schools than at any time in the history of the Boston system. Their missions and authority were spelled out in detail in the court's orders, and they were explicitly linked with planning the future of the schools by requiring every school to file a lengthy annual report, prepared between parent councils and school staff, on enrollments, attendance, student achievement, facility quality and maintenance, human relations, and program plans.

The Home and School Association objected to the councils because its leaders felt threatened with disestablishment. Generally, however, there was little discussion about the parent participation plans, perhaps because in Boston there were no precedents and therefore no one could imagine these plans would lead to the decline of the patronage and influence practices so endemic to this city.

Judge Garrity had included the Home and School Association as a party to the remedial phases of the case. This body of parents was concerned with more than its own future. Its concerns extended to proposing a remedy, arguing against the court plan, and appealing court orders on several occasions. The value of their inclusion was great. Association members were constrained to work within the system of justice and their views offered worthwhile divergence from those of the plaintiffs, the state board, and, on occcasion, the school committee. In the course of hearings, thanks to the gifted advocacy of Home and School Association attorney Eliot Fremont-Smith, it was possible to discern quickly what remedies were devoid of controversy among reasonable people and what ideas were sensitive.

The main argument presented by Fremont-Smith was sounded repeatedly from the opening hearings in 1975 until late in 1977, when the association began to withdraw. It appeared in motions, legal briefs, a planning proposal, giant map displays, and in an elaborate effort to appeal the entire court plan. It became a yardstick for measuring opposition to or support for other proposals, as Fremont-Smith viewed issues. His argument was that *desegregation must be limited in scope to the schools cited in the liability opinion.* As that comprised perhaps twelve schools operating in 1973–1974, the argument was certainly aimed at reducing the scope of the remedy to one-tenth of that anticipated by other parties.

There is reason to think this notion grew up out of exchanges between Fremont-Smith and the sociologist James Coleman, whom the attorney tracked down to a vacation hideout in a remote rural area in West Virginia. Coleman had not studied the Boston case but he was then active nationally in the search for new ways to counter court remedies. In 1976, he accepted an invitation from prominent antidesegregationists in the Massachusetts legislature, including one who had helped to foment violence in South Boston.

Like all arguments, this one had its tiny grain of truth: No one had shown during the liability hearings that every school in the system was segregated. The plaintiffs had shown, however, that segregative policies of the committee were both intentional and systemic in their consequences. Neither Coleman nor Fremont-Smith, in fairness, was an opponent of school desegregation. Coleman was concerned with remedies that did not polarize urban politics through conflict and that did not empty them of their white, middle-class households. Fremont-Smith, who later gave noteworthy service in attempting to mediate conflicts in South Boston, wanted a remedy his clients could accept.

Arguments by other parties, what is more, were equally narrow and were delivered less eloquently. Mayor White's attorneys played what Judge Garrity came to call "your broken record." It consisted of arguing that nearly every aspect of the court plan was too costly for a city verging on bankruptcy. School committee attorneys specialized in variations on a single theme: The court lacked the authority to do whatever it prepared to do.

STUDENT ASSIGNMENTS

The court team recommended that students whose parents preferred community district schools be assigned on an individual basis. The concept was derived from Dentler's experience in adapting a computer program to assigning students in Harrisburg, Pennsylvania, schools in 1971 and from Scott's experience in designing a student record system at Boston University. It proposed to assign students on the basis of ID number, address, school grade, and ethnicity to the nearest available school that would yield a composition with the ethnic ratio variances set for the district. This method optimizes everyone's chance of assignment to a relatively nearby school. We also related the method to the facilities and boundaries of Boston. Scott found a list of schools that had been defined as fire unsafe or otherwise unfit for school use over the years. The list had been composed by the Public Facilities Commission, and we used it in connection with developing the assignment method. Similarly, Scott reviewed maps of the Boston wards, the Catholic diocese, railroad lines, and rivers.

The Massachusetts Board of Education filed an extremely detailed critique of this recommendation and others, however. Among its criticisms was an argument for avoiding individual assignment methods and using a *geocode* method instead. The plaintiffs, the school department, and the city made similar arguments. Judge Garrity adopted their points of view and ordered the geocode method.

A geocode is a mapped unit of the city, much like a census tract or a precinct, comprising several blocks of real estate. In Boston, geocode units were mapped in 1972 for use by the police department to communicate the locations of calls for radio patrol cars.[6] The geocoded maps had been sold to the school system for use in Phase I. The parties to the case had come to understand and rely upon the 830 geocode units as the preferred basis for planning. Their shared notion of a method was to assign clusters of geocode units within each school district to particular schools, using the already prepared data on prospective students *residing* in each geocode unit, by ethnicity and grade level.

We were adamant in our view that technically superior and more responsive methods had been devised in other cities, but Judge Garrity held to the wisdom of adopting that which expanded, however slightly, the area of consensus among the major adversaries in the suit. The geocodes offered one attractive feature that the judge stressed, too: "Geocode assignment," he stated, "unlike individual or address assignment recommended by the masters, allows students to attend school with their immediate neighbors of all races." The point remained somewhat theoretical in a city where less than one in ten geocode units contained a mix of families by race and ethnicity, but theories have their attractiveness when custom is involved.

A complete analysis of student assignment operations is presented later in this book. Here, we stress the planning features of this matter. Development of the guidelines for assigning students proved to be the most demanding intellectual task confronting the court. None of the planning proposals had treated this problem more than cursorily. Assignment of students in 1974 had been carried out hastily using incomplete guidelines, with poor results in terms of errors and delays. When the masters retired from the case, therefore, Judge Garrity assigned Tom Hayes, the law clerk who had assisted the masters, the task of formulating guidelines on a full-time basis. It took him, even with a mind that worked as logically and smoothly as that of a chess master, about 400 hours to complete the puzzle.

The puzzle solution was derived from (1) analyzing the logic of the plan's features, which included the complications that would result from processing parental applications that listed up to three school preferences; (2) fitting assignment rules to variable ethnic ratios that had to be worked out and tested along the way; (3) devising a method of fitting students from within geocode units to the seat capacities of schools within districts; (4) enabling the clustering of bilingual students on an individual basis, with allowances for interdistrict movement for them and for students with handicaps and disabilities, and (5) making all of the above-mentioned features consistent with city-wide school choices and preventing ways of drawing off students and thus segregating isolated community schools while filling the magnets.

Solving the puzzle also involved creating a special grandfather clause for high school seniors and setting rules for medical, programmatic, and desegregative transfers following initial assignments. Above all, it was essential to devise rules that could hold up every time new and changing conditions intervened. Hayes's guidelines, reviewed and reworked by Judge Garrity, his regular law clerk Terry Seligman, and the two of us, thus became the "set piece" of the plan. Fitting the rules to the computer program and closing gaps between them and the real conditions imposed by the state of student records were accomplished by us in collaboration with two members of the Boston School Department Data Processing Center, Jack Haran and Alfred Tutella.

The guidelines are much more than a puzzle. They are the key to implementing the *equity* aims of the major portions of the plan. Thus, their development was the result of the combined efforts of a dedicated team of lawyers and educators. No other federal school desegregation case on record has achieved as thorough, explicit, and equity-centered a series of assignment guidelines. (True to the most remarkable traditions of the countercultural era in Boston and the legacy of Henry Thoreau, the very gifted Tom Hayes returned to his permanent job as an ice cream scooper at Steve's Ice Cream Parlor soon after completing this part of the plan.)

OTHER ELEMENTS OF THE PLAN

The permanent plan issued on May 10, 1975, contained features not already mentioned. For example, it directed the closing of twenty-two schools and required that ten others closed in 1974 be removed permanently from use. It required the prompt completion of school construction activities at various sites and called for erecting additional new schools, all as part of a design to equalize the quality of facilities and their geographic availability to students. It also called for the repair and renovation of other structures.

Supplementary orders extended the reach of the plan to other vital matters during 1975 and 1976. Safety and security policies and procedures were developed when it became apparent that local and state authorities were likely to plan inadequately. Teacher and administrative desegregation guidelines were prepared. The latter included procedures for community screening of candidates for every permanent position that became vacant.

The effect was to increase greatly the ethnic mix of administrators and, at the same time, to increase the quality of selection and diminish selection through nepotism and patronage.

IMPLICATIONS OF INADEQUATE PLANNING

The *Brown* decision had been aimed at guaranteeing simple justice. Typically, from 1955 to 1970 a school district would be shown to have maintained good facilities and staffs for white students and dilapidated buildings and less qualified, less well-paid staffs for black students. In the Deep South and border states, equity often meant closing two or three of the most deteriorated facilities and then unifying the others. However, by the time of the Denver case, equity had become more complex a term by virtue of dense urban settlements, multiethnic student populations, and diversified curricular programs. In some cases, as in Nashville, the complications grew out of transportation logistics.

But no federal case had the complexities common to the Boston challenge. Dentler had helped plan the desegregation of the New York City school system in 1964, when it was still demonstrably feasible to do so. As David Rogers's study, *110 Livingston Street,* showed, however, the New York City Board of Education was not forced to remedy its wrongs. That city and cities like Philadelphia, Chicago, Cleveland, and Los Angeles are much more difficult to design desegregation plans for than is Boston. But among them and the nation's other largest city systems, only Boston has thus far faced the imperative to redress its wrongs in a system-wide way.

A court is not a planning agency. It lacks qualified and sufficient staff and it cannot work through or mediate diverse subcommunity interests in the ways that urban planners can when, for example, they plan new housing developments or highways or parks. Yet in Boston the court had to act like a planning agency for want of one. None of the proposals submitted by the parties began to be sufficient by constitutional, educational, or technical standards. Even the best of them from a legal perspective—the entry from the plaintiffs—was a shallow and hastily prepared draft version of possibilities.

Had the court settled for a lesser degree of thoroughness, educational equity for all children and youth would have suffered in the long run. No mere reshuffling of bodies will prove conducive to eliminating the ravages of decades of discrimination. If a prompt and sure remedy was to be devised, the court's agents learned they would have to devise it themselves. The *Keyes* decision had made plain the will of the Supreme Court, which was to develop and require the implementation of truly workable plans. It was that ideal we aspired to achieve.

One implication of the court's active role in the planning of Boston school desegregation will become clearer in later chapters. It is that, for a time, the gulf between the school committee and city hall as defendants and the court as their judge was greatly widened. The defendants had not authored the plan. They were the managers and defenders of a system that was unstructured, crusted with decrepitude and public neglect, dual in nature, and underfinanced in all but salaries for regular teachers and administrators.

How could an acting principal, supported by one telephone and one secretary and housed in a deteriorating and fire unsafe schoolhouse, assimilate the plan and act affirmatively? How could the plan's deep reforms be comprehended by those who had been appointed to headquarters positions over the years by reason of nepotism, fealty to board members, or even by purchase of their positions? How could parents, whose elected officials had denounced the court as tyrannical and demonic for two years, take in the positive and even transformative features of the plan and its likelihood of enhancing the life chances of their children? Could the public believe that a truly worthwhile plan for equalizing and reforming public education could come up out of the intergroup conflicts, racial tensions, and political rampages that had stormed across Boston during 1974 and early 1975?

Just as the substance of the liability opinion had become obscured in 1974 by preoccupation with what immediate remedy would be ordered, so the court plan's substance remained obscure for most of 1975. We held a press conference on May 10, 1975, in order to distribute the court memorandum and order and to explain its contents and to answer questions. Media reporters concentrated on only three topics: How much did the order differ from the masters' report? How many students would be bused? and How many white families might flee Boston? Later in the summer, *Boston Globe* coverage of the plan became detailed and instructive for parents, teachers, and students.

But as the opening day of school approached, hundreds of reporters descended on Boston, and all but a handful of them were assigned by their editors to report on incidents of tension and violence. Very few had read the plan and not more than three or four agencies had people in them who were able or willing to explain it to anyone else. Only as issues surrounding compliance with the order were joined in court hearings did the particulars of the plan begin to seep gradually into the public consciousness.[7]

There were also very few voices raised in support of the court plan. The Massachusetts Board of Education and its commissioner, Gregory Anrig, himself a seasoned planner of school desegregation, endorsed it. Governor Michael Dukakis and his Secretary for Educational Affairs, Paul Parks, announced their support. Roman Catholic Cardinal Humberto Medeiros defended it, as did various Protestant and Jewish religious leaders and a dozen civic and social agencies.[8] Boston Teachers Union leaders, who had called for a one-year moratorium on implementation of the plan, did not attack it. This was encouraging in itself, because in April 1975, at the invitation of the union, Scott gave a preview of some elements of the plan at a meeting of 300 teachers who were union building representatives. He found himself shouted at, cursed, and jeered by an angry mob.

The legions of those who attacked the court plan were, in contrast, a noisy army. They included the mayor, the city council, the school committee, the coalition named ROAR and its three "information centers," the Home and School Association, most Boston members of the state legislature, the *Boston Herald-American* (at that time the daily with the largest circulation in Massachusetts), and all but one of the weekly neighborhood newspapers. Misinformation about the plan was disseminated daily through every medium. Judge Garrity received an avalanche of letters from officials and citizens, most of them urging withdrawal of the order or a delay of one year in implementation.

This, then, was the context that surrounded reception of the court desegregation plan. The context extended well beyond Boston. It came to include President Gerald Ford, who announced his belief in the rule of law while he denounced the court plan as a serious mistake. Denunciation and opposition were rarely aimed at the substantive ingredients, except for obsessive attention to the fact that the plan ordered the desegregation of *all* schools in the system (save for a few in East Boston), and that it entailed the *busing* of over 20,000 students.

MISSING ELEMENTS

It is doubtful whether any school desegregation plan ordered by a state or federal court in the years from 1954 to 1975 was as comprehensive, inventive, and detailed as the 1975 court plan for Boston. In the welter of political and civic confusion that followed its issuance, however, this achievement was seldom noted. Critics and appreciators alike also failed to observe what was missing from the plan.

For example, the plan did not specify the machinery for implementation. It called into being an Office of Implementation within the school department, as proposed by chief planner John Coakley, but it did not specify much about its mission, structure, or functions. It called for affirmative action in order to remedy the ravages of discrimination, but it prescribed no program of race and human relations training that would equip administrators, teachers, and municipal civil servants with the means to take affirmative action.

In the hearings before the panel of masters, the president of the Boston Teachers Union, John Doherty, had stated that teachers would need help because "We don't know how to teach *them*." Master Charles Willie asked for clarification of this testimony and was told what he knew but wanted to have as part of the record: The overwhelmingly white and insular cadre of 5,000 teachers did not know how to teach black and other minority students. More importantly, the union asked for training in how to teach ethnically mixed and academically diverse rather than homogeneous groups of students in their classrooms. This and similar tasks were left to the devices of the school committee. The brief and shallow training that resulted was worthless.

The plan had invoked a complicated network of participants, from the bar association, to business and industry, to the colleges and cultural agencies, to parent councils. Still, it overlooked inclusion of black, Chinese, and Hispanic civic organizations, and members of some of these groups felt left out and cut off from the implementation process.

In short, the plan was long on legal remedies, demographics, geographic boundaries, facilities, and organizational structures. But it was short on providing for "practical" remedies involving race relations, curriculum and instruction, and the content of participation. What was missing came to matter more and more poignantly as the school committee perfected a strategy of protracted inaction on anything that was not a direct court order. Every circumstance, from ignorance of the plan, to scope of public opposition fanned by elected officials, to media emphasis upon violence, to a strategy of avoidance that made whatever was missing from the plan an opportunity for nonfeasance, thus conspired to *delay* or confound implementation.

LESSONS FOR PLANNING

A poor school desegregation plan will not equalize or improve learning opportunities for children. A good plan may not have this effect, either, because it may be thwarted in its execution. Yet, good planning is a necessary precondition. We are convinced that the court plan was a good one for many reasons, but if someone plans for another city in another time, how can we help them learn from the Boston experience?

Our first inference is that a school board that has to be brought to trial and convicted of segregation before it acts to remedy past wrongs on its own initiative will not prepare a good plan. There are, however, a few exceptions, such as Minneapolis, Minnesota, that come to mind. Generally, though, a school board will lack the determination and the competence to plan a remedy, and in these cases, planning will have to be conducted by another source.

The plaintiff is also not likely to submit a good plan. Energies for this party go to proving liability. What is left to expend on planning goes to critiquing proposals from others. In the Boston case, the plaintiffs commissioned planning only when it seemed the case might flounder for want of a plan by the school committee. The product was a cautious plan; it concerned *only* student redistribution. To deal with other issues would be to risk reversal on appeal or charges of intent to control overall public instruction.

Although other parties should be added to a case in order to prevent error and to widen the base of civic involvement, the first lesson is that, just as federal litigation is a last resort, the role of the court as plan author must be acted out if all other options fail. The quality of the court plan in turn will depend on the quality of the judge's understanding and interest. From the perspective of legal history, this is the classic circumstance in equity cases. Nothing peculiar is involved. Public school systems are no more complex than a thousand other matters crying out daily for well-planned remediation by judges.

Judge Garrity used the resources traditionally used by the judiciary. He expanded the range of parties; hence, the attorneys and their firms and clients became planning agencies. He appointed experts—a routine procedure. He appointed masters—a less common yet long-standing recourse of courts. He also secured a special-duty law clerk and put him to good use on student assignment rules and made regular use of such significant sources of information as the Community Relations Service staff of the U.S. Department of Justice (directed regionally by Martin Walsh), U.S. marshals, and the FBI. While opposition leaders liked to project the court's actions as being an isolated, remote, and detached type of justice, the facts were very different. In addition to these diverse sources, Judge Garrity had the benefit of unsolicited correspondence from thousands of citizens and he studied the press and assiduously attended to television reporting.

Working under the burden of a political polarization that began developing ten years prior to the court suit, the court acted as the "next best" forum for planning. The best forums, local public agencies such as the school department and city hall, were closed off from use by the school committee. Under these conditions, the court proved to be exceptionally adequate to the challenge.

The entire team of court workers who were empowered to find facts, including the masters and Judge Garrity himself, failed in one substantial respect: They did not get valid, reliable, and complete information on the school system. Instead, to the detriment of the plan, they relied on data provided by the defendant without demanding proof of its veracity or making adequate checks. One of the cruelest lessons of the Boston case has been that the best plans cannot be built upon ignorance or incorrect data on school assignments, on programs and procedures, and on staff and facilities.

We believe that a court and attorneys for plaintiff are, in this regard, victims of structural constraint. Agents of the school system must be treated with civility and even respect if they are to be expected to implement the remedy. The legal fraternity is constrained against creating a new breed of "white-collar desperados." In the Boston case, no one was ever punished, although witnesses, providers of reports, and officers of the schools charged with liaison habitually gave incomplete and misleading information.

The standard of full and forthcoming disclosure, including acknowledgment of ignorance, should be fully enforced. No quarter can be given in finding the facts about enrollments, personnel, programs, operations, administration, and finances. The remedial planning process should be one in which the climate is cleared of deception, pretense, fronting, and guesswork. Most of the serious flaws in the court plan that have materialized in a five-year period of implementation can be traced back to insufficient and incorrect information.

One other kind of flaw in the court plan stemmed from an intellectual failure, we suspect, and that was the emphasis on structural remedies to the point of neglect of *functional* concerns. If learning opportunities are to be equalized, teaching practices must be changed. We know much from good educational research and development in the 1960s about effectiveness in teaching in urban schools and how to foster it, but we stood shy of intervening in this domain. Race relations programming was neglected. Guidance counseling was left to run its customarily stupefying course. Retraining of staff to meet changing patterns in multiethnic instruction was not designed into the plan.

The literature on school desegregation is replete with evidence that desegregation in itself will not modify school achievement.[9] A good desegregation plan will also be designed to affect the educative process directly. Our plan affected the structural conditions that underlie that process, to be sure, but direct intervention into teaching was avoided.

The legal foundation for this avoidance is fairly firm. It is that a public agency is to be left to perform its chartered mission with its customary "regularity." In other words, a court may shape the standards or ends of practice, but it is to avoid intrusion into the means, save where complaints are raised and a showing of evidence is made. In Boston, the NAACP, as the initiating client, exercised its historic strategy of avoiding implication in the locality's sway over practice. There were a few exceptions made, as with an effort to make South Boston High School safe for black students or to close it down. Otherwise, the only parties ever to refer to *functions* were El Comite and the Boston Teachers Union.

We think the legal foundation can be changed, and we think we see the way to do it, in the illumination given to hindsight. Educators, ourselves included, will have to demonstrate through a showing of facts the causal connection between the elimination of racial/ethnic discrimination and affirmative action toward reforming public instruction. Lawyers, like other professionals, lack perspective on pedagogy. The educational literature has not filled the gap between the cold structural features of desegregation and the vital functioning of teaching and guidance. When that gap has been filled (we hope through the efforts funded since 1973 by the National Institute of Education), it is likely that court plans will extend to include a reform of pedagogy.

Finally, the Boston case shows, in our opinion, that a good desegregation plan should be very comprehensive. The court plan approximated this goal but fell short in several aspects. Components were added later, always result-

U.S. District Court Judge W. Arthur Garrity, Jr. in his chambers.

The Panel of Masters, February–April 1975. Upper left, retired Massachusetts Supreme Court Justice Jacob J. Spiegel, presiding officer; upper right, former State Attorney General Edward J. McCormack, Jr., associate presiding officer; lower left, former U.S. Commissioner of Education Francis Keppel; and lower right, Harvard University Professor Charles V. Willie.

Gregory R. Anrig, Commissioner of Education, Commonwealth of Massachusetts.

Thomas Atkins, president of the Boston Chapter of the National Association for the Advancement of Colored People (1972–76), former member of the Boston City Council, and a prime mover as an attorney and a political leader in mounting the case against the Boston School Committee. Boston Globe Photo

Sandra L. Lynch, Counsel for the State Board of Education, Commonwealth of Massachusetts.

Boston Globe Photo

Court-appointed experts (1975–80) Marvin B. Scott, former Boston University associate dean of education, and Robert A. Dentler, former Boston University dean of education. Boston Globe Photo

Charles Leftwich, associate superintendent of the Boston Public Schools and manager of desegregation operations, 1973–77.

Boston Globe Photo

John R. Coakley, chief desegregation planner for the Boston School Committee (1974–75) and associate superintendent and senior advisor in charge of the Department of Implementation since 1977.

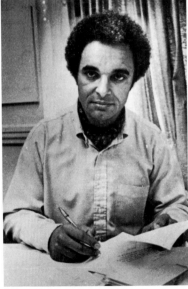

James P. Breeden, executive director of the Citywide Coordinating Committee (1976–77) and senior advisor to the superintendent for planning since 1978.

Boston Globe Photo

The Boston School Committee in April 1974. Left to right: Paul R. Tierney, Kathleen Sullivan (Alioto), Chairman John J. Kerrigan, John J. McDonough, and Paul J. Ellison.

Courtesy of the Boston School Department

ing in confusion, delay, and problems of technical contradictions between earlier and later directives. A comprehensive plan for desegregation will deal, in a single document, with student assignments, personnel desegregation at all levels, facilities, programs, districting, administrative design, allocation of authority, citizen participation, security, transportation, public information, implementation, monitoring, race and human relations training, student organization and codes of discipline, budget and costs, and the reform of teaching and guidance counseling. Fragmentation of planning causes loss of momentum, multiplies court disputes, and generates new problems along the way. Any plan requires alterations over time. A comprehensive plan may be subjected to better periodic review and more rational revision than a partial plan.

A POSTSCRIPT ON THE POLITICS OF PLANNING

Even court-based planning is ultimately a political act, for it is a process that affects the allocation of resources and values.[10] In the Boston case, the politics of planning a remedy grew out of the nature of the Panel of Masters. Retired Justice Spiegel was identified with service to the court, but the other three masters had constituencies of their own. This was wholly natural and appropriate, certainly, and it would be fairly impossible to appoint federal masters who lacked eminence based upon memberships and connections with reference groups of great influence.

The consequence, however, was that three of the four masters expected their plan to be adopted by Judge Garrity. They worked energetically during their seven-week tenure to build an envelope of political and civic support for their plan. They viewed their task in part as that of throwing a rope bridge (anchored on one cliff in constitutionality and on the other side by public acceptance) across the chasm created by school committee defiance.

When Judge Garrity modified even 10 percent of their proposals, in the light of new arguments and evidence, the small bridge snapped. Newspapers such as the *Boston Globe* celebrated the masters' plan and deplored the changes. City hall spokesmen cheered the one and denounced the other. Various interest groups announced a crisis of betrayal.

The masters retired from the case too early to be able to grasp the need for changes. Their bridge would not have withstood subsequent pressures against city-wide desegregation in any event, but the masters could only see the short-term implications. Judge Garrity also did not remain in close enough continuous contact with his team during the seven weeks; thus, he could not stem the disappointment caused among three of the masters when he tried later to ease the shock. Indeed, he made a point of standing apart from the masters and did not discuss their findings of fact or law, or their plans with them until after they filed their report. In his view, this was proper judicial conduct. Moreover, it took us, as the experts who continued to advise the court, four more weeks of work in order to accept the necessity for revision.

Hindsight persuades us that a team effort is essential to desegregation planning. The team should be obligated, however, to have frequent exchanges with the presiding judge, and its members should be retained until a *final* court order is issued. Judge Garrity's team achieved an extraordinary level of creative productivity. Its results were not the fruits of "groupthink," for the seven members displayed divergent ideas and sought out diverse external sources.

But a powerfully effective group effort generates deep ego investments in the product, especially when the task is accomplished under great cross-pressures and on a tight schedule. The team that produced the final court plan included Judge Garrity, his regular clerk, Terry Seligman, the special clerk, Tom Hayes, and the two of us. Martin Walsh contributed to special portions of the plan. For the sake of comprehension and resolution of tensions extraneous to the question of merit, the team should have included the masters. None of us foresaw this in January of 1975, and by April, the Panel of Masters had retired, by prior agreement.

NOTES

1. *Final Report of the Masters*, U.S. District Court, District of Massachusetts, in *Morgan v. Kerrigan*, March 31, 1975.

2. In his "Recommendations of the Special Master on Status Reports," Daniel R. McCarthy wrote, "On September 30, 1977, following hearings on school closings, [my] report set forth a series of findings . . . regarding the lack of effective planning and coordination in such important functions as transportation, computer utilization, and accounting and financial management,' as well as failure to utilize modern management tools and techniques in the operation of the school district . . . [Now] it does not appear that the defendants have heeded the findings or followed the recommendations . . . which the Special Master viewed then, and still views, as vital to proper desegregation implementation." *Robert A. Reed et al., v. James A. Rhodes et al.*, Case No. C73–1300, U.S. District Court, Northern District of Ohio, Eastern Division, July 30, 1979.

3. The committee and department moved to a renovated, much-improved facility at 26 Court Street in 1977. One year later, most of the furnishings were in place.

4. NAACP Legal Defense and Educational Fund, *It's Not the Distance, It's the Niggers*, New York, 1972.

5. For a good essay on community districting, see Mario D. Fantini, "Afterword," in Naomi Levine, *Ocean Hill–Brownsville*, Popular Library Edition, New York City, 1969, pp. 137–155.

6. After selling the geocode maps to the school committee, the Boston Police Department stopped using them. Apparently, they had little orienting value and no pinpoint accuracy for patrol cars. We never did learn the technical rationale underlying delineation of the units.

7. J. Michael Ross et al., *The Boston School Desegregation Crisis: An Historical and Narrative Account*, Part IV, National Opinion Research Center, Chicago, Illinois, 1978.
8. U.S. Civil Rights Commission, *Desegregating the Boston Public Schools: A Crisis in Civic Responsibility*, Washington, D.C., August 1975.
9. Nancy St. John, *School Desegregation*, John Wiley and Sons, New York City, 1975.
10. Robert A. Dentler, *Urban Problems*, Rand McNally, Chicago, Illinois, 1978.

STUDENT ASSIGNMENTS 3

CRUX OF THE PLAN

THE SOCIAL AND EDUCATIONAL POLICY STRANDS in every school desegregation plan are woven together around the method of assigning students. No matter how many other considerations may be taken up in a plan, and no matter how many commentators concentrate on those considerations—which range from the goods and evils of busing to studies of achievement outcomes among students —the point of a school desegregation plan is above all to eliminate the deliberate separation of students by race and ethnicity from equal access to educational opportunities.[1]

As we stated earlier, a plan that lacks a sound method for assigning students will not prove workable. This method becomes the measure of quality in both planning and implementation. There are other quality measures, as we shall show in later chapters, and Chapter Two showed the pains taken by the court in the Boston case to perfect a good assignment method. This chapter is concerned with what that method revealed about the Boston school system and about the quality of implementation.

BACKGROUND

As Judge Garrity's liability judgment stated, prior to 1974 Boston public school students had for decades been assigned to specific schools on the basis of expediency and group influence. A neighborhood assignment system had been preserved for some neighborhoods but not for many others. In those where the system had been preserved, families with influence could make alternative arrangements if they wanted their children to attend schools outside their neighborhoods.

Thousands of students were assigned annually to schools distant from their homes. Others who sought favorable assignments were sent to walk-in neighborhood schools they did not wish to attend. Each year, arrangements changed often enough so that parents without special access to information were unable to make long-term plans for their children. Thousands of other families also used the public schools one year, moved their children into non-public schools the next, and then arranged for their readmission to public schools the following year or some years later.

Because there were thirteen different grade structures operating by 1972, students might attend as many as seven schools, some for only one year, in moving across the system from grades 1 through 12. For some students—especially those who were labeled gifted or slow learners—tracking systems by alleged ability were maintained, while for others no tracks were available. As far as we can determine, the notion of a rational, fair, and rule-based system of student assignments was less believable among Bostonians familiar with the public schools than was the notion of honest and clean city government.

The parents in some neighborhoods were satisfied with the assignment arrangements they had achieved from 1940 to 1970. They were not, however, satisfied with the physical conditions of *their* schools (they had every reason to think of the schools within a two-mile radius of their homes as *their* schools, not the city's). These neighborhoods included East Boston, Charlestown, South Boston, parts of Hyde Park, and West Roxbury. These were firmly consolidated, virtually all-white ethnic enclaves.

Some of these neighborhoods were old and some, like West Roxbury, were young and growing. There, a network of small neighborhood schools had been built to accommodate the children of upwardly mobile middle class families with wage earners who were merchants, white collar civil servants, politicians, technicians, and service professionals and managers.

In East Boston, school facilities were old and very dilapidated, but parents expected their children to be able to attend school somewhere on that narrow split of land. They showed little concern with or interest in the schools of the rest of Boston. The struggles in East Boston were aimed at getting better facilities for that neighborhood.

Insularity within these neighborhoods was extreme. Even in the early 1970s we met adolescents who believed that people from other neighborhoods were strange, different, and dangerous by definition. The insularity was neither singularly ethnic nor socioeconomic: Irish-Americans from Charlestown were isolated from Irish-Americans from the same income and occupational strata in South Boston, for example. Roxbury and the South End were not objects of avoidance by residents of other enclaves for racial or social class reasons alone, by any means. The insularity was a matter of historically reinforced geographic isolation and subcultural evolution.[2]

Roxbury and the South End had themselves been enclaves of this kind at one time, but after World War II, each became an area of rapid in- and out-migration. Jeremiah E. Burke High School, for example, was the last high school to be erected in Boston between its completion in 1934 and the building of English High in 1973. Burke was designed to accommodate Jewish girls, for it stood in the center of a stable, highly developed, and insular Jewish neighborhood. The fact that its entryway is built to look like the nave of an Anglican cathedral appears to be a symbol of the assimilation motif that underlay public instruction in Boston. But the important point is that Roxbury itself did not become a predominantly black and Hispanic settlement until 1955, two decades after Burke was built.

If an urban ecologist were to divide Boston into its twenty-two residential neighborhoods (the number varies with different assumptions about what comprises a neighborhood), he or she would find that in 1970 only six of them were racially and ethnically mixed. More than that number were bounded by a racial frontier—a location where one block was virtually all black and the next block was all white, but these are not unsegregated neighborhoods.

Under this ecological condition, the concept of children and youth moving out of their neighborhoods and into "alien" ones each day seemed fantastic as well as dangerous. The exceptions were selective. White students had long been bused to Boston Technical High School in the center of black Roxbury. That school was lodged in what had been Roxbury Memorial High School, until Roxbury became a black community. At each level in the system, but especially at the high school and middle or junior high school levels, students traveled outside their neighborhoods in annually increasing numbers, but by special arrangements they traveled to virtually all-white or all-black schools. Under these conditions, system-wide desegregation seemed unimaginable.

Phase I reduced greatly the number of predominantly black and other minority concentrations, while leaving intact some eighty-five all-white schools. Phase II thus loomed before the white public as an unthinkable transformation of conditions. During one court hearing the attorney for the Home and School Association, Eliot Fremont-Smith, presented maps to show that *if* students were assigned system-wide to the school nearest them, the schools would appear to be *more* segregated than under their school committee assignments in 1973. His argument was that assignments already mitigated the residential effects of extreme residential segregation. What Fremont-Smith and Cantrowitz, his demographer, did not know, however, was that thousands of other students were assigned to more distant schools *by race*, so that either way—by neighborhood proximity alone or by the gerrymandering of attendance zones, segregation prevailed. The difference was slight and the alternative of assignment to equalize access was the one policy not considered.

RACIAL BALANCE PROPAGANDA

After the state legislature enacted the Racial Imbalance Act in 1965, political leaders, policy scientists, and educators began to question the concept of racial balance. Its critics stated that the concept implied that the mere reshuffling of students by race was desirable. What it really implied, however, was that a certain racial mix produced by employing the principles of statistics, was legally and educationally sound. It implied quite firmly that the absence of such a mix was itself a violation of the law.

The constitutionality of the state act was upheld on several occasions between 1966 and 1974, and the distinction between the state legislature's concept of racial balance and the federal court's concept of desegregation was never fully comprehended by a majority of the public. As the U.S. Supreme Court had made plain in at least two cases, the Constitution had nothing to say on the issue of racial balance, while it did proscribe deliberate racial and ethnic separation of public school students.

When the court plan was issued, however, and those who understood some parts of it scanned the reports, they merged with that large group of citizens who understood nothing about the plan to conclude that it was a racial balance order. After all, it followed Phase I, when the state law had been implemented on a statistical basis. It hinged on things called variable ethnic ratios. It prescribed the racial and ethnic composition of student bodies in every school in the Boston public system.

As the student assignment process got underway in June of 1975, opposition to the guidelines built up like a giant summer thunderhead on the basis of a prevalent belief that a numbers game had been ordered and was taking shape. The ethnic ratios for each district, the detailed guidelines, and the application booklet, as well as the prospect of computerized processing of applications, all combined to fuel this gathering storm of opposition. That the order would impinge upon even the elite examination schools suggested to many opposed to it that discriminating standards of selection were about to be confused with discriminatory standards.

Local news coverage of the plan was exhaustive but not comprehensive. The Boston Bar Association produced and disseminated a well-exposited analysis of the case and its place in the context of the law, but this document was rather densely reasoned and required a fairly high degree of literacy from readers. Between May and September of 1975, then, a growing public awareness of the wide scope of the plan and its effects on assignments developed against a backdrop of ignorance about the legal differences between racial balance and desegregation and about the rules for assigning students under the new plan. At our request, Muriel Cohen of the *Boston Globe* prepared one very complete report on who would go where to school, but with this one exception: Press coverage concerned politics, not law or the details of assignments.

IMPLEMENTATION BEGINS

The order said little more about implementation than that student "assignments shall be made by a staff unit designated by the Superintendent, under the supervision of court representatives," the latter meaning the court experts. In previous parts of the order, the court had referred repeatedly not only to the superintendent but also to an entity it called the school department.

All of this sounded sensible enough, to be sure, and it meant that the court intended to refrain from taking part in direct administration of the system. After all, far less well-funded and well-staffed public school districts throughout the Deep South and the border states had risen for twenty years to such a directive to handle implementation themselves, and Boston had just completed most of the Phase I school year. Some group, surely, had manned the public machinery of implementation.

In fact, the school committee had in April cashiered its superintendent, William Leary, chiefly for this reason: he had, indeed, attempted to implement the law. Leary was a complete lame duck by the time the court issued its permanent plan. A new superintendent, Marion Fahey, had been appointed, but she was scheduled to take charge on September 1. How knowledgeable she would prove to be about desegregation was unknown, as her direct experience with Phase I was relatively slight.

A second fact was rather well understood among the parties: There was no such entity as "the school department." Certainly, there were administrative personnel assigned to headquarters, but no unified chain of command existed, and the court plan required that a chain be created immediately and that it be built up out of that mythical department. What the court actually meant was that the school department was to designate everyone who worked on the system payroll as a member of an organization—a civil bureaucracy—and to distinguish clearly between that organization and the school committee itself.

But the system had operated for years as if committee members were administrators and as if top administrators like the superintendent, business manager, chief structural engineer, and custodial engineer were coequal agents serving not only the will of the committee but also the wills of individual members to whom each was more or less beholden. Teachers and other field staff thus did not define themselves as members of a public service department. Headquarters personnel defined themselves as working for one or another of the chief agents. For example, chief engineer Anthony Galeota had separate municipal statutory authority to plan and contract for school repairs and minor renovations. He also had seventy headquarters staff members working under him to do his, not the superintendent's, bidding.

Certain other headquarters units did not report in any clear way to any of these chief officers, but had a strange historical autonomy of their own, with their own lines of communication to the schools. What there was of true bureaucratic structure tended to be unified through "Superintendent's Circulars," complicated written directives sent to all administrators and posted in all schools on an irregular basis. The circulars covered every imaginable facet of policy, program, and operations.

Superintendent Leary had very little time in which to act. The court plan was published on May 10. The first deadline on its timetable was for the filing of a "Print-ready copy of the Orientation and Application Booklet for parents and students," no later than May 19. It was to be published in seven different languages, mailed to all parents and guardians on May 27, and returned for processing by June 6.

Leary rose to the occasion. He turned to his own administrative assistants, men who had helped him thread his way through Phase I and who were themselves without clear career prospects since Leary's contract was not being renewed. He also turned to John Coakley, the staff planner for the school committee, and to the members of the Educational Planning Center.

With the help of bilingual teachers in the system, the booklet (in all seven languages) was prepared on time. The school committee disassociated itself from the booklet in 1975, and its opening section emphasized the fact that the booklet was the product of court orders. A year later, however, the committee members scrambled to get their names printed on the title page of every issue, once they realized that parents really studied the booklet and that it constituted a genuine catalog of the educational offerings and facilities of the system. What is more, the booklet became important to the committee members because they could orient themselves to the particulars of a system some of them barely understood.*

By the first week in June, however, Leary found he had a mutiny on his hands. Joseph Carey, director of the Educational Planning Center, and Robert Murray, associate director, refused Leary's appointment of them to head up

---

*In a 1976 television show moderated by reporters Rowland Evans and Robert Novack, Dentler, representing the court, discovered that school committee members Louise Day Hicks, Kathleen Sullivan, and Paul Tierney did not know how many buildings comprised the system, how many students were enrolled, the ethnic composition, and many other rudimentary facts about Boston public schools.

the Student Assignment Unit, which the court had ordered be created to staff assignment operations. Others on lower echelons resisted further involvement in assignments. Leary turned to Coakley and to his own administrative assistants, Edwin Lambert and John Halloran, to carry out the task. Later, he placed the system's only black associate superintendent, Charles Leftwich, another of his own appointees, in overall charge of implementation.

Implementation, such as it was during the first months after the court order, was based not at school headquarters, but at a nearly deserted military base on a huge wharf in South Boston. This had been the home for the Educational Planning Center. It was a location that offered safety from protests and protection of the application forms that were pouring in from Boston parents. Most of all, the location enabled the school committee to disassociate itself utterly from the implementation process.

Two vital operations were conducted from the South Boston base; mailed-in applications were opened, classified, and partially coded (see Figures 3.1 and 3.2), and staff began the task of mapping out the geocode units that would be assigned or attached to each school within the eight community school districts. We had been assigned by Judge Garrity to supervise these operations, which we did on a daily basis. In the period from June 1 through June 29, we came to realize that staff members did not know how to set up or carry out the most elementary sorting, classifying, mapping, or analytical procedures. There were individuals who were competent and even gifted, but for three weeks, nothing resembling an operating table of organization took clear form. Responsibility for errors, delays, and even for the receipt and dissemination of supervisory communications was impossible to locate.

As the mail continued to be opened, however, something important happened. It became evident that of the 67,000 parents who had been sent the orientation and application booklet, more than 42,000 had responded, even though filing an application was not obligatory. In addition, the preference rankings were carefully completed and many contained penciled-in notes about the needs and interests of students. Typical was the mother who wrote along the margin of the form, "My George don't hear good. He don't talk good. What have you got for George?"

For the dozens of exteachers assigned to work on the applications, maps, and assignments, the message was soul stirring. After all of the conflict, after years of uncertainty and neglect, parents wanted very earnestly and positively to interact with their public schools. They were demonstrably prepared to participate in the assignment process.

THE DATA PROCESSING CENTER

As the applications were batched and classified, they were transported to the system's data processing center, located five miles away at Boston Technical High School in the center of Roxbury, for keypunching and translation onto IBM computer tapes. In the course of relocating supervision from the military base to this center, we realized that the court timetable, requiring that proposed assignments be filed with the court on June 20, would not be met.

The data processing center itself was only a few years old. It was not connected by cable and terminals with city hall or school headquarters. Indeed, it was isolated in every way from the sources and the users of its services. Its director, James Daley, was the former head of the mathematics department in the Technical High School upstairs. His professional experience with computer programming was limited and his disposition toward student assignments for purposes of desegregation was as negative as that of most other senior officials in the system.

Within a very few days it became evident that neither the fledgling assignment unit nor the staff of the data processing center was capable of implementing the assignment guidelines. Student records were in grave disarray, as they had been for a decade. Initial computerization of those records had improved their quality greatly, yet they were in temporarily unusable condition. And, they remained incomplete. Students were still listed who had already been discharged, other students were still listed three and four times under redundant identification numbers, addresses were still wrong, and zip codes were still unavailable. And often, where addresses and names were in order, the records had listed students incorrectly as to school or grade or age. Most fundamentally, data on race and ethnicity were riddled with errors.

These, like other mistakes, were not the fault of data processing, nor could they be corrected without elaborate and protracted communications with school principals in the field. With the schools running toward the end of the school year, and with principals, teachers, and clerks scheduled to take off for vacation within a few days, the records had to be relied upon in their impossibly invalid and unreliable condition.

This was when we began to realize that there were not 85,001 students enrolled in the Boston public schools—the number of names provided the court early in April on a printout from the computer and the number of seats provided for students by court order. Nearly 3,000 names were "cleaned" from the Alpha list three weeks later, as end of year reports on missing and withdrawn students were filed. Associate Superintendent Leftwich and administrative assistants Lambert and Daley took this as routine. At first fearing our supervision, they volunteered no explanations for the flux of records or for their error-ridden nature. As far as most of the committee members were concerned, this is how things had always been, and from their point of view, student records had never been in such good shape.

It should be noted that on a direct order from the court, Scott hired thirty temporary secretaries and installed them at tables at 26 Court Street, the new headquarters of the school system, before that building came into use. Under his supervision and with administrative procedures he devised, they reviewed, verified, and corrected entries on the Alpha list of students in an

FIGURE 3.1

Kindergarten Application Form, 1979

BOSTON PUBLIC SCHOOLS
APPLICATION FOR STUDENT ASSIGNMENT: YEAR 1979-1980
KINDERGARTEN I and II
STUDENTS NOT CURRENTLY ENROLLED

For office use only

1. Pref. 1 2 3 4 5 6

I. Results of LAU Home Language Survey
   A. Based on the results of the LAU Home Language Survey, does the student require a bilingual educational program?
      Yes_____ No_____

   B. If the answer to question A is *yes*, parent/guardian must fill in the appropriate Bilingual Application (blue form) only.
      If the answer to question A is *no*, parent/guardian must fill in this application only.

II. Personal Information (Please print)   Date_____

   Name of Student Last _____ First _____ Middle Initial _____

   Sex   M_____ F_____   Date of Birth   Mo_____ Day_____ Yr._____

   Address _____
              Apt. No.   Street No.   Street   Section of City   Zip Code
   Home Phone_____ Grade for September, 1979_____

   Name of Parent/Guardian   Last _____ First _____ Middle Initial _____

   Race or Ethnic Group. (Check one of the following):

   Black   _____   Hispanic   _____   Native American _____
                                                         (American Indian)
   White   _____   Asian   _____   Other _____

III. Choice(s) of Assignment:
   Directions: Mark number 1 next to the school of your first choice.
               Mark number 2 next to the school of your second choice.
               Mark number 3 next to the school of your third choice.
               Sign this application at the bottom.

                 NO CHOICES FOR MAGNET SCHOOLS OR PROGRAMS CAN BE GUARANTEED

   Half-Day Programs
   20_____Community District School
   14_____Curley Elementary
   17_____Haley Elementary
   19_____Hernandez Elementary
   30_____Jackson-Mann Elementary
   32_____Ohrenberger Elementary
   33_____Trotter Elementary

   Extended-Day Program
   21_____Community District School
   34_____Guild
   35_____Hale
   36_____Hennigan
   37_____McKay
   09_____Lyman (restricted to residents of District 8 or black and other minority students)

Signature of Parent/Guardian_____ Date _____

Verifier must attach two proofs of address, and a Birth Certificate. _____
                                                          Signature of Verifier, District/School

                              Keep bottom copy for your personal records

FIGURE 3.2

High School Application Form, 1980

BOSTON PUBLIC SCHOOLS
APPLICATION FOR STUDENT ASSIGNMENT
HIGH SCHOOL LEVEL
STUDENTS NOT CURRENTLY ENROLLED

For Grades 10, 11, 12

See Reverse Side
for Humphrey Center

For office use only

L. Pref. 1 2 3 4 5 6

I. Results of LAU Home Language Survey

A. Based on the results of the LAU Home Language Survey, does the student require a bilingual educational program?

Yes _____ No _____

B. If the answer to question A is *yes*, parent/guardian must fill in the appropriate Bilingual Application (yellow form) only.

If the answer to question A is *no*, parent/guardian must fill in this application only.

II. Personal Information (Please print)   Date _____

Name of Student   Last _____   First _____   Middle Initial _____

Sex   M ____ F ____   Date of Birth   Mo. ____ Day ____ Yr. _____

Address _____
Apt. No.   Street No.   Street   Section of City   Zip Code

Home Phone _____   Grade for September, 1980 _____

Name of Parent/Guardian Last _____   First _____   Middle Initial _____

Last School of Assignment: _____
School Name   City   State

Race or Ethnic Group. (Check one of the following):

Black _____   White _____   Asian _____   Hispanic _____   Native American _____
(American Indian)

III. Choice(s) of Assignment:

Directions: Mark number 1 next to the school of your first choice.
Mark number 2 next to the school of your second choice.
Mark number 3 next to the school of your third choice.

NO CHOICES CAN BE GUARANTEED

20 ____ Community District School
71 ____ English High School
72 ____ Boston High School
74 ____ Copley Square High School
75 ____ Madison Park High School
76 ____ Umana School of Science and Technology (entry at grades 9 and 10 only)
80 ____ Business Education at East Boston High School (entry at grades 9 and 10 only)
82 ____ Agri-Business and Natural Resources Occupations at West Roxbury High School (entry at grades 9 and 10 only)
85 ____ Autobody or Sheet Metal at South Boston High School (entry at grades 9 and 10 only)
81 ____ Automotive at Brighton High School (entry at grades 9 and 10 only)
84 ____ Architectural Woodworking/Furniture Finishing/Upholstery at Dorchester High School (entry at grades 9 and 10 only)
88 ____ Machine Shop at East Boston High School (entry at grades 9 and 10 only)
83 ____ Machine Shop at Hyde Park High School (entry at grades 9 and 10 only)
86 ____ Electrical at Charlestown High School (entry at grade 9 and 10 only)
87 ____ Printing at Boston Technical High School (entry at grades 9 and 10 only)
89 ____ HUMPHREY CENTER - ENGLISH HIGH (entry at grades 10 and 11 only)
90 ____ HUMPHREY CENTER - MADISON PARK HIGH (entry at grades 10 and 11 only)

STUDENTS CHOOSING 89 OR 90 MUST CHOOSE ONE, TWO, OR THREE OF THE PROGRAMS
BELOW: INDICATE YOUR ORDER OF CHOICE BY MARKING "1" "2" and "3"
___ GRAPHICS MEDIA   ___ COMMERCIAL MALL   ___ CONSTRUCTION
___ HEALTH   ___ METALS FABRICATION/MANUFACTURING

FOR DESCRIPTIONS OF PROGRAMS SEE APPLICATION FOR HUMPHREY CENTER (REVERSE SIDE)

Signature of Parent/Guardian _____   Date _____

Verifier must attach Two Proofs of Address and Language Forms.

Signature of Verifier, District/School _____

effort to compensate for the list's deficiencies. The procedures he installed were still visible on blackboards in headquarters two years later.

Incidentally, most commentators on urban school desegregation have never worked directly with student records. They do not have a sense of the impact of big-city dynamics upon enrollments, assignments, promotions, and programs. Even a meticulously empirical and systematic analyst such as Christine Rossell, who has conducted important studies of the white flight issue and served on the Citywide Coordinating Committee in Boston, has never immersed herself in the record files.[3] As a result, commentators and advocates think of state attendance records as reliable and valid indicators.

In fact, such records are seldom accurate. Families move as often as three times a year. Children do not begin to attend school until October. Names are given incorrectly. Families merge and break up at high velocity. Temporary withdrawals are endemic. Suspension rates are high. Illnesses take a vast toll among the urban poor, and intrafamily disputes or neighborhood antipathies flare up and make school-going a temporarily dangerous voyage.

Conversely, public schools are pathetically underequipped for charting student turnover. Some straggle on with one secretary and one telephone as the resources put into the breach for a student body of 1,000. Classroom teachers tire of filling out forms that flow from headquarters like a paper avalanche. Court orders to control this flux rationally bounce like small rocks down the steep sides of an erupting volcano.

These limitations were not known to the public. Assignment decisions had to be made under tight security during a period of political turmoil, and the press could not get an accurate story on why assignments were behind schedule. More crucially, the one competent computer programmer in the little center was Jack Haran, a temporary employee who had to carry out the task of fitting the court's guidelines into a series of appropriate programs. Several times during June and July of 1975, members of the school committee harassed Haran. They notified him that his position had been abolished. They terminated his employment. At one point, they even directed him to stay out of the data processing center.

Haran hung in, however. He worked an average of eighteen hours a day throughout June of 1975 and developed the computer programs and operations that made implementation of the guidelines possible. It is to Director James Daley's credit that he did not drive Haran out of the center. It was the associate director, Albert Tutella, who supported and fostered Haran's work and became the administrative activator that made it fruitful. Haran's perseverance proves that every enterprise must locate somewhere within its ranks someone with the skills, the intellect, and the doggedness of will to make fulfillment of an objective possible.

Working round the clock, seven days a week, the assignment unit staff, the mappers, the data processing center staff, the supervising court experts, but above all Jack Haran, found a way to render sensible the proposed assignment of 80,000 students. On the Fourth of July Judge Garrity spent the day with his clerk, Terry Seligman, and with us, personally reviewing the assignments and making last-minute changes in the maps before the computer was turned on to prepare the mailers notifying parents of the outcomes of the new assignment process. The court's aim in May had been to send out the assignments before the public school year ended. That deadline was missed and the news went out to join the gathering storm.

LEARNING BY DOING

The first round of assignments in July of 1975 told the court most of what it would learn in greater depth over the next four years about the deeper difficulties associated with implementing school desegregation. First, the court discovered that its assignment guidelines were predicated on the existence of adequate records and adequate data processing capabilities. Indeed, the guidelines were legally and technically highly sophisticated. While they entailed no more than twenty-five general decision rules, these required an additional fifty specific decision rules to be applied during the assignment process.

The student records, in contrast, needed constant scrutiny, repair, and reworking, just to be kept accurate and up to date. Still missing from the processing system, for example, was a method for verifying the accuracy of a student's identification number, name, sex, age, ethnicity, address, or zip code. Programmatic data on grade level, special needs, bilingual status, and the like were even less verifiable.

Naturally, it did not take long for members of the court to learn that the student assignment rules were too sophisticated to be fitted simply or directly to the data on the student population. In action anthropology, the equivalent would have been for planners to spend months designing a water system for installation as a plant in a remote locality, only for them to find upon arrival that villagers had yet to learn, let alone to accept, the value of boiling water before consuming it.

The court also learned that the authority, responsibility, and resources needed to manage student records and prepare student assignments had never been lodged within a single unit of the school system. Even under the new mandate for an office of implementation with an assignment unit, authority and responsibility remained scattered. One group assigned students to the kindergartens, another department assigned students to special education classes, and still another assigned students to vocational education programs. A very new and cross-pressured little unit was in charge of bilingual screening and assignments. Not until the court ordered the creation of a large, overarching Department of Implementation in the spring of 1977 were these divergent agencies obligated to coordinate their activities.

The court also learned that few public school personnel were competent to design, let alone to maintain and modify, a student record and assignment system. The few who, like Jack Haran, Charles Leftwich, and Albert Tutella, materialized from within the ranks and, from pride of craft, undertook the task, were banished or otherwise punished by their superiors or by members of the school committee.[4] Public school districts do not select administrators and technicians on the basis of their ability to perform such tasks. They promote teachers from within their field ranks, and very few teachers know much of anything about information management systems. Those who do learn, later wish they had not done so.

Very few persons associated with the court case comprehended the profound instability of the Boston public schools. Only insiders with long familiarity knew that each year thousands of parents seek admission of their children sometime between August 15 and October 1. If assignments are prepared and mailed out before that period, those designs for composing student bodies for each facility made in June are skewed severely by the late arrivals. In addition, high school teacher assignments and course schedules cannot be completed until late in August.[5]

Before the court intervened, these sources of delay, confusion, and error were interpreted as customary. Parents with patronage or access, through nepotism, to the schools, as well as those few with special knowledge of model programs, could jockey about for advantageous assignments. By mid-October of each year, the entire system would stabilize in ways that seemed adequate for many parents, while thousands of others had no channel for grievance or influence and resigned themselves to silence or alienation.

Court intervention exploded these customs. Those who had achieved some small advantages for their children saw themselves set back. They organized to attack the orders. Those who expected an improved set of opportunities did not know the particulars of the assignment procedure and wondered whether others had gained where they had lost anew. Still other parents heard of promising magnet schools for the first time and applied, only to fail to win seats in the computerized lottery. And in the first year, parents got assignments in the mail to schools at locations they had never visited. The community districts, after all, merged parts of predominantly black Roxbury with seven out of eight districts. Even where the distances were small in terms of city blocks, the perceived social distances were vast. When parents called to seek explanations or to apply for transfers, information agents of the school committee, some of them hostile to the court plan, would provide no information, except to say that the assignment was the result of a court order.[6] Later, they began to add that *we* had made the assignments personally and would allow no changes.

TRANSFERS

Where neither rhyme nor reason had guided the sending of learners to one school or another before 1974, the court plan brought both. The reasons were explained in the order, the rules were harmonic from district to district, and within a month, many parents began to learn the notes. Applications for transfers, allowed under half a dozen conditions, inundated the assignment unit. From July through September of 1975 the number of requests soared to 5,800. Early in October we began to analyze these in detail, for the assignment changes were so great as to generate disorder in teacher staffing and transport planning.

Before the 1976–77 school year Judge Garrity tightened the gate on transfers, based on our study and advice. Even with this change, the volume of applicants was overwhelming. A more exact analysis of student records conducted that year showed that they were still error-ridden and redundant. These errors were in some cases being exploited by parents whose quest for a "better assignment" had continued to be incessant. In addition, falsified medical excuses were cropping up; students were receiving one assignment, withdrawing, and then seeking readmission to a different school. Assignment unit staff seemed steadfast, but they could neither clean the records nor catch up with the many changes (see Table 3.1 and Figure 3.3).

As a result, Judge Garrity directed us to monitor every single assignment made after court approval in each June. Our supervision became increasingly intense. Scott specialized in reviewing and approving every proposed student reassignment and every new student arrival, with Dentler substituting occasionally. Between January 1977 and January 1980, Scott reviewed and approved about 65,000 new admissions, readmits, corrections of error, medical and desegregative transfers, and programmatic changes—a number then equal to one year's total enrollment.[7] Thus, annual turnover of student assignments, *apart* from promotions in grade, graduations, and new entrants indentified by June, equaled 25 percent. When we began the one-by-one monitoring, we expected to stem the tide. While the records were finally cleaned and a reliable assignment system devised, the rate of change did not slow down.

By June of 1978, an effective Department of Implementation had achieved impressively rational control over assignments. Albert Lau, a gifted former bilingual teacher, built a superb record management system, utilizing computer facilities the court ordered installed in new school headquarters. John Canty, a gifted former English teacher, perfected a sound procedure for processing assignment applications. With all of this reform, however, student movement in and out of Boston public schools has persisted.

By 1979, when we gained the time to look up from the grindstone of monitoring, we began to understand the reasons for these movements. A major reason is that the *authority structure* basic to schooling fell into extreme decay between 1965 and 1975. Before that decade, students in some Boston public schools wore uniforms. They rose and stood by their desks and said "good morning" in unison when an administrator or other dignitary visited. Sexes in secondary schools were segregated. Truant officers with police powers tracked down truants. Misconduct was disciplined harshly.

TABLE 3.1

**Students and School Personnel
Assignments, Reassignments, and Transfers,
1979–80**

Category	Black	White	Other Minorities	Total
Corrective				
Assignment errors	303	137	133	573
Programmatic				
Special Needs	463	308	125	896
Bilingual	89	69	681	839
Programmatic transfers	883	602	353	1,838
Desegregation transfers	163	78	66	307
Sibling transfers	86	106	79	271
Other			3	3
Total	1,684	1,163	1,307	4,154
Medical	21	36	9	66
Demographic				
New to Boston	2,950	2,825	2,886	9,661
Readmissions	552	740	590	1,382
Change of address	2,024	677	914	3,615
Total	6,524	4,242	4,290	15,056
Grand Total	8,532	5,578	5,739	19,849

SOURCE: Department of Implementation.

The pieties of civic conformity were part of every daily lesson plan. The "good working people" could be distinguished from the "shiftless unemployed" by the adherence of the former to the authority of the system. This structure changed radically in the 1960s.

Teacher unionism climaxed in 1971 and contributed to this change. As poor wages, poor working conditions, and long hours of overtime without pay

FIGURE 3.3

Student Assignment Printout, Madison Park High School, 1980

```
ANALYSIS OF STUDENTS BY RACE BY GRADE                                    PROGRAM    AVAILABLE      PROGRAMMATIC        DATE 04/11/80
ASSIGNED ENROLL 04/12/80                                                 CAPACITY   SEATS          ROOM ALLOCATION

1210 MADISON PARK HIGH                                                   1-13                      BILINGUAL      12
DISTRICT 9    COURT CAPACITY   SEATING CAPACITY  2400                    48        14     BILINGUAL  MAINSTREAM     8
                                                 HIGH    2010            240        4              SUB SEPARATE   6
              AVAILABLE SEATS  + 54    SUBSTANTIALLY SEPARATE
                                       BILINGUAL
```

GRADE	BLACK	WHITE	ORIENTAL	HISPANIC	INDIAN AMERICAN	TOTAL BY GRADE	BLACK	WHITE	OTHER		BLACK	WHITE	OTHER	TOTAL
							PERCENTS				TRANSPORTATION			
09	447	270	6	122	2	847	52.77	31.88	15.35 *		224	252	42	518
10	334	222	8	88	0	652	51.23	34.05	14.72 *		185	204	43	432
11	238	151	4	65	4	462	51.52	32.68	15.80 *		112	136	40	288
12	147	122	3	27	2	301	48.84	40.53	10.63 *		72	109	16	197
SCHOOL TO DATE	1166	765	21	302	8	2262	51.55	33.82	14.63 *		593	701	141	1435
PERCENTAGES	52	34	1	13	0	100	45.00	39.00	16.00 *		41	48	9	100

1979-80 IDEAL K-13 PERCENT

```
                     BLACK  WHITE  ORIENTAL  HISPANIC  INDIAN AMERICAN  TOTAL BY GRADE          ENROLLMENT
BILINGUAL TOTAL       128    11       0        105          0             244       *  ASSIGNED    1166  765  331  2262
VOCATIONAL ED TOTAL     0     0       0          0          0               0       *  DID NOT REPORT  7   14    3    24
EXTENDED DAY TOTAL      0     0       0          0          0               0       *
ADVANCED WORK TOTAL     0     0       0          0          0               0       *  ACTUAL      1159  751  328  2238
SPECIAL NEEDS                                                                        *
  MAINSTREAM          148    61       0         29          1             239       *
  SUBSTANTIALLY SEP.   41    16       0          4          1              62       *

                                                                                    *  TRANSACTIONS  FROM 04/06/80 TO 04/12/80
                                                                                    *                     BLACK  WHITE  OTHER  TOTAL
                                                                                    *  NEW ADMISSIONS       0      1      0      1
                                                                                    *  TRANSFERS IN         2      0      0      2
                                                                                    *  DISCHARGES           2     15      2     19
                                                                                    *  TRANSFERS OUT        1      0      0      1

RATIOS 1-13        BLACK  WHITE  OTHER *  BLACK * *    STATUS WHITE   OTHER
RANGE                50     43      18         8      +    126     +   141           *  TRANSACTIONS  FROM 07/01/79 TO 04/12/80
HIGH PERCENT                                                                         *                     BLACK  WHITE  OTHER  TOTAL
  RATIO            1005    864     362 * *                                           *  NEW ADMISSIONS     105    369     46    520
IDEAL PERCENT                                                                        *  TRANSFERS IN       106     70     36    212
  RATIO             905    784      16   322 * -   92  +     46                      *  DISCHARGES         118    388     84    590
LOW PERCENT                                                                          *  TRANSFERS OUT       17     94     17    128
  RATIO             804    704      14   281 * - 193  -     34      +    60
```

67

went out, dedication to social controls went with them. By 1975, teachers had achieved favorable terms. Their pay exceeded that of assistant professors in nearby colleges, their working day ended at 1:30 or 2:00 p.m., and they could often take second jobs for extra pay. Secular modernism had arrived. A schoolteacher could now live as well as a plumber and could care as little about details as a plumber cares about repairing one leaky faucet.

Parents in increasing numbers began to shop around for the "best" schooling arrangement. The shopping was not always for quality of instruction, by any means. It could be for convenience, friendships, comfort of social fit, or any other consumer preference. A kind of voucher mentality evolved, parallel to student transfers from college to college in the same era.

At the same time, parents learned to organize, mobilize, and redress grievances. New state laws gave parents and children rights that countervailed the traditional power of school administrators. The private sector flourished with "free schools." Parochial schools hired lay teachers and "went modern" (if only slightly) in the process. The state opened a public experimental school in Roxbury. The city sponsored alternative schools. The rise of teacher unionism was in synch with the rise of consumerism. Expelling students was once a common practice, but by 1973, the number of student expulsions for misconduct had plummeted to zero. Absenteeism and tardiness among students had soared, and the costs of hiring substitute teachers for the rising rate of teacher sick days had begun to become prohibitive.

In this changing context, a school assignment notice that reached a parent by mail seemed a bit like a coupon for a sale at the supermarket: If you didn't like it, you didn't redeem it, and you called around to see what other coupons were available.

ROCKS AND HARD PLACES

The assignment process, in its evolving clarity and accessibility, stimulated these trends. Parents got a catalog and application blanks. There were open houses where staff advertised their buildings and programs. Special programs cropped up like blossoms in the city's dust. New facilities and renovated classrooms came on the market.

Unlike the supermarket, however, not all products were available to all shoppers. The rules were stringent, and their implementation brought many parents to a fever pitch of frustration laced with adaptive cunning. For high school students, for example, seats were in short supply. The rules enabled the assigners to place students *out* of their community districts in high schools unfamiliar to them. Others got within-district assignments, only to realize this still meant placement out of one's beloved neighborhood.

The four high schools whose students caused 90 percent of the violence in and around all buildings in the system from 1975 through 1979 were scenes of conflict over assignment rules.

South Boston High, the most chaotic setting in Boston in the 1970s, accommodated its white neighborhood residents, to be sure, but it also hosted hundreds of black youths from Roxbury and a smaller group of bilingual Hispanic students, bused in together each morning.

South Boston High was loved by the families on the hill and at the foot of the hill on which it stands, not for its educational worth but for its insularity, its ethnic, communal homogeneity.

The black and Hispanic youths who were assigned to the school seemed to Judge Garrity to be like "shock troops," bearing the violent brunt of neighborhood reactions to their movement onto "Southie soil." The barrenness of the educational program inside, moreover, and the fact that most faculty were natives of South Boston whose ignorance and hostility matched that of the street-corner toughs, made the trip not only brutal and terrifying, but also futile.

While elementary schools nearby and indeed throughout the South Boston district desegregated peacefully *and* offered decent instruction for all who entered, the high school became a stage for protracted conflict.

Hyde Park High School assignments followed a similar pattern. A formerly white school became half black through districting and because of a changing racial frontier in the increasingly black residential area of Roslindale. Hyde Park, too, was a low-grade facility and offered poor programs, and the district superintendent and headmaster could have vied for first place in a contest for distinction as most incompetent. Staged violence became a specialty there and assignments helped foster the crisis.

Charlestown High School, located across from the Bunker Hill Monument, looked in 1975 like a movie set for the film *Blackboard Jungle*. The facility was a wreck; its programs were observably poor and it was slated for replacement. Not only did black students have to arrive by bus via bridges over the river that sets Charlestown apart from the rest of Boston, an equal portion of Charlestown whites were assigned to Roxbury High School in the opposite direction. Here, the conditions for reactive ugliness were ripe, but two things mitigated violence. First, hundreds of the whites from Charlestown assigned to Roxbury High did not actually attend; they dropped out or transferred to parochial schools nearby. Second, the headmaster, Frank Powers, was a former basketball coach who commanded respect, maintained tough disciplinary standards, and did not tolerate displays of racial hatred. While protest marches took place, few gang blowouts occurred within the old school. What a bitter paradox it was, then, that a black student football player for Jamaica Plain High School, Daryl Williams, was shot in the neck and paralyzed while playing in a varsity game at the new field of the fine new Charlestown High School a few blocks from the old building in October of 1979.

East Boston High was the fourth most frequent site for violence. There, white residents were displaced to other schools in order to prevent overcrowding and to make room for minority students wishing to enroll in a special business education magnet program. Assignment rules exacerbated the tension in this school, but most student violence was the result of political agitation by adults, and the headmaster managed to welcome black and other minority youths and to mount a program worthy of a trip into hostile ethnic territory.

Other high schools did not manifest tension and violence of this kind or intensity. Similarly, elementary and middle school regular assignments nowhere fostered serious intergroup conflict.* About one-fourth of the elementaries showed definite and marked avoidance and withdrawal by whites, especially in 1975 and 1976. Some of these were like Maurice J. Tobin School, which was based next to a black and Hispanic housing project and attended by white children assigned to travel four miles from their all-white neighborhood. Others were like Randall G. Morris, where whites could walk to school from a distance of two to four blocks, but refused to do so when black children were bused in from Roxbury.

THE QUEST FOR ADVANTAGE

Most community district school assignments, then, were accepted without public clamor. The struggles that bubbled up from the cauldron of assignments had far more to do with those seeking access to magnet schools, special programs, and schools with strong reputations for excellence, or some other consumer preference.

Vocational programs illustrate the struggle. These were housed in ten of the system's eighteen high schools. Nearly every one of the progams was a bastion of white male fraternalism, however. Students could be assigned to these programs only if their parents applied, however, and minorities stayed away (and went unwelcomed) until 1978. In 1976 and 1977, the court asked us to limit enrollments until court guidelines were met. As a result, the vocational programs—many of them languishing anyway for want of quality, fit to the labor market, and lack of vitality—were threatened with extinction. Those who loved them—the vocational teachers and the stalwart if dwindling band of white parents—protested vehemently. They believed their programs were being held hostage by the assignment rules, and indeed they were. In 1978, the Department of Implementation found the means to recruit minority students, and the teachers began to welcome blacks and girls alike. Self-interest triumphed, but only after three years of great stress.

Indeed, there is no doubt in our minds that the court plan and its implementation through assignment of students resulted in a massive and positive reform of vocational education in Boston. As the number and diversity of learners were expanded greatly, the quality and variety of programs began to improve and expand as well. Public neglect, school committee indifference,

---

*An important exception was Patrick F. Gavin Middle School in South Boston, where white students and a few white teachers made daily life miserable for six black teachers.

and an outdated curriculum and teacher force had been kept half-alive by the annual infusion of federal funds allocated by the state. The radically insistent demands for sex and ethnic desegregation at long last broke through the rock of custom and made a revival of services feasible.

DISJUNCTURES

Two kinds of sharply painful disjunctures, one caused by exogenous demographic forces and one by forces inherent in implementation of the assignment rules, broke repeatedly across the city from 1975 through the 1977–78 school year. The court rules were designed to be self-adjusting. If the ethnic composition of a district changed during a year, the racial/ethnic ratios prescribed by the court changed too. Student bodies changing toward violation of the guidelines were to be redesigned by revising the set of residential geocode units attached to those schools.

In spite of the intentional flexibility, about 30 out of 155 schools manifested enrollments each year that defied the logic of the orders. Typical of these was the Joseph Lee Elementary School. A new facility with a good staff and sound programs, Lee was nonetheless haunted by having opened under a great cloud of controversy about desegregation in 1972. As a result of political manipulations of its initial enrollment policies, Lee became defined for most white parents as a black school.

Lee remained segregated in student composition from its opening through 1980. The court ordered the school department to take what it called "special measures" at Lee and other schools in 1977, but these came to nothing under the deliberate inaction of John Coakley. The measure that could have worked—revision of the geocode units—was resisted with inexhaustible cunning each year, always in the name of "maintaining stability."

As we shall show in the next chapter, momentum in the court case collapsed for this very reason in May 1980 when, under the guise of facilities planning, attorney for the plaintiffs, Larry Johnson, joined the school committee in calling for a stay before the U.S. Court of Appeals.

Once mapped in June 1975, the geocode units went unchanged except when schools burned down or were closed. The entire policy aim of readjusting attendance zones within districts in response to changing population patterns was defeated, giving the court plan, in the course of implementation, a grotesquely rigid character.

CONCLUSIONS

Segregation began with the rigid sequestering of students in the service of the *status quo*, which for many Americans appears to have been designed to mete out literacy, numeracy, and social advantage to some and to deny it to others. Desegregation in Boston began with a plan aimed at shattering that design and replacing it with one that equalized access. In the course of implementation, the means for defeating the aim were developed. These included student withdrawal and transfer, a pitting of magnet admissions against community districts, and, above all, the rigid sanctification of the geocode unit maps.

When the court moved against these means each year, it was outmaneuvered, and as the means were perfected, the school committee fostered a wide consensus among all of the parties, with the sole exception of the Massachusetts Board of Education, in support of the permanence of the maps. Great progress toward equal treatment in student assignments was achieved, but it fell short of reaching about twenty-four schools, when it became apparent that more change was required than the attorneys for the plaintiffs were willing to demand.

A strong contributor to this collapse was the confusion generated each year by the assignment procedures. While they improved annually in accuracy and promptness, they were also frustrating in the extreme. Parents could not understand them, and those that did often manipulated the rules like some Americans do income tax regulations. Assignment operations began under heavy security and never shed that original aura of secrecy. As the Department of Implementation perfected the operations, John Coakley began to have something strategic to offer to Superintendent Wood and some school committee members; namely, a way of mobilizing public fear of change as a device for resisting further desegregation.

As Edmund Burke warned in the eighteenth century, where assignment remedies were not quickly and sharply implemented, confusion evolved and a rationale for foreclosing further court intervention took shape. If the geocode units go unchanged from 1980 to 1985, the Boston schools will be resegregated. Each year, the number of segregated schools outside of the city-wide magnets will increase, until the most common pattern will be monoethnic schools. If this takes place, those who warned of this outcome will achieve the prestige afforded to prophets and seers.

There are three remedial alternatives adequate to preventing this, however. One is *insistence* upon compliance with court guidelines, which would force geocode remapping. A second is a court change from geocodes to individual student assignments. These two entail renewed judicial activism, at a time when the case is in the last scene of its last act. A third alternative, the one Robert Wood has pinned his hopes upon, is the re-entry of thousands of students, most of them white, as a result of the system's "new magnetism." In that event, we could expect a revival of the economy of Boston as the engine generating the magnetic energy.

The strategic singularity of student assignments persists in any event. Its persistence confirms the vision of those civil rights workers who made the *Brown* decision the cornerstone of their effort in 1954. Who will go where to school really does ramify across every other feature of the polity. In the spring of 1980, Dentler gave the after-dinner speech at the annual banquet of the Harvard chapter of Phi Delta Kappa, the Phi Beta Kappa of education. After he spoke, State Senator William Owen, a black leader from Roxbury who had just been inducted that night as an honorary member (thus agreeing to help in integrating the fraternity), spoke up from the floor. "I'm opposed to desegregation and integration of the schools," he said. "What you've been talking about won't accomplish what is really important. None of the poor kids in Boston will get to be president of John Hancock Insurance or of Harvard anyway, and that's what counts."

We are not at all sure Senator Owen is right: Whoever *does* become president of Harvard will have to be well-educated, and where he or she gets admitted or assigned to school will most surely affect that education. We suspect there is nothing at all incidental or accidental about the emphasis placed, under segregation and desegregation alike, on who goes where to school.

NOTES

1. According to Judge W. Arthur Garrity's memorandum of May 10, 1975, in *Morgan v. Kerrigan*, Civ. No. 72–911–G, "The goal of the court in formulating a remedy for intentional segregation of the schools is to eliminate government-imposed isolation of blacks within the school system. Largely as a result of school committee actions, most students in Boston attend schools that are either 'black' or 'white.' The remedy in this case must convert this 'dual system' to one 'without a white school and a Negro school, but just schools.' This does not mean that all schools in the system must show the same or nearly the same ethnic compositions, but rather that the remedy should eliminate assignment patterns that leave some schools so disproportionate in their ethnic makeup that they are in affect 'Negro' or 'white' schools—to use the language of *Green v. County School Board*."

2. Alan Lupo, *Liberty's Chosen Home: The Politics of Violence in Boston*, Little, Brown, Boston, 1977, p. 79.

3. We made this point several times in conversations with Rossell and even offered to share the complexities with her directly. She and other researchers responded by emphasizing the importance of official statistics such as state records. She also thought that close association with "educators" would diminish her scientific competence.

4. Leftwich was fired in 1977 because he tried to establish a Department of Implementation that would have some independence from the superintendent and the school committee. Tutella was ostracized for a year until he quit, with Haran, in order to join Leftwich in Cleveland, where all three were appointed by Judge Battisti but then isolated and finally driven out by the school board. In contrast, those who resisted the court actively, from John Coakley to Robert Murray and others, were promoted within the Boston School Department.

5. The schools are locked from late June until mid-August, save for a few used for summer programs.

6. Until 1977, the Information Center was run by persons with strong ties to political leaders in South Boston. Some staff regulars were ROAR activists.

7. In the period from June 1979 to May 8, 1980, for example, 4,094 students received programmatic transfers and 65 got medical transfers, the number in this latter group having declined from repeated use in previous years. In the same period, there were 14,827 students added: 9,548 of them "new to Boston"; 1,704 readmits, and 3,577 changes of address. Over the same period, 12,600 students withdrew from the rolls.

THE SCHOOL FACILITIES

4

THE SIGNIFICANCE OF SCHOOL FACILITIES

SCHOOL BUILDINGS HAVE BEEN CENTRAL TO THE PROCESS of public school segregation and desegregation in the United States since the 1850s. William Lloyd Warner's classic study, *Who Shall be Educated?*, includes the question, *where* shall they be educated?

Public schools consist of teachers, students, staff, equipment, and materials that are located in physical as well as social space centered within particular buildings. Since 1965, we have begun to understand that programs can be conducted "without walls." These continue to be very rare. Thus, as desegregation consists of changing answers to the questions of who shall attend school, and where, so the location, condition, size, and planned use of a building is pivotal to desegregation planning and implementation.

State-mandated dual systems in the Deep South created the legal conditions that led to the *Brown* decision. In many of those systems, at least until the 1950s, black schoolchildren were assigned to dilapidated, virtually unusable buildings, while whites were assigned to sound, attractive, relatively new structures that black students often had to pass on the way to their shacklike school buildings.[1]

An early fundamental aim of school desegregators thus became that of equalizing access to the better school buildings and generating political pressure to replace the shacks white students were assigned to attend with better facilities. As the impact of the *Brown* decision moved northward between 1958 and 1964, organizations such as the Urban League conducted studies that found minority segregated schools in many American cities were older, more dilapidated, and less well-equipped than white segregated facilities. By the time of the Boston case, nearly every federal court remedy had come to consider school closings, repairs, renovations, and replacements as tools for securing equal protection.

THE BOSTON SITUATION

Boston is, by North American standards, a very old and economically depressed central city. The issue of school facilities had become critical ten years before the advent of the federal suit in 1972. In his widely read book, *Death at an Early Age*, Jonathan Kozol reported in bitter detail on the extreme disrepair of school buildings in the Boston system. He had not known those conditions had been assayed by experts and commissions appointed by the school committee and city hall from 1944 through 1969. Altogether, eight such reports were filed and made public; they recommended the closing of a total of sixty-two schools as unfit.

Of the 201 facilities still in use in 1973, nearly 6 in 10 had been erected between 1847 and 1911. Most of the remainder had been constructed between 1913 and 1922. Many built in the nineteenth century were fire-unsafe, all-wood structures. And many of those constructed between 1870 and 1903 had wood frames, floors, and roof structures, and were faced with cheap masonry. These were classified as "not fire resistive" by the city Public Facilities Commission. Some 55 of the 62 facilities that had been recommended for closing (and some of them had virtually been condemned) were still being used. A few of the schools seemed to observers to be held up by little more than their rusting exterior fire escapes.

Most of the schools, with some noteworthy exceptions at the secondary level, had been sited on the cheapest available lots. Not more than a dozen elementary schools built before 1950 had outdoor play space. None, other than those built after 1965, contained indoor gymnasiums. Residential areas in which many of the schools were once located had long since deteriorated, leaving the schools behind on decaying streets lined with boarded up stores and empty frame houses.

And, as we have stated earlier, maintenance and repair operations had become well-developed facets of the patronage system of the school committee during the era of the Great Depression. Repair operations were the purview of the chief structural engineer. He also reported directly to the committee and managed a full-time staff of seventy who did no repair work, but prepared forms for letting contracts to outside firms. A building administrator with influence at school headquarters could get a repair completed through this apparatus within a single school year, or even during a summer. The ordinary *acting* principal, temporarily and nominally in charge of a facility in six out of ten buildings, could expect a delay of three years following the filing of a requisition.

The oldest, most dilapidated, and least well-maintained and repaired facilities were located in the oldest sections of Roxbury and Dorchester. Some in Chinatown, the South End, the North End, and East Boston also competed for high places on the list of the most unfit buildings in the system.

The poor conditions of facilities in these areas was partly a matter of ethnic succession in the normal course of the urban ecological process: As a residential locale aged, its more advantaged, mobile households would leave, to be replaced by the most mobile households from the next socioethnic stratum in the population. Ethnic succession was reinforced, in part, by the highly patterned, consistent withdrawal of maintenance and repair services from the older, declining locales and the reconcentration of such services in the politically more influential and responsive, developing neighborhoods.

Under these circumstances, there were few forces at work to create pressure to close facilities classified as unfit or fire unsafe. What resources there were at hand from 1940 to 1965 thus went toward the development of new neighborhoods in West Roxbury and, to a far lesser extent, Hyde Park. Poorer, less mobile, and less politically influential families worked to keep the facilities they had. Not losing what little one had nearby seemed the outermost reach to be attained.

Chinese-Americans, for example, were almost wholly segregated in their enrollment in the Quincy Elementary School, constructed in 1847 as the nation's first multiclassroom public school building. Their families and the teachers made as much as they could of this "opportunity," and many Chinese students from this school went on to distinguish themselves in the city's three elite examination schools.

Their achievements proved the point that the 1966 Coleman Report, *Equality of Educational Opportunity*, had made: Quality of facilities plays a negligible role in affecting academic achievement. We will never know, however, what extraordinary talents were depressed or wasted within Boston's Chinese-American community by virtue of life within a dingy, dangerous, creaking old schoolhouse.

In the years from 1965 to 1971, Mayor Kevin White's administration injected new ingenuity, hope, and resources into the replacement of school facilities in Boston. A network of elementary schools with playgrounds, gymnasiums, and swimming pools was planned, and some were erected. Internationally distinguished architects were commissioned to plan new facilities.

State funds began to pump into the city the means to finance the erection of magnificent, prize-winning structures.

By 1970, however, these promising developments began to come to a halt as state funds were blocked because the school committee refused to commit money to facilities that would optimize racial balance. It was at this turning point that a fantastic opportunity for deep reconstruction of public education in Boston was rejected by an antidesegregationist majority of committee members. These were typified, for example, by long delays in construction of a new Quincy Elementary School in Chinatown, which was designed as a multipurpose community service facility of truly excellent quality.

STATE BOARD RULE

In 1974, the Massachusetts Board of Education published its own *Short-Term Plan to Reduce Racial Imbalance in the Boston Public Schools.* Unlike previous plans such as Superintendent William Ohrenberger's plan of 1965, this one addressed the issue of school facilities in a forthright fashion.

The state plan asked these key questions: Are the seat capacities of schools adequate for the numbers of students to be assigned to them? Are the facilities adequate enough to support programs for particular grade levels? (Remember that by this time the system was operating facilities with thirteen divergent and confounded grade structures.) Will students, under the new plan, be assigned to facilities that are equal or superior to those they currently attend? The plan demonstrated how pivotal facilities are to desegregation planning. It concluded by recommending the closing of ten of the oldest and most deteriorated, unsafe structures in the system. This became the plan adopted by Judge Garrity as Phase I for 1974–75.

PHASE II PLANNING

The Panel of Masters and the two experts received no recommendations for school closings from the school committee or the plaintiffs, but they did get a list of fifty-five facilities from the Public Facilities Commission, and this list became the basis for the masters' report.

The masters recommended permanently closing the schools that had been temporarily closed during Phase I. We studied the list with care and noted that three-fourths of the schools on it had been listed in at least seven of the eight reports and plans for closings and replacements since 1944. These schools were sampled for visitation, and Scott ensured that photographs of the exteriors and interiors of many of them were available for examination by the masters. Over a period of six weeks, Scott toured approximately seventy buildings.

In addition, the masters settled upon the principle of establishing a uniform grade structure as a corollary to the principle of equal protection. They adopted, after examining several proposals from the parties, a K–5

elementary, 6–8 middle school, and 9–12 comprehensive high school structure. This principle, combined with that of community districting, required us
to calculate technically which facilities would best support programs at these
levels and to estimate how many seats would be needed within each district at
each of the three levels. Technical analysis in March 1975 disclosed that the
system contained a surplus of at least 3,000 seats at the elementary level and
a shortage of at least 2,000 seats at the high school level.

In pursuit of an equalized, comprehensible, and serviceable system, we
learned that the system was rife with annexes and portable classrooms.
These had been introduced during the 1960s (some came earlier), partly in
order to enable racial segregation within surrounding neighborhoods. In
some, the annexes were larger than the buildings to which they were
ostensibly attached. Some were former Roman Catholic facilities that had
been purchased or rented. Others were rented from the city or from private
firms. With a few exceptions, we found that most of them were unfit for school
use, and that they fostered segregation.

The worst of these were called portable "demountables," temporary
structures of a cheap and flimsy sort that were hauled to a school yard or an
empty lot and put up on cinder blocks. Often, these demountables had been
vandalized into severe disrepair and were poorly maintained. Most had been
scheduled originally for use over a three-year period, which had then been
extended gradually to a decade or more. They were preserved because they
were useful to the committee in maintaining student segregation. Capacities
of white schools could be enlarged so that students would not be assigned to
nearby black schools, some of which were underutilized. Complaints about
overcrowding at some black schools could be met by avoiding desegregative
assignments and adding portables.

Although the Boston schools virtually stand in the long shadows cast by
the Harvard School of Design and the Massachusetts Institute of Technology
School of Architecture and Planning, many of the schools we recommended be
closed were found to have been built by fools, knaves, or both.[2] Some hallways
did not connect with classrooms. Some classrooms were built without access
to hallways, except through other classrooms. Additions had been built onto
deteriorating structures without correlating the new sections with the old, yet
both portions were kept in operation. The more schools we visited, the more
convinced we became that some of those *not* on the list were unfit to remain
open.[3]

It became apparent within a few weeks that necessarily drastic actions
regarding school closings would fall most heavily upon the black and Hispanic
residential neighborhoods. Some facilities were therefore left standing. The
closing of others led to later ramifications in the distribution of busing
obligations between white and black neighborhoods. In other words, where
black schools were closed, heavy busing had to be introduced. Black students
were bused to adjacent white neighborhoods where the equally heavy busing

of white students *out* of these schools was necessarily introduced as well. Both the plaintiffs and the state board criticized the masters' preliminary report and final report for proposing to close too many previously black facilities. Judge Garrity later mediated these criticisms and made changes in the plan in order to ease the transportation burden for black and white groups alike. At the same time, he increased the burden elsewhere by changing district boundaries.

In order to test the technical analyses of the experts, the masters took testimony from the chief structural engineer of the schools, Anthony Galeota. He reported that all school facilities on the active list were structurally sound, but he also noted that some of them were built of wood and were considered unsafe by the fire marshall. (One of the schools burned to the ground while the masters were gathering this testimony and attempting to refine their data.)

Most noteworthy is the fact that agents of the school committee never came forward to actually contribute judgments based on long familiarity; most of the facilities had been in use for more than fifty years, and not more than a handful had been closed by the committee or the city before 1974. Yet, the agents of the federal court were left to grope in the dark, aided by very little more than the one list submitted by the Public Facilities Commission and by the data provided by the State Education Department.

Equally baffling, given the age of the system, were the reams of conflicting data on the seat capacities of the buildings. It became evident that some administrators reported inflated numbers and others deflated them, depending upon the whims of committee members and local constituencies. These estimates also played a part in maintaining segregation.

The Phase I plan contained a list of estimated capacities compiled from various official sources over the years. Some of the numbers differed by as many as 400 seats from one source to the next. It was as if the physical condition and seating capacity of every building had to be exhumed archeologically, when in truth at least fifty school administrators at headquarters, only a few blocks away from the courthouse, were thoroughly familiar with the facts.

In addition to gaining capacity estimates, we also obtained enrollment and attendance reports. Dentler prepared a card file that listed the diverse seat capacity estimates on each school, together with date of construction and a few other particulars. Later, he used this in order to set a seat capacity limit on each facility, arriving at the limit by averaging the numbers on each card and then finally testing his estimates on helpful agents from the State Education Department.

In the course of our searches, we found buildings that were listed as not in use but were in fact inhabited by teachers and students. We learned that as late as March 1975, when a building was scheduled for closing, it was not emptied of equipment and materials, shut down, locked up, or otherwise secured. The facilities that were turned over to the city were customarily rehabilitated or sold for use for other purposes. In some instances, those that were retained by the school committee were left standing in deteriorating neighborhoods to be vandalized or set on fire.

Scott visited one building that had been listed as closed more than a year earlier. He found the upper floors had been closed but that the first two floors were in active use as a school. Arrangements for school closings were often made by field administrators, with little involvement of anyone at head-quarters other than the chief custodial engineer.

These findings led the masters to recommend that schools closed for school use by the court be promptly turned over to the city. Months later while touring closed facilities for Judge Garrity, Scott found that some of them had not been shut down; heating, plumbing, lighting, and water systems were still working, doors had not been locked, and windows had not been boarded up.

Many of the schools recommended for closing by the Public Facilities Commission had been included on the assumption that they would be replaced by new structures. A good example was the Carter Temporary School, built of cinder blocks to house 100 students on the site where a much larger, magnificent elementary facility was to be erected in the Roxbury locale with state funds. The site itself was part of the Madison Park area of the city, where planning for renewal and redevelopment began, according to city hall annals, in 1960.

Construction of the new Carter School was delayed for a decade. By the time of the federal suit, the decline in births that began in 1967 and that reduced elementary enrollments beginning in 1973 made the school unnecessary. The court ordered the temporary structure replaced, nonetheless, as part of furnishing Roxbury with a few decent school structures. Later, it accepted stipulations from the state board, the plaintiffs, and other parties, including the school committee and city hall, that set aside the construction directive. In addition, it accepted the school committee's request to continue to use the cinder block Carter Temporary as a permanent facility to house severely handicapped, substantially separate, special needs children.[4]

Nearby, the city and state had planned construction of Madison Park High School. It was to be the very ultimate in comprehensive, multipurpose campus school design and construction, designed by Marcel Breuer and Associates to serve up to 5,000 students. The site was prepared and the foundation laid in 1969. However, mistakes were made in the foundation work and construction activities were delayed time and again by city hall for other reasons. This facility was not ready for use until September 1977. Its scale was reduced from 5,000 to 2,500 seats. The original architectural plans were modified until the result bore only an external resemblance to the original design.

In contrast, West Roxbury High School took less than three years to build. The difference was due in part to the fact that West Roxbury houses the politically influential white middle- and upper-middle-class constituents of city hall officials and the school committee members. In part, too, West Roxbury was cheaply and conventionally designed and inexpensively constructed on open space that abuts a huge sanitary landfill.

THE PHASE II ORDER

On May 6, 1975, following the masters' recommendation that closed schools be turned over to the city, Judge Garrity ordered the school committee to permanently close twenty-two schools taken from the Public Facilities Commission list, and to permanently close the ten other facilities that had been shut down temporarily during Phase I. Acknowledging that the closings were related to fitting seating capacities to numbers of students at each level in each district, and to eliminating the most unfit schools from the roster, Judge Garrity noted these legal considerations:

> A major reason for closing schools is that desegregation is more easily and economically achieved through the consolidation of student bodies. Many of the city's elementary schools in black areas have in the past been overcrowded; many elementary schools in white areas have been under-utilized, e.g., when a new school was constructed to replace an old one in a predominantly white neighborhood, the school committee accommodated parents protesting the closing of the old one by keeping them open. Should school facilities be uniformly used to capacity, an excess of several thousand available seats at the elementary school level would remain. Thus a number of the older elementary schools can be closed, with accompanying savings of the cost of operating and heating those schools. Elementary schools will be kept open whose locations enable busing to be minimized overall, and which permit the more efficient assignment of students by geocodes.... Uniform utilization of facilities throughout the city will also tend to equalize the availability of the system's resources to all students.[5]

The judge's reasons gave no notice to our conviction that equity itself demanded that indecent, fire-unsafe dungeons should not await the children and youths who boarded yellow buses and traveled fifteen to thirty minutes each morning in search of an education.

None of the court records tell the story of the A. Palmer Elementary School in Roxbury, for example. Scott visited this school, erected in 1885, in February of 1975. He found it was surrounded by a huge black metal fence. The front door creaked and groaned when opened, making Scott feel as if he were entering a house of horrors. On the second floor, children sat on old chairs and couches that lined the hallway, trying to complete remedial reading tasks in the dim half-light that filtered through a dirty old skylight set in the roof just above them. The light was too dim to enable Scott to take pictures of the hallway, even with flash attachments.

Palmer's roof was sagging and leaking; the lower and upper floors were dirty; paint and linoleum peeled away from the classroom and corridor walls; toilet facilities were broken, uncleaned, and flooding over; and the grounds surrounding the school were cluttered with paper and trash. As compensation for broken windowpanes in classrooms, the ancient furnace pumped heat into the building at a furiously uncontrolled rate, producing a temperature of 85°F. Within a few months, the school was torched by arsons or vandals. It had been left on the list of schools to be kept open because it was superior to other facilities, and because it was central to the Roxbury area residential settlement.

IMPLEMENTATION

The basis for including school closings, repairs and renovations, and construction of new schools in the court orders was laid in the Phase II order. These became a set of tools for pursuing desegregative remedies and for attaining educational equality of opportunities. The Phase IIb and III orders extended this convention, adding ten more schools to the closing list, requiring repairs and renovations where parent councils and field administrators reported urgent and continually unmet needs, and building replacements where they had been sketched in previously by the city in its 1967 and 1968 plans.

Between August 1976 and April 1977 it became apparent to the experts and the court that something new and different would have to be introduced if the school system was ever to meet the criteria for judicial disengagement. School closings, after delays, failures to secure buildings and remove equipment and materials, and much wrangling over timing and details, became quite efficient by 1976. Implementation of the other orders dragged on interminably.

Take, for example, Jamaica Plain High School. Part of this school was built in 1879; the remainder was added in 1898. By 1972, the upper floor was too unsafe to be used, and enrollment capacity was limited to 750. City planning of a replacement began at the neighborhood level in 1958, but nothing definite took shape until 1973, when the state board agreed tentatively to finance the renovation of the Boston Gas Company plant for use as a replacement.

By that time, incidentally, the utility of, and the equipment for, the cooperative vocational programs at Jamaica Plain High had disappeared. The program had two parts, floraculture and agriculture, both introduced in about 1922 when part of Boston was still actively engaged in truck farm gardening, wholesale flower production and supply, and related commercial services. The band saw installed in the workshop of the school in 1922 was still in operation in 1973. The small collection of hand tools was kept under lock. Students could be observed learning to do drawings of farm outbuildings.

Floraculture was taught with dried plants and strawflowers, as no flowers were grown or imported.

Although Judge Garrity ordered the replacement of Jamaica Plain High with the renovated Gas Company building to become effective September 1976, the change did not take place until 1979.

The Jamaica Plain Community District population consisted of more than 2,000 public high school students. Even when magnet school choices were subtracted, the old facility could not possibly guarantee seats to all eligible residents. By 1976, the school's vocational programs had been terminated and the faculty relocated to the new West Roxbury High where a revised program in agribusiness services was begun. But 1,200 students had to be assigned to the dingy old facility in Jamaica Plain in 1976, leaving neighborhood residents feeling as though positive changes would never come to their part of the city.

In the same district, the court had ordered its only school pairing in response to a plea from the school committee to leave open the Longfellow Elementary School. The court, which had directed that the school be closed, except for temporary use for kindergarten classes if such were needed in the immediate area, directed the William Lloyd Garrison School in the black neighborhood to pair with the Longfellow in the white neighborhood.

Within a few days of the opening of school in 1975, Garrison was set on fire and some of its classrooms and part of its roof were destroyed. By November, it became apparent that the Longfellow School was flourishing. Neighborhood whites and bused blacks alike were enrolled and attending in large numbers. However, white students did not travel to the partially destroyed Garrison School, nor did the school department act to repair or restore the building. Black students continued to attend through the year. The court then ordered the Garrison closed permanently and left the Longfellow open.

Early in 1975, the state board financed the purchase of more than a quarter of a million dollars' worth of heavy machinery for use in Boston Trade High School. The court ordered continued use of this facility as a magnet school. It required the addition of an academic faculty and program as part of ensuring that every high school in Boston would provide a comprehensive education, and it ordered improvement of the plant.

In August 1975 we found that the school had not been repaired or renovated and that the machinery had not been installed. During a court hearing, the chief structural engineer promised to arrange a quick face-lifting of the school, an event so unusual for any school located in Roxbury that one television news journalist, Gloria Gibson, filmed the inside and outside of Boston Trade High before and after its cosmetic improvement.*

*Her filming led to the sudden repair activities. Without Gibson's coverage subsequent to the hearing, we think the promise to repair could have gone the way of many similar promises— toward limbo.

In December 1977, two years after the face-lifting, Scott made a brief visit to this facility, just to check on developments. He found that the machinery had been installed but that it could not be plugged in and put to use because electrical outlets had not been installed. He also found that the plumbing had been allowed to rupture and go unrepaired; water was pumped continually onto the roof and seeped down the inner walls, lodging in the flooring beneath the newly installed heavy machinery. Part of the floor was too weak to be walked on. Drawing upon Scott's findings, Judge Garrity stopped the assignment of ninth graders to Boston Trade for 1978. Superintendent Wood later called for its closing in 1980.

Delays and mistakes in repairs and renovations became so frequent that in the fall of 1975, Judge Garrity ordered that all repair requisitions, work orders, and contracts be sent directly to him for review. At hearing after hearing, Chief Structural Engineer Anthony Galeota pledged to "get right to it" and to "work a little magic in no time," whenever he was challenged about delays and neglect. Although Galeota professed cheerful readiness to help the court, it was impossible to guess what would in fact be accomplished without constant surveillance of his progress.

New buildings were part of the pattern of delay as well. We accepted the report of the city in defining a magnificent new facility in East Boston as constructed and ready for occupancy. The court ordered that it be used as a scientific and technical magnet school under support and assistance from Massachusetts Institute of Technology, Wentworth Institute, and Massport Authority.

A year after the school was opened under the name of Mario Umana High, both Wentworth and Massport reported that the facility was grossly unequipped and that the city was unwilling to complete the task of equipping it. In addition, faulty lighting may have contributed to the drowning of a student in the Umana pool in its first year of use; his body was not noticed in the dim light during a swimming class. Extensive renovations followed the tragedy.

Four months after a new elementary school named Mattahunt opened in Hyde Park, Scott visited it and found that the teachers and children were wearing coats, gloves, and earmuffs indoors because the wrong blower fan had been installed and the heat did not get from the boiler room to the class-rooms. The swimming pool had water in it but had yet to be used because the filter systems had been improperly installed. Roads were not built to provide easy access to the new school, either.

Completion of new facilities seems to have been related to the bidding procedures used by the city. Allegedly, very low bids are placed with the fore-knowledge that when the city clerk of the works signs off on a "completed" construction project, various subsequent construction and equipment contracts will have to be let in order to bring the building up to usable levels. In this way, according to some informed sources, public construction can be done at what appears to be the lowest cost, yet subsequent contracting can be arranged to the mutual advantage of political officials and contractors.

In his April 1977 Phase III order, Judge Garrity required the creation of a transportation and facilities unit within the newly mandated Department of Implementation. The principle behind creation of a joint transportation and facilities unit was that busing is intended to get students to something of value at the end of the ride. The unit was to coordinate and oversee the implementation of school transportation, repair, renovation, and construction orders.

The judge also ordered the development of a Unified Facilities Plan to cover the decade from 1977 through 1987. He directed its development through joint efforts by the school superintendent and the chief structural engineer, the city public facilities department, and the state board. The order was aimed at laying a basis for disengagement of the court by obligating otherwise separate agencies to plan together and by setting forth for review and argument all of the closings, repairs, renovations, and building replacements projected for each coming year over a ten-year period.

The new plan, published in September 1977, was imperfect. Fuzzy on the long term and unintegrated in its parts, it also lacked community input about school closings. Judge Garrity delayed review once again, at the request of several of the parties, to enable public hearings on the plan in January.

There seemed in 1978, for the first time in the history of Boston, some prospect that school facilities would begin to become somewhat equalized in quality, habitable, and reasonably maintained. The Citywide Parents Advisory Committee was to serve as a permanent monitoring agency for fulfillment and annual updating of the Unified Facilities Plan, and the permanent Department of Implementation was to coordinate fulfillment with close regard to student assignments, transportation, public information, and overall desegregation of the system.

THE NEW POLITICS OF SCHOOL CLOSINGS

Public reactions to school closings in 1974 and 1975 were mild and adjustments to the effects of closing thirty-two facilities were swift. When portables and annexes were closed in 1976 and 1977, moreover, reactions were limited to two types: opposition to any closing and support of additional closings.

Administrators, teachers, and parents coalesced in an effort to prevent the closing of the Whittier Annex to Dorchester High School. The high school suffered from overcrowding and the annex seemed to the coalition to be essential. When the coalition threatened to boycott classes, the court permitted the John Greenleaf Whittier, a former elementary school, to remain open after it received assurances that the annex's heating, plumbing, and electrical systems would be repaired.

A year later, the same issue was joined. This time, students were confined like hostages to the school auditorium pending resolution, and we went out to visit. We found that Whittier was being used to segregate black students and to segregate ninth graders from upper-grade students. In addition, the school was suffering from a "repaired" heating system that brought the temperature in all rooms up to 92°F on a cold day in October. This time, the court scheduled Whittier for closing at the end of the year.

In the process, the teachers and parents discovered they could achieve changes in court orders. The school committee's receipt of permission from the court to call back the superintendent's facilities plan in November 1977 in order to seek community review intensified the impression that the ancient politics of avoiding school closings needed modernizing. It became clear that no force would be firm enough to withstand *organized* and vocal coalitions mobilized to veto planned closings.

Soon, however, planning became equated with opposing closings, and issues of scheduled replacements, renovations, and repairs were neglected. Therefore, as the school committee took School Superintendent Fahey's 1977 plan to the neighborhoods, the new politics of avoidance emerged. No revised version of that plan was ever submitted to the court.

By the winter of 1979, the court faced an impasse we had warned Judge Garrity would develop since 1977. Some 26 elementary schools in 6 of the 9 districts were segregated, 15 of them from 1975 through 1979. At the same time, there were from 9,500 to 10,000 excess seats in the elementary grade facilities. About 4,000 of these were the result of faulty enrollment data dating back to 1975. At that time the court ordered the provision of seats for all registered students and the school department published student population estimates based on massive withdrawals from the Boston public schools in 1975 and 1976 and birth rate declines that began to become precipitous in 1967. Finally, the geocode units attached to schools in 1975, which were to be revised periodically, were left unchanged. As a result, the court-ordered fit between schools, seats, and numbers and ethnicities of students was in extreme disarray.

By 1979 case law had made it clear that no court can play "the Hounds of Heaven." It cannot order a remedy and then revise the remedy when population movement, birth rate changes, and real estate changes take place.[6] In the Boston case, the tools for adjusting the system were provided in the court plan. Ceiling capacities on enrollments in a school could be lowered by the system. Geocode units could be revised. The racial/ethnic composition guidelines for each district changed each year to reflect natural demographic movement. What the court did not anticipate was that its tools would be left to rust in their box.

If the court intruded too far into facilities planning, then the new coalitions charged that Judge Garrity was seeking to act to cover up failures in his

Phase II 1975 Plan. Those parents using the schools began to assert themselves imaginatively as the valiant agents of moderation who had stayed with the system through its years of turmoil. Boston Teachers Union leaders came forward to speak for the teachers as stoic heroes of the desegregation struggle. If Judge Garrity ordered more schools closed, he would betray the moderate and stoical majority. By implication, he would also be vulnerable to legal appeals.

If the court did nothing, however, the prophecy of Louise Day Hicks and John J. Kerrigan, who warned that desegregation would fail in Boston, would come true. Twenty-five years after the *Brown* decision of 1954, for example, the case in Topeka, Kansas, reopened because the public schools there had never achieved desegregation. Many antibusing spokespersons in Boston prophesied failure or resegregation as the ultimate outcomes there.

Two other developments contributed to the impasse over school closings. The court plan greatly improved the quality of usable buildings and equipment between 1974 and 1977. At the same time, the plan fostered decentralization, greatly heightened parental participation, and laid the conditions for the emergence of a coalition of teachers and parents concerned about quality education. The moderate and stoical majority had elected a moderate school committee in November 1977, and that committee appointed a liberal superintendent. The entire new coalition, with its new politics of resistance to closings, was predicated upon the student assignment plans ordered by the court in 1975. To close more schools, then, would be to sabotage the new coalition.

Mayor Kevin White, as one of the defendants, had argued since 1975 that the court plan—once the court modified the masters' plan—was fiscally unaffordable. In October 1976, the mayor began a campaign to press for the closing of fifteen to twenty more schools and for reducing the teacher force on the grounds of fiscal prudence. Mayor White moved that the court should approve these cutbacks in time to implement them by February 1977.

In rejecting White's motions as undesirably disruptive, Judge Garrity placed the court in a precarious situation. Mayor White could claim profound foresight if the court found it necessary to do his bidding two years later, and others could appeal or criticize the court on the grounds that its actions were contradictory. If the court took no action in a circumstance where desegregation was still unaccomplished and where the costs of maintaining 10,000 excess seats and a teacher/student ratio of one to thirteen were staggering for Boston, the court would appear not only to be a captive of its own past policies but indifferent to the public fisc as well.

Just as in 1975 the media had not transmitted the message of the imperatives of constitutional law to the public, as late as 1979 the press and TV had not publicized the fact that excess seats existed. The numbers of underutilized schools, featherbed teachers, and substandard schools were not the data that sold newspapers or built Nielsen ratings. The connections between the law, desegregation implementation, and the economic future of Boston went unreported.

This was not the fault of journalists. It was the result of city-wide silence about the vast changes overtaking Boston in the final quarter of the twentieth century. Those leaders who did speak up, such as the enlightened Governor Michael Dukakis, were defeated at the polls in 1978 by advocates of the *status quo ante*. Bathed in a medium of misinformation and avoidance of reality by political, economic, and educational leaders, parents and teachers were not equipped to appraise the implications of failure to prepare for the future.

In February of 1979, Judge Garrity tried again to set the stage for this future. He asked the Department of Implementation to show how it intended to desegregate students in preparing assignments for September 1979. One of the useful effects of this request was to clarify precisely how many excess seats were projected for every school (see Tables 4.1, 4.2, and 4.3). Superintendent Wood joined Chief Planner John Coakley and others in arguing against revising geocode units for 1978, and for preserving stability.[7] The trade-off, however, was a commitment to submit a long-range Unified Facilities Plan with student assignment changes in the fall of 1979.

Planning this time fell to James Breeden, a black educator and civil rights leader who had directed the Citywide Coordinating Council (created by the court) in 1977 and 1978. Breeden was now senior officer for planning and policy in the Robert Wood administration. With coparticipation from the State Education Department and city hall, he began his planning in April 1979.

This time, the planning effort seemed more flexible than it had ever been. Breeden knew the law, local political history, the court plan, and the craft of planning. He had the confidence of the court and a mandate from Wood to support him. He had access to all school data and the good will of Massachusetts Education Commissioner Gregory Anrig to assist him. He also knew how to preplan so as to elicit the views and preferences of interest groups and affected parties.

What Breeden did lack, however, was a base of support among the white school establishment. He had been active as a foe of segregated and educationally inferior public education in Boston since the early 1960s when he was Episcopal Canon of the Greater Boston Diocese. He began study for a doctorate at Harvard in the early 1970s and spent several years in Africa working on educational development projects. In addition, he changed his residence from Boston to Lexington. When Wood appointed Breeden, he had to carry with him to 26 Court Street the burden of previous disputes with John Coakley and others in the Department of Implementation, disputes that grew out of his leadership role in the Citywide Coordinating Council.

Judge Garrity ordered the new plan to be submitted no later than December 1, 1979. Breeden had to go public with it earlier, however, in order to elicit community views, and this put the school committee, the city council, and the November 2 mayoral elections between him and his final version.

When we saw a draft in August, we reported to Judge Garrity that excellence in planning had come to Boston at last. Breeden had mustered help from students at MIT, Harvard, and elsewhere. New enrollment projections were prepared. Data on seats and building conditions were collected and ordered sensibly. Critical concerns were sifted, arrayed, and then carefully considered in making inventive judgments about how to desegregate the school system as well as to upgrade quality and to conserve stability for the system across the future.

Two approaches to public review were used by Breeden. During the summer of 1979, he requested and received recommendations from committees within each of the nine districts. South Boston Community District 6 refused to recommend *any* changes, but Community Superintendent Joseph McDonough breached the district's silence and forwarded suggestions of his own. During October and November, Breeden arranged a series of public hearings at which school committee members did not participate as panelists. Indeed, they avoided discussing the plan so assiduously that one member, Paul Tierney, said he could not vote on November 30 because he had only seen Superintendent Wood's proposals the day before. When members were present at discussions, they spoke against closing schools. Committee member Kathleen Sullivan Alioto, for instance, appeared at one hearing and queried aloud whether Breeden's plan was designed to benefit blacks at the expense of whites.

TABLE 4.1

Excess Seats in High Schools by District, 1979

District	Capacity[a]	Enrollment[b]	Difference	25% Cushion	Excess Seats
1	1,171	1,129	42	11	31
2	946	1,328	− 382	− 95	− 477
3	1,102	1,351	− 249	− 62	− 311
4	1,104	953	151	38	113
5	2,064	1,877	187	47	140
6	1,118	1,034	84	21	63
7	1,386	1,166	220	55	165
8	1,344	1,160	184	46	138
9	12,350	10,950	1,400	350	1,050
Total	22,585	20,948	1,637	411	912

[a]Capacity figures are from the Department of Implementation's Space/Program Matrix, March 1979.

[b]As of December 1979.

TABLE 4.2
Excess Seats in Middle Schools
by District, 1979

District	Capacity[a]	Enrollment[b]	Difference	25% Cushion	Excess Seats
1	1,416	1,197	219	55	164
2	1,658	1,421	237	59	178
3	2,196	1,647	549	137	412
4	1,496	1,383	113	28	85
5	2,809	2,849	-40	-10	-30
6	1,872	1,734	138	35	103
7	1,792	1,288	504	126	378
8	1,081	857	224	56	168
9	3,600	3,291	309	77	232
Total	17,920	15,667	2,253	563	1,690

[a]Capacity figures are from the Department of Implementation's Space/Program Matrix, March 1979.

[b]As of December 1979.

For all of its apparent excellence, the Breeden plan had two deficiencies. First, the court had asked for a plan that would elminate at least 5,000 of the more than 10,000 excess seats in elementary grades (see Table 4.3). Breeden met this target for 1980, but only barely. When, as a sop to the school committee, Wood reduced the list, he cut out five schools with more than 200 seats. He also discarded Breeden's alternate plan to list thirty-two other buildings as "support" schools subject to closing between 1981 and 1985, if needed. Second, the plan did not offer restabilizing hope; it did not show where "displaced students" would go in the future or why the projected upgradings would make the readjustments worthwhile.

These deficiencies were not the result of poor planning by Breeden. The first was an outcome of instructions from Wood to limit political risk by going for the allowable minimum of closings. The second grew out of the gulf between Breeden and Coakley, who the court charged with planning revised geocoding and transportation to show the technical and desegregative feasibility of the plan. Although the work was easy to do and was in draft form

TABLE 4.3

**Excess Seats in Elementary Schools
by District, 1979**

District	Capacity[a]	Enroll-[b] ment	Difference	25% Cushion	Excess Seats	Utilization
1	3,420	2,211	1,209	302	907	.74
2	4,650	3,064	1,586	396	1,190	.75
3	4,954	2,825	2,129	532	1,597	.68
4	4,202	2,675	1,527	382	1,145	.73
5	7,788	5,566	2,222	555	1,667	.79
6	5,582 ·	3,087	2,495	624	1,871	.67
7	4,360	2,541	1,819	455	1,364	.69
8	2,344	1,510	834	208	626	.63
9	5,722	4,076	1,696	424	1,272	.78
Total	43,072	27,555	15,517	3,878	11,639	.73

[a]Capacity figures are from the Department of Implementation's Space/Program Matrix, March 1979.

[b]As of December 1979. K_1 and K_2 half-day students were counted as half students, and the seat capacity matrix was calculated by the same method.

early in October, it was not disseminated until December 1, and then in a very incomplete form.

More crucially, Coakley's Department of Implementation chose to align itself with the teachers and parent leaders organized to protest the plan. The department did not make extensive revisions in geocode attachments in order to optimize desegregation, explaining that the results would be "too disruptive." Instead, several old, previously rejected planning ideas were dusted off and presented by the department to illustrate that it was resourceful in responding to public clamor.[8]

In December 1979 the court began hearings on an emasculated version of the Breeden plan and on unsatisfactory submissions from Coakley. Wood's last-minute effort at emasculation did not net him a school committee endorsement. A motion for approval failed on a 2–1 vote in favor, with two of the five members abstaining. Endorsing Wood's proposal were Kathleen Sullivan Alioto and John D. O'Bryant, the only black member of the committee since the Reconstruction era.

In spite of what seemed to be insurmountable obstacles, the foundation for resolving the issue of facilities had by now been laid. The Breeden plan, the seating and program space matrix and improved enrollment records from the Department of Implementation, and the much-improved computer technology for mapping geocode unit attachments, facilitated soundness of judgment.

Judge Garrity's aim in reviewing the facilities plan was to lay a solid basis for future action on both schools and student assignments and then to ring down the curtain on the case he had been involved in for eight years. There would be a few other details to attend to, he announced, but the Unified Facilities Plan and related assignment revisions were to enable the court to disengage itself from school desegregation planning. Instead, the hearings dragged on from December to May 1980, and their subject matter became the *bete noire* of desegregation.

Coakley's assignment plans did not go the required distance. Along with Wood and attorney Simonds, Coakley formed a protective barrier around what he labeled a moderate reassignment approach. Its moderation consisted of making virtually no changes in the geocode maps save for the small handful of schools Wood proposed to close. It sapped the desegregative purpose of closing schools and fell far short of eliminating 5,000 of the 10,000 excess elementary seats.

As these realities became apparent, the other parties formed their first strong coalition, The Joint Plaintiffs, in an effort to prevent the closing of a single school. Larry Johnson, the plaintiffs' attorney, became the chief spokesman for the coalition, putting his black parent clients in the strange new bed of the Boston Teachers Union and the Boston Association of School Administrators. El Comite was there, too, as was the Citywide Parents Advisory Committee, the parent advisory body created by the court.

The Joint Plaintiffs advanced two main arguments. They claimed that the United Facilities Plan misstated the number of seats in each school by failing to count rooms used for such ancillary but important purposes as Title I programs, speech therapy, remedial reading, and music and art sessions. They submitted studies by parents and teachers showing a grave lack of correspondence between the Department of Implementation space matrix and the real uses space was serving. Next, they argued that school facilities should be equalized before more facilities were closed. They listed the many schools lacking libraries, cafeterias, and other minimal amenities. Both counts were termed evidence of the failure of the joint planners to do educational, as distinguished from physical and financial, planning.

Judge Garrity sent Wood, Breeden, and Coakley back to the drawing board. He could see from advisory analyses we provided that the system was awash with excess seats, that the figure of 10,000 was conservative, and that the arguments were devised in order to maintain the assignment *status quo ante*. Nevertheless, the court had never made independent judgments about facilities and seats other than to establish maximum allowable capacity for each building in 1975. These ceilings had often been lowered on motions from the defendant. Accordingly, the judge directed replanning that took the claims of The Joint Plaintiffs into close account.

As a result, the Department of Implementation (DI) made "new measurements" of schools that had been built and used 100 years earlier, and seats disappeared by the thousands (see Figure 4.1). Indeed, the new space matrix accommodated all claims and came out almost magically with an excess that would be cut in half *if* Wood's list of schools (and no others) were closed. The DI also reissued its moderate reassignment approach and added, with dire warnings, approaches of the kind the court ordered.

When the hearings resumed, it became obvious that the changes were no less objectionable to the teachers, administrators, and parents. Attorney Johnson renewed his call for a delay in facilities planning. In April, Judge Garrity issued an order and a long memorandum intended to break the stalemate. He approved Wood's list of closings, rejected some other features of the plan, and added two schools to Wood's list in order to spread the burden of the closings equally across the districts. In addition, he asked for further work on an assignment proposal from the DI.

Superintendent Wood revolted. He announced from every rooftop, and on television, that Judge Garrity "had gone too far" and that his experts were agents of inflexibility who had to be expunged. A week later, school committee defense attorney Marshall Simonds moved for a stay and appealed the orders, calling for a return to the 1979 space matrix and assignment plan. In argument before Judge Garrity, Larry Johnson opposed the stay and the appeal. That was on Friday. By Monday, before a three-judge appellate, he said he had changed his mind. Only State Attorney Robert Bohn, speaking for the Massachusetts Board of Education, opposed the stay; hence, it was granted.

Our informed but unproven assumption is that Wood achieved a trade-off with Johnson: In exchange for supporting or not blocking a stay, The Joint Plaintiffs were promised a full share in "educational planning." Johnson had explained earlier to each of us that he believed the case was about to enter a new phase, one in which equalization of facilities and programs would be the major issue.

Our impression is that Johnson was influenced powerfully by the ideas growing out of the Atlanta and Dallas cases, where plaintiffs traded off desegregation for power shares and policymaking positions. Those cases converge partially, as well, with the ideas of two Harvard professors, Derek Bell and Ronald Edmonds. Bell, a law professor, had once been an active attorney on the staff of the NAACP Legal Defense Fund. He argued many school desegregation cases, including *Inglewood* in Los Angeles, until he had conceived a new interpretation of the *Brown* decision. Edmonds was among the first educators to publicly attack the Phase II plan in Boston. These very prominent black professionals share the view that desegregation itself is

94

FIGURE 4.1
Sample Page from Space/Program Matrix

SPACES: A = 26, B = 15, C = 8, D = 0, K = 25/25

PROGRAM/SPACE ALLOCATION	A	B	C	D	K	TOTAL SPACES	ANCILLARY — LIBRARY R R	ITIN T I	H.E./SH.	ART/MUS.	READING	ESAA/636	ANC. TOTALS (Bil/Rg)	PROGRAMMATIC SPACES/SEATS	PROGRAMMATIC TOTALS (Bil or Rg / Seats)	NON-PROGRAMMATIC TOTALS (Bil or Rg / Seats)	ASSIGNABLE CAPACITY	UNASSIGNED ROOMS
District VII	A	B	C	D	K		R R	T I					Bil or Rg	(seats)	Bil or Rg / S E A T S	Bil or Rg / S E A T S		
Bancroft	13	0	2	0	1	16	3	E	E 2 1	1		1	Bil 1 / Rg 7	1 / 50 (K-S)	1 / 50	5/3 / 5/130, 3/90	270	0
Blackstone	34	8	5	6	6	59	1 / 3	1 / 6	2 1 2	2		2	Bil 1 / Rg 17	6 / 48 (SW); 2 / 40, 4L / 150 (K-S)	Bil 2 / 40; Rg 10 / 198	7 / 140; 15 / 390	768	7*
Bunker Hill	10	0	0	0	1	11	1 / 1	1 / 1	A 1 1	1			Rg 5	1 / 50 (K-S)	1 / 50	5 / 130	180	0
Eliot	18	1	0	0	1	20	2	2	2	1	1		Rg 5	2 / 16 (SW); 1B / 50 (K-S)	3 / 66	2 / 40; 10 / 260	366	0
Kent	25	2	5	0	5	37	1 / 2	1 / 4	1 1 2 1	2	1		Bil 1 / Rg 12	6 / 48 (SW); 3L / 100 (K-S)	9 / 148	7 / 140; 8 / 208	496	0
Hurley	16	2	6	1	1	26	1 / 2	1 / 6	6 1	1		1	Bil 1 / Rg 10	1 / 50 (K-S)	1 / 50	4 / 80; 10 / 260	390	0
Quincy	27	11	2	1	5	46	1 / 3	1 / 3	1 1 3 1	3	1		Bil 1 / Rg 13	3 / 24, 4 / 80 (SW/WS); 3 / 120, 3L / 100 (K-S)	Bil 3 / 120; Rg 10 / 204	7 / 140; 12 / 312	776	0
Prince	17	1	1	0	0	19	1 / 1	R 1	1	2			Bil 1 / Rg 5	4 / 100 (ADP)	4 / 100	4 / 80; 5 / 130	310	0
Warren-Prescott	22	0	0	0	2	24	1 / 2	A 1 2	1 1	2			Rg 8	3 / 24 (SW); 2 / 100 (K-S)	5 / 124	11 / 286	410	0
													Bil / Rg				3966	7
													Bil / Rg				446	

*approx.

unimportant but that deep reforms in the delivery of public instruction are crucial. They see desegregation as diverting attention from what is most important, equalized learning.

The logical *cost* of their policy preference is, of course, a renewal of some features of the patterns of separate but equal. That cost has been accepted in Boston by Larry Johnson in his allowance of segregative student assignments for 1980–1981. When pressed by Judge Garrity to acknowledge this openly, Johnson did so on the court record in May 1980.

In equity cases, the plaintiff's counsel governs the scope of the remedy. If Johnson wants three-quarters rather than a "full loaf" of desegregation, that is what his clients will get. In accepting a stay of Judge Garrity's orders, moreover, Johnson put the District Court in what Judge Garrity called "hibernation." The U.S. Court of Appeals may act in June 1981 on the appeal filed in May. Meanwhile, the United Facilities Plan is inert, students will be segregatively assigned under an order allowing but not approving this action, and other business will languish until 1981 — if it is taken up again at all.

Thus, the issue of facilities planning, associated with student relocations, at last broke the grip of the court. The likelihood that the remedy suit will revive around the issue of facility equalization seems to us to approximate zero. The Boston schools case climaxed in 1975 and reached its major, near-final anticlimax in 1980, after three years of trying and failing to consolidate the fit between facilities and desegregative assignments.

SOME IMPLICATIONS

The Coleman Report for the U.S. Congress published in 1966 affirmed the results of forty years of educational research when it concluded that physical facilities and equipment only negligibly affect the quality of teaching and learning in public school systems in the United States. When contrasted with such factors as the social and economic background of the student, the student's self-concept, the group mix of the student body, and the quality of daily teaching, school plant quality has little cumulative impact on achievement.

As with most generalizations, however, this one depends rather heavily upon the presence of a few minimum standards. A school plant should meet fire safety standards. The indoor temperature should be maintained somewhere between 60°F and 80°F during the cold season from November to March. There should be ample lighting by which to read books and blackboards. An exit to a corridor or to the outdoors should be available in each room. There should be toilet and washbowl facilities that tend to work on most school days. Broken windows should be replaced, especially in winter, and holes in roofs and ceilings ought to be repaired. We could get more particular than this and suggest that learning materials be available as well as state that blackboards and desks (or tables and chairs) are classroom essentials.

The impact of court planning and monitoring of implementation has been, in this respect, more profound than any other force ever exerted upon the school system. The most dangerous and unfit dungeons were ordered closed and repair and maintenance operations were stimulated tremendously, with the facilities in greatest need finally receiving attention. Major renovations and construction projects planned by the city and the state were resumed; some were even completed on schedule or only two to three years behind schedule. Rational, joint planning for the future was insisted upon by the court and mechanisms for review and monitoring, as well as desegregative coordination, were established.

This transformative impact resulted in the development of a set of minimum standards for schoolhouses, such as a ceiling on the number of students that can legally be assigned to each building. Still, the structural conditions that led to the Boston nightmare have gone unchanged. Some buildings are kept spotless, well heated or cooled, and well lighted, while others deteriorate into trash heaps.

In addition, administrative problems still exist. The membership of the Public Facilities Commission does not include a single school committee member or agent. It answers to the mayor alone. The state board finances renovations and construction, but its authority to intervene and affect conditions directly is exceptionally weak. Planners in the school department ostensibly serve under the superintendent, but their tiny staff does not include any professionals trained in engineering, architecture, city planning, or construction.

As a result of these deficiencies, school facilities are managed in the tradition of a shell game at a carnival. The suckers—teachers, parents, and children—cannot win against the house odds. The operatives resemble paid shills, who live within their salaries but make the house arrangements for others. There are thus several autonomous games working at the same stand. There are custodial appointments by the school committee, work orders and contracts for repairs, architectural engineering and bidding management for new projects and renovations by the Public Facilities Commission, and legislative and statehouse participation in the financing of new construction projects. The return potential of all of these combined is too great to estimate. Equal and minimally decent facilities, equipment, and materials for all of the city's public schools will be achievable only when the state or the city, as a polity, cancels the game.

CONCLUSION

The effects of desegregation are almost always profound. Desegregation can force those affected by it to seriously consider what they regarded as acceptable school facilities for their children *before* desegregation took place. It may also force those affected to re-evaluate their success in fulfilling this vision over the years.

Because Boston has one of the oldest public school systems in North America, these effects become more dramatic in this city. Desegregation has had similar effects in the much newer buildings of Los Angeles as well, however. Extremities of deferred maintenance, cheap siting, and poor architecture and construction are noteworthy disclosures and they unfold to view from Alabama to Cleveland, and from Boston to Pasadena, once the call for equal protection is sounded.

The Coleman Report, itself a landmark research by-product of school desegregation, confirms forty years of research evidence that suggests that there is little if any connection between quality of facilities and quality of learning. This finding has enduring truth. It also helps us place our emphasis upon other policy and program factors. The finding may be, in another sense, an artifact of elaboration of the *status quo*: Facilities may be so unimportant because we have made them so, just as curriculum is not influential for the same reason. In other words, the evidence is an analytically valid description of what exists. We have attended very little to formulating what might become influential.

Copley Square High School in Boston may illustrate the point. It occupies two old brownstones in the Back Bay neighborhood, which is central to the city in many ways. The facilities can accommodate only 550 students and a faculty of 30, and even then they are crowded and very hard to keep clean.

Still, the program fits the plant. The academic courses are college-oriented and rigorous, but they are augmented by off-campus studies and diverse work and project experiences. Morale is high, student applications for entrance are numerous, and achievement outcomes are fairly impressive.

Copley Square demonstrates how unimportant the facility can be compared to program and faculty. It also demonstrates, however, how important the facility can be. The brownstones are ideally sited for off-campus projects. Attending them means entering a vibrant part of the city that reveals adult urbanites at work. The building itself, while a bit shabby and cluttered, has the singular advantage of appearing to be a cross between a chic pair of townhouses and the offices of a research or advertising firm. Finally, the scale is fitting for the program, which celebrates the growth of individualism. At yet a third level of meaning, Copley Square High invites us to imagine how much better a school it might become if its plant and equipment were made to serve its program.

The absence of playgrounds, gymnasiums, lunchrooms, practice rooms, art and craft shops, TV and other instructional media equipment, libraries, offices for teachers, and usable rest rooms—all commonplace in Boston schools—does not cause poor academic achievement. But their absence, like the siting of a new high school next to a city dump, transmits clear messages to teachers and students about the unimportance of schooling. These messages certainly have the power to depress motivation in some students.

Desegregation also discloses our national ignorance about other educational design standards. Is the factory our model? How many students should fit into each box? When is a building underutilized? Does it affect the learning of children when they are gathered on one floor and two others are closed off and left in disrepair? When does a building become obsolete? When is it unsafe? When tough decisions must be made about who goes where to school, our false pride about variety crumbles. While no one would actually advocate the end of design diversity, our collective inability to set some standards makes it very difficult to make responsive choices.

In the course of making such decisions, what is more, we realize that public schools are not built for the sole purpose of serving students. They are built in order to affect land values, to sustain the builders and contractors, to cultivate funds and votes, and to make jobs for adults. When a court orders equalization, the deepest layers of inequality founded on exploitative self-interest are apt to be laid bare. On the eve of desegregation, Boston, and later Cleveland and Chicago, was found to be verging on bankruptcy. In the midst of court-ordered reform of occupational education in Boston, the associate commissioner for occupational education was convicted of fraud and theft of public funds, in concert with many educators serving as consultants. New school construction lags years behind schedule as costly "mistakes" plague the contractors. Repairs are requisitioned but left undone for years.

Thus, school facilities are a mirror in which we behold ourselves as indifferent to the needs and interests of children, eager to profit at someone's disadvantage, incapable of simple agreements about standards, and ready to rationalize the whole as educationally unimportant, or to sentimentalize the deteriorated school across the street because it is our beloved "neighborhood school." The image we see in the mirror is not that of Boston; it is one of every metropolitan area in North America.

A court is the next to the least preferred place for making social policy. The worst place is on the battlefield. A court is not a planning agency nor is it a good substitute for elective and appointive administration. In the educational ruins of Boston, it was the last resort and the only source of hope for reformative justice. Its achievements, too, are therefore reflected in the mirror of school facilities.

In a five-year period, the court closed forty buildings and approximately thirty annexes and portables. These were, *without exception*, unfit, outmoded, and antithetical to good teaching and learning. In the same period, the court forced the construction of about eight new, superior schools, the renovation of ten others, and the repair of another fifty. There is no doubt in our minds that these were highly desirable and necessary contributions to the public interest.

At the same time, the very intervention of the court confounded the policy of desegregation, reducing its ability to make reasonable collective decisions on its own. The side effects of intervention—of doing that which elected leaders refused to do—have clouded the image in the mirror. Many Bostonians can no longer perceive the situation of their city, and many more have concluded mistakenly that the children are worse, not better off, than before. It may take the rest of this century for the clouds to roll away.

The side effects offer compelling reasons why other public school districts should design and install equities of their own, in preference to being taken to federal court. In Minneapolis, for example, the school board gave such compelling evidence of readiness to remedy its segregative wrongs that the court awarded three years for advance work leading up to implementation. By going to court in defiance of the Constitution, in contrast, Chicago will risk self-destruction.

These effects do not justify judicial inaction or avoidance, however. A court remedy will, in all cases, have deep impacts on facilities. Those who think of the problems as a matter of merely redistributing students have failed to attend to the issue. In Boston, where school buildings ranged from architectural glories to antiquated hovels, the court remedy has been, from necessity, so pervasive as to modify the map of the city and change the locks on the lockers in the halls. The vastness has proved incomprehensible to most citizens.

In one of her first speeches after being appointed U.S. Secretary of Education, Shirley Hufstedler called for a new approach to quality desegregated education. She urged the relocation of school facilities from residential neighborhoods to work sites, noting that millions of mothers now work full time and that the work site is more integrated than the neighborhood.

We think her policy proposal is inventive and highly desirable. It will converge with trends in preschooling, alternative, and career education in valuable ways. The meaning of the Boston case, however, points to the strength of political as well as capital investments in public school facilities. If public education is not to continue to deteriorate over time into a quaint yet irrelevant leftover from 1911, and if it is to be brought into the more electronically and occupationally integrated society of the 1980s, some method of educating parents must be devised.

Currently, there is great electoral "mileage" left for leaders to continue disguising the fact that the children have disappeared and that the buildings will not suffice for the future. Even an urbanist of the stature of Robert Wood staked his local career on the fantasy that legions of child-rearing families will return to Boston.

NOTES

1. James S. Coleman, in his 1966 report, *Equality of Educational Opportunity*, challenged the commonly held assumption that the schools black children attended were inferior to those attended by white students. The survey found surprisingly small differences between predominantly black and white schools. In their review of this finding, Frederick Mosteller and Daniel Moynihan stated, "Obviously, this was disconcerting. No one then thought the result would be close . . . ." *On Equality of Educational Opportunity*, New York, 1972, pp. 8–9.

Few reviewers (Dentler included, when he published the first review of the landmark study) noted that twelve years after *Brown*, many Deep South and border state districts had cleaned up their facility inequities. Midwestern and western states did not have those inequities except in big cities not included in the sample. New York City refused to participate and Boston was not in the draw.

2. We mean this rather literally. In a few decades, builders seem to have been selected for their competence since some facilities built between 1880 and 1911 are excellent. However, in other periods, selection procedures, both political and financial, favored high orders of incompetence or the outer reaches of cheapness—or a combination of both.

3. Our investigations never induced action by the court to intervene on a single facility independent of findings from the Public Facilities Department, but they influenced substantially the point of view of the masters and, later, the judge.

4. Carter Temporary has survived all changes, including subway construction running within a few feet of one of its walls. We predict that it will be standing and in use in the year 2000.

5. Phase II order, Part II, pp. 77–78.

6. In its *Spangberg* decision on Pasadena, the U.S. Supreme Court ruled that the district court could not try to extend desegregation by changing its plan after resegregation set in. Home and School Association attorney Fremont-Smith made much of this in the Boston case, and Simonds tried later to do so, but both ignored a key feature of the decision: it concerned an effort to prevent minorities from becoming the majority in any given school. In short, it ruled against a quest for racial balance. The Boston plan was not based on this precept.

7. As with school closings, Judge Garrity did not calculate the number of excess seats. This was done by the Department of Implementation.

8. One such plan was called the beacon schools concept. It was a warmed-over version of a part of Coakley's 1975 plan that had been rejected by the masters and entailed proliferating magnet schools within the eight community districts. Another was called the linkage concept. Each declining facility would be linked with a viable one, and students would be guaranteed seats in one or the other facility if and when one had to be closed. Over a six-year period Coakley's range of inventiveness was confined to the quest for magnets on one end and a passion for what he called "stability" on the other. This range expressed succinctly the planning imaginations of thousands of voters, however, and should not be ascribed solely to him. He was the reed bending in the winds.

TRANSPORTATION 5

BUSING AS A TOOL IN DESEGREGATION

BUSES HAVE BEEN USED as a means of conveyance for many centuries. Whether the vehicle carrying passengers was drawn by oxen, horses, electricity, or gasoline engine, the basic purpose and design of the bus has changed very little over time. Early in the twentieth century, the bus took on extra importance in American life. For the millions who could not afford to own a Model T Ford, travel by bus became the best alternative. By the 1920s, the bus had begun to serve as the universal mode of transportation for the nation's rural and urban poor.

In rural America, riding the bus became the natural way of getting to and from public school, and the bus remains the prime means of bringing the children and youth of the countryside together, in increasingly centralized locations, for common learning experiences. In most rural counties, the practice of maintaining separate schools and of making black students pass one schoolhouse to attend classes in another ended during the 1950s. And in the nation's suburbs, the relatively fair and impartial drawing of attendance zones within which students are transported daily by bus has been a routine practice for thirty years.

In some of the largest central cities, however, the practice of advantaging some students and disadvantaging others through the siting of school facilities and the provision or denial of transportation has tended to persist.

The myth of the neighborhood school is central to this persistent practice. Some neighborhood constituencies have managed to establish political hegemony over facilities erected at public expense but maintained to service some residential blocks and not others. City-wide schools have been maintained and transportation provided for those privileged enough to gain access, while other students have been set apart from either of these arrangements.

In many big cities, these patterns suggest that there is a strong ecological correlation between the residential distribution of ethnic minorities and the location of quality schools. It is no accident, therefore, that the term busing came to be synonymous with policies that threatened these long-standing practices of educational advantage. Survey research has demonstrated repeatedly over the years that almost no one cares about the matter of busing itself.[1] What a majority of parents have cared about intensely is the danger they felt to be inherent in the advent of busing, coupled with mandatory assignments that scattered students to locations the majority of them had successfully avoided in the past.[2] Even those within the majority who continued to be assigned to the schoolhouse across the street from home cared intensely about the possibility that new strangers would now arrive at that school, conveyed on yellow buses. Every urban school desegregation process depends for its successes and failures, therefore, upon transportation planning and implementation.

TRANSPORTATION SYSTEM COMPLEXITIES

Contrary to popular thinking, the operation of a contemporary school transport system involves far more than the mere provision of yellow buses. In Boston today, for instance, the school department arranges with various carriers for the daily transportation of about 39,000 students, or more than half of the total student enrollment. Services are purchased from five different vendors for bus, van, and station wagon services at a cost of more than twelve million dollars a year.

There are, in fact, seven types of student transportation. Regular transport is daily service to and from schools for students in grades 1 through 12, and is provided by yellow bus vendors from corner-to-corner pickup points covered by hundreds of 65-passenger vehicles. A second service is delivered by the regional transit authority, the Massachusetts Bay Transportation Authority (MBTA), whose subways and buses carry high school students by the thousands each day under special reduced fare arrangements. High school students also ride MBTA vehicles to a central point where they are met by yellow school buses and carried the remainder of the distance to and from school.

Isolated transportation services consisting of station wagons, vans, and minibuses that pick up students living a long way from regular routes and other students makes up a fourth type. Until 1980, the Boston schools planned this last service on a door-to-door basis, but it has since become a corner pickup arrangement for reasons of economy. Kindergarten students are treated separately from other elementary children (for reasons understood only by Bostonians), and this has resulted in a fifth type of service, operated until 1979 as a door-to-door service and then revised to a corner pickup arrangement.

Students with special needs who are assigned to substantially separate classes receive a sixth type of transport service. Station wagons and vans, many of them equipped with gear to assist persons with disabilities, are operated on a door-to-door basis. The seventh type is a miscellany: transport services for special programs operating at some schools, physical education and varsity athletic team buses, vocational education transport services to and from work sites and job skill training facilities, field trip buses, buses for emergency use, and late buses for students detained after school for any reason.

THE LOCAL HISTORY OF BUSING

A journalist reporting on busing in Boston in 1973 might have concluded, if he had only a few hours to research the story, that the city schools were based on a neighborhood system and therefore required little student transportation services. He or she might have heard that about 1,000 students were carried on school buses from remote residential locations, and that another 1,000 handicapped students received door-to-door taxicab and van service. What that journalist would have missed were the many chartered buses that came and went each day from the two Latin schools and Boston Technical High, and the 27,000 other students who traveled daily via the buses and subways of the MBTA on passes supplied by the school department.

A Transportation Department within school headquarters planned and managed this fragmented yet large-scale set of transport arrangements. It was directed by Henry Hurley, a former school bus driver, and contained a staff of about ten who not only handled this service, but also assisted some school committee members in the conduct of a variety of private special services. These included scheduling tax form preparation, selling insurance, and providing legal advice to teachers. When the court ordered that Phase I of school desegregation begin in June 1974, the Transportation Department operations were expanded and the department was relocated in an aban-

doned schoolhouse on Beacon Hill. It was set apart from other system operations, yet it had the ambience of a city firehouse located close to the seat of all
heavy forms of public business, the statehouse.

It became apparent that implementation of Phase I would not result in
the busing of more students, but that the time had come for introducing busing
through contracts with vendors. After all, under state law, busing costs were
reimbursable by the state not only for long-distance trips but for desegregation and for safety purposes related to desegregation.

Three-year contracts were thus signed with three vending carriers—
Hudson Bus Lines, Brush Hill Auto Body Inc., and William S. Carroll Inc. A
fourth carrier, Rewhit Transport, Inc., was added later. An important and, for
some interests, highly profitable decision had been reached. Unlike dozens of
other large central-city school systems throughout the nation, Boston did not
purchase a fleet of vehicles nor hire a corps of drivers and maintenance
workers. It drew instead upon vendors, leaving to them the uncertainties of
weather, scheduling, repairs, and the bonding of drivers. The school committee did not inform the public of the fact that no vendors existed in the Boston
area with these capabilities, or that it had decided to avoid investment in and
reliance upon the MBTA.

In 1974 the distances students were permitted to be bused were severely
limited by restrictions written into the state's Racial Imbalance Act, on which
the Phase I plan was based. In addition, fewer than half the schools in the city
were affected by the Phase I plan. Therefore, the newly emerging system of
busing was not grossly overtaxed, all routes were covered, and transportation did not appear for a time to loom as a major source of future problems.

THE PHASE II PLAN AND BUSING

The permanent court plan, however, made new and vaster demands on
this fledgling operation. All schools were now included in the busing plan.

Busing distances within community districts were limited to an average
of not more than 2.5 miles, and the longest allowable bus trip was limited to 4.9
miles. Bus travel times, said the court plan (based almost word for word upon
the masters' report), were to average between ten and fifteen minutes each
way within community districts. The longest trips anywhere were to take no
more than twenty-five minutes each way. Buses were to be provided for every
elementary school student who lived more than one mile from his or her
assigned school, and for middle and high school students who lived more than
two miles away from their assigned schools.

The court assigned us as its liaison agents in the planning of all aspects
of the Phase II busing operation. We were to work with the Boston School
Department's Associate Superintendent for Support Services, Charles
Leftwich, and after we had reviewed the results with Judge Garrity, the plans
were to be reviewed for final additions or corrections by members of the
newly formed Community District Advisory Councils (CDACs).

Our first discovery was that the Transportation Department staff did not include anyone capable of planning. We saw Henry Hurley at only two short meetings; he was caught up in the conduct of "more vital business" with committee members and bus company managers. Our meetings were handled instead by the department's assistant director, George Fallon, known affectionately as "Ace." Ace did not give any evidence that he knew much about transportation planning. For many years he had served as a classroom teacher and then as a minor functionary within school headquarters. He rose to this high post by providing imaginative special services not related to busing.

The coordination of busing plans for each of the nine districts in the court plan was in the hands of a single man, and each man drew a map of where the buses might travel and where they might make their daily pickups. This approach made it possible to simplify the planning task because each "planner" could act as if his district was a thing apart. It also resulted in extraordinary compounding of costs.

Little progress could be made until August because the department's assignment unit was unable to complete the planning of assignments until July, and routes for buses could not be planned until these were available. At the same time the transport planning began, moreover, thousands of parents filed applications for student transfers, leaving Hurley's men uncertain about who might be going where in September.

Somehow, a set of routes and schedules was prepared before mid-August. The court reviewed the crude entries and then asked for CDAC reviews.

Much to our amazement, CDACs and other interest groups historically opposed to busing began to press hard for greatly expanded services. The standard of safety was stretched to its outermost limit as bus after bus was added to the list; some of them would travel less than six blocks. On instructions from Hurley, his men factored nearly all of these additional requests into the 1975 plan. The estimate we had submitted to the court was that about 24,000 out of 85,000 students would need transporting under its Phase II plan. As the busing plan was redesigned to meet this novel upsurge in demand, the number rose to about 27,000.

Very little time was left for practice runs or other preparations by the vendors. They were left scampering for extra vehicles and new drivers up until the last two days before the schools opened. When they did open, the multiplication of errors was a wonder to behold. Thousands of students were left stranded at pickup points because buses never came. Less fortunate students boarded buses on schedule but were then driven about the city for as long as an hour and a half in search of schools that were usually less than 2.5 miles away from the pickup points. Some districts had their streets choked temporarily with buses that made their runs without the burden of riders. Thousands of assignments had been changed and thousands of students had withdrawn from school or were kept home by parents as an expression of protest. Other districts had too few buses, and so on.

Back at transportation headquarters, these crises seemed to Fallon and his team mere challenges to be worked out by further mapping, calls on walkie-talkies, and a great deal of chasing about to "clear up small snafus," as Ace assured us. And indeed, within two weeks, the newly emerged system seemed to have taken hold. Buses could still be seen making their runs without passengers, to be sure, but most students made increasingly accurate connections with one bus or another and Boston began to put its program of busing on what Scott liked to term "automatic pilot." Judge Garrity's skepticism never diminished, however, after he learned from his senior clerk that the clerk's daughter had ridden for an hour and a quarter one way in order to get to a magnet middle school located only two miles from her home. He prophesied more trouble to come, and he was right.

FOUR YEARS OF LITIGATION

In March 1976, the Boston School Committee and City Corporation Counsel began to investigate the performance of the bus companies based on suspicions of overbilling. By early fall of 1977, County District Attorney Garrett Byrne sent these officials a fifty-five-page analysis of billings showing that the four companies first hired in 1974 had overcharged the city by $923,000, and that $787,000 of this amount had already been paid them. The excess charges were due to charges for alleged extra trips during Phase I, for early dismissals of students during Phase II, and for standby buses used during student and neighborhood conflicts in the fall of 1975. Most of the overbilling was done by two vendors, Brush Hill and Rewhit Transport Inc., but all four were implicated.

In the fall of 1977, while state court litigation got underway around these charges, the school committee filed a second complaint, this one against Richard Zimmerman, the president and treasurer of the Lexington Taxi Company. The committee charged the company, later known as Transportation Management Corporation (TMC), with fifteen counts of malfeasance for nonservice.

In one of the counts, TMC was charged with having claimed to bus special needs students who did not exist and others who had long since withdrawn from the schools. In another, the company was charged with having reduced the maximum carrying capacity of its vehicles from nine to eight passengers, with corresponding increases in its charges amounting eventually to $1.2 million, even though the contract with the school committee had not changed.

TMC countered by suing the Boston School Committee, stating that unless the committee dropped its suit and paid the bills for extra runs made when loadings were reduced, the company would (1) repudiate its contractual obligations and sell its assets, including vans and minibuses; (2) fail to renew its performance bond; and (3) cease to provide services.

In turn, the committee sought an injunction to prevent TMC from taking these steps, in view of its discovery that no alternative companies could provide transportation for more than 2,500 special needs children. In addition, the committee moved that the state court appoint a temporary receiver to manage and conserve the assets of the company.

While this case was taking shape, the Massachusetts Education Department had begun to rigorously scrutinize billings from the school committee for reimbursements; many challenges were made as a result of faulty or unverified records, and these disputes continued from 1977 through 1980.

In January of 1980, parents brought a class action suit against the school committee. Seeking financial compensation for damages, the parents charged that the faulty transportation system deprived children with special needs of educational services. These charges were the result of TMC's failure to deliver timely, accurate, and consistent transportation to and from schools. The parents' suit also charged that the school committee was violating its obligation to carry out federal and state court orders. In 1978 a state superior court ordered TMC to provide services under the terms fixed in 1977, which included transporting kindergarten as well as special needs students.

What is most revealing about the court order for desegregation planning is the inclusion in that order of directives to the school department's director of the implementation unit to plan and establish all of the routes and pickups for all vehicles furnished by the corporation. The court also required that the routes and schedules to be used be fixed no later than one week before they were to be implemented, and that no child undergo a bus or cab ride of more than one hour. If any ride lasted for more than one hour for more than ten days in a row or if any ride resulted in student tardiness for more than ten percent of the time in a two-week period, the transportation director was required to revise the schedule. (There is no correspondence between these standards and those set forth in the permanent order of the federal court.)

In considering the school committee's complaints against TMC, the state judge found in favor of most of the school committee complaints. He barred TMC from selling its equipment and increased the span of control over busing accorded the school transportation director.

In another litigation in state court, Brush Hill sued for payment by the school committee of an unpaid series of transport bills dating back to 1974 and amounting to $453,900. The company also alleged that it had found it necessary over the years to expand the security protection of its buses and had incurred extra costs of $96,477. Payment of $200,000 was also requested by Brush Hill because, the company stated, "civil strife" had resulted in the extra repair costs for damage to its buses.[3]

This case is still pending, but in filing its defense, the school committee admitted to failure to pay the vendor in full. At the same time, the school committee filed a new set of charges, this time aiming them at the Peerless Insurance Company. The committee accused the bonding agent, located in New Hampshire, of overcharging—by $376,000.

In still another suit, the Cambridge Taxi Company in 1978 sued the city, the school committee, several persons in the Department of Implementation, and the Transportation Management Corporation. According to this complaint, Miguel Torrado, the transportation engineer who had succeeded Henry Hurley and others, labored to convince bidders on busing for handicapped students to reduce the amounts of their competitive bids. When Cambridge Taxi was awarded a contract, he and others demanded the company further reduce its offered price.

According to Cambridge Taxi, which was granted the contract but later lost it to TMC, Torrado and attorneys for the Boston City Law Department used the initial awarding of the contract to the taxi company to convince TMC to drop its suit against the Department of Implementation in order to be favored with the contract.

This suit has not yet been resolved, but we have learned several important things from studying the filings. One is that the Boston City Law Department, not the school department, controls the process of fixing contracts for bus services. While Torrado and others from the Department of Implementation were involved in the bidding processes, all decisions were made by city hall lawyers. Another is that Cambridge Taxi had made a price proposal of $6.90 per pupil per day, when the price for an identical service in Brookline, the closest suburban district to Boston, was $2.83.

Until we studied these filings, we could not understand why School Superintendent Robert Wood suspended Miguel Torrado in 1978 without explanation. That action had seemed bizarre to us, for Torrado had brought the transportation unit out of its Hurley era and into the contemporary period by applying skills in transport planning. Indeed, during his time in the job, the Department of Implementation had begun to computerize student assignments and transfers and to integrate these with transportation routing and scheduling plans (see Figure 5.1). We still do not know whether his suspension was due to the allegations made in the Cambridge Taxi litigation or to the risks he took in trying to computerize kindergarten busing. Those risks resulted in a brief period in 1978 when massive mistakes in schedules and pickups were made.

Overbillings, services failures, breakdowns in bidding procedures, and problems in performance bonding were not the only sources of bitter court battles during these years. In another kind of action in 1977, Hudson Bus Lines sought a preliminary injunction to enjoin and restrain bus drivers from threatening or engaging in any work stoppages at their garages and from

FIGURE 5.1

Computer-Printed Transportation Notice

```
* * *  OFFICIAL TRANSPORTATION NOTIFICATION  * * *

                ROBERT      MOY
SHALL BE TRANSPORTED TO -
    2010  EDWARDS MIDDLE          28   WALKER ST      CHARLESTOWN
    GRADE   08

ON THE MORNING OF WEDNESDAY, SEPTEMBER 5, 1979 BY -
    BUS NO.  7151    BEFORE  07-00 A.M.
    TREMONT AT HERALD

REPORT TO THE PICKUP LOCATION ABOVE FIVE MINUTES BEFORE THE TIME
STATED ABOVE.  SHOW THIS NOTIFICATION WHEN BOARDING THE BUS.

THE RULES AND REGULATIONS OF THE BOSTON SCHOOL DEPARTMENT MUST
BE OBSERVED FOR SAFETY REASONS.  THE BUS DRIVER AND BUS MONITOR
ARE THE RESPONSIBLE SCHOOL DEPARTMENT PERSONNEL.  FOLLOW THEIR
INSTRUCTIONS.  ALLOW THE SAME AMOUNT OF TIME FOR THE RETURN
TRIP HOME.

FOR FURTHER INFORMATION, PLEASE CALL 726-6555.

                               2010   485159
                               MOY              GAN CHEUNG
                               MOY              ROBERT
                                  15 EMERALD CT          APT.    B
08/23/79 195916   114841       SOUTH END        MA 02118
```

```
* * *  OFFICIAL TRANSPORTATION NOTIFICATION  * * *

               SOOKCHEE JEN MUI
SHALL BE TRANSPORTED TO -
    2010  EDWARDS MIDDLE          28   WALKER ST      CHARLESTOWN
    GRADE   06

ON THE MORNING OF WEDNESDAY, SEPTEMBER 5, 1979 BY -
    BUS NO.  7151    BEFORE  07-00 A.M.
    TREMONT AT HERALD

REPORT TO THE PICKUP LOCATION ABOVE FIVE MINUTES BEFORE THE TIME
STATED ABOVE.  SHOW THIS NOTIFICATION WHEN BOARDING THE BUS.

THE RULES AND REGULATIONS OF THE BOSTON SCHOOL DEPARTMENT MUST
BE OBSERVED FOR SAFETY REASONS.  THE BUS DRIVER AND BUS MONITOR
ARE THE RESPONSIBLE SCHOOL DEPARTMENT PERSONNEL.  FOLLOW THEIR
INSTRUCTIONS.  ALLOW THE SAME AMOUNT OF TIME FOR THE RETURN
TRIP HOME.

FOR FURTHER INFORMATION, PLEASE CALL 726-6555.

                               2010   557531
                               MUI              CHI KEUNG
                               MUI              SOOKCHEE JEN
                                  48 PAUL PL            APT.    A
08/23/79 195916   114842       SOUTH END        MA 02118
```

refusing to drive regular school bus routes under their contract. This action resulted because hundreds of drivers who had been hired by the vendors to perform the new transport services began to organize for unionization in 1976. Struggles developed and raged for a year, not only between managements and drivers but between rival unions.

Just before Christmas in 1977, the drivers began to picket, to devise work stoppages, and to strike. The court found that the drivers did not have the right to strike as employees of a set of vendors working under pre-existing and fixed municipal contracts. At the same time, the court ruled that the drivers should have the right to engage in union representation elections supervised by the American Arbitration Association and the Massachusetts Labor Relations Commission. The drivers *did* achieve union representation of their choosing and they did not threaten the viability of busing again until October 1980.

Here was the picture, then, of a city devising outrageously costly contracts with incompletely equipped and insufficiently bonded vendors who in turn hired drivers on ambiguous terms and in some instances hired drivers who should have been screened from this line of work. As late as May 1980, some handicapped children and youth were still being denied adequate van and taxi transportation to and from public schools in Boston. Four years of unremitting and costly litigation has yet to resolve a number of the issues underlying this botched scene.

REFLECTIONS ON LESSONS LEARNED

Miguel Torrado was the first person we met who advanced a serious and well-planned design for purchasing and operating a fleet of buses and vans. In our capacity as court representatives, we discussed this with him and associates in the Department of Implementation several times in 1978, but his plans were never reviewed in earnest by others in the Boston School Department hierarchy.

Late in 1979, however, the idea took root in the mind of Robert Wood, and the school committee committed itself to considering the idea as a matter of policy, promising to contract an independent study. The committee did not go so far as to consider hiring and managing drivers, nor was there talk of shifting full authority from the city hall law department to the school department, two policy moves essential to bringing rationality to the busing arrangement.

Our guess is that under the twin forces of inflation and recession, with city hall moving to cut back its entire work force in desperate efforts to prevent bankruptcy, the policy will not be implemented. The opportunity for action was lost somewhere between 1970 and 1980, but we may be mistaken. What emerges from the mire of Boston politics is often very slow in taking usable shape, yet it is also true that it somehow or sometimes heaves into being after years of intrigue and debate.

During the decade of the 1970s, the subway system of the MBTA was racked by equivalent shocks of overpayment, faulty equipment purchases, massive breakdowns, and political and litigative chaos. This creates a backdrop for what can be seen through the rear view mirror of hindsight. It tells us that this was a period when a new and efficient school transport system could hardly be created under conditions that were breeding chaos in the region's largest public transit authority.

Federal court foresight, including our own as its agents overseeing transportation planning, was as feeble as everyone's in 1975 and 1976. Court hearings that bore on the topic, for instance, were preoccupied with the unavailability of late afternoon buses and field trip services, issues of trivial import compared to massive schedule failures. Neither the plaintiffs' nor the intervenors' attorneys ever made a motion for serious remediation of the manifestly failing busing system.

The court did not probe the issue, although the local newspapers reported periodically on parent complaints and on the state court litigations. Attorney Larry Johnson did move once for more buses and more protection for minority high school students, and some small improvements were made. On another occasion, in reviewing busing plans in 1979, we found that in some schools the start of classes had been changed from 8:00 a.m. to 7:20 a.m. and 7:35 a.m., meaning students had to rise at 6 a.m. each morning to get ready. This change was planned by the Department of Implementation in order to economize on bus runs. We learned that many teachers liked the arrangement because they could leave for second jobs at 12:30 p.m. each day, but Judge Garrity intervened and held to 7:50 a.m. as the earliest time classes could commence. Even this hour seemed to us a hardship and a deterrent to school attendance, but we heard no chorus of support from parents or administrators.

Judge Garrity also took pains to stand aside from labor disputes and celebrated the fact that this and other issues were being dealt with in state superior courts. All of us missed the important point, however, that busing was pivotal to fulfillment of the court desegregation plan and that it was not being provided in a satisfactory fashion.

AN INDEPENDENT TRANSPORTATION SYSTEM STUDY

The school committee commissioned the management consulting firm of Cresap, McCormick and Paget, Inc. to study the school transport "system," and that firm filed its initially confidential report with the committee on Halloween 1979 (see Table 5.1).

Much can be learned from the contents of this study which was, in our opinion, conducted in an expert and socially responsible manner, and we have drawn on some of the firm's data in devising tables for this chapter. The report does not document or summarize the variety of severe disruptions and chaotic disorders the system was heir to during its five years, but its criteria, conclusions, and recommendations demonstrate the awareness of the analysts and provide future planners with informative guidance.

TABLE 5.1

**Students Transported to Boston Public Schools
with 1983-84 Projections**

| School Year | Assigned Enrollment | | Number (Percentage) Transported[a] | | | | | |
	Total	Kindergarten	Isolated	Kindergarten	Special Needs	Regular	Car Check[b]	Total
1974-75	85,805	11,111	960 (1.1)	100 (0.9)	1,000 (1.2)	n.a.	n.a.	—
1975-76	82,932	10,225	1,100 (1.3)	900 (8.8)	2,000 (2.4)	n.a.	n.a.	—
1976-77	76,180	8,423	1,200 (1.6)	1,800 (21.4)	2,200 (2.9)	n.a.	n.a.	...
1977-78	75,338	8,588	1,250 (1.7)	2,350 (27.4)	3,070 (4.1)	26,000 (34.5)	6,000 (8.0)	38,670 (51.3)
1978-79	72,358	8,264	960 (1.3)	3,100 (37.5)	3,150 (4.4)	25,300 (35.0)	6,500 (9.0)	39,010 (53.9)
1979-80	68,762	7,276	494[c] (0.7)	3,067[c] (42.2)	3,483[c] (5.1)	25,300 (37.4)	6,500 (8.9)	38,868[c] (56.5)
1983-84	54,151	6,585	0-400 (0.7)	2,800-3,100 (42.5-47.1)	2,800-3,700 (5.2-6.8)	20,000-25,000 (36.9-46.2)	6,000 (11.1)	31,600-38,200 (58.4-70.5)

SOURCE: Cresap, McCormack, and Paget, 1979.

NOTE: n.a. = not available.

[a]Percentage of total assigned enrollment, except for kindergarten, where percentage is of total kindergarten enrollment.

[b]Token or pass used on Massachusetts Bay Transit Authority vehicles.

[c]Estimated.

Seven "transportation delivery system design criteria" are presented in the study: student safety, system responsiveness to changes, reliability in delivering timely and appropriate service, adequate management controls, management structure simplicity, protection against service disruptions due to contractor failure and weather, and cost-effectiveness. In its summary of findings, the study reveals the gaps that exist between these criteria and actual performance:

> The Transportation Function Lacks Sufficient Focus and Impact.... There is no one position that is clearly accountable for transportation.... Issues are addressed on an *ad hoc* rather than a systematic basis....

> Within the Department of Implementation, Clearer Definition of Priorities in Transportation Operations Needs to be Reflected in Job Definitions.... The specific responsibilities of routing and scheduling, complaint handling, and working with special needs problems are inadequately focused.

> Transportation Planning is Short Term and Not Adequately Comprehensive or Coordinated.... The operations and costs of transportation are not explicitly considered in assigning students to schools.... The constraints of cost, long-term projections, and related decisions, such as the Unified Facilities Plan and the new Occupational Resources Center, are not sufficiently integrated into the planning effort.

> The Cost-Effectiveness of Routing and Scheduling is Limited.... Current standards for service require a large number of pickup points and routes. Contributing to this number are the separate kindergarten route and the one-half-mile standard for maximum walking distance to pickup point (one-fourth of a mile for kindergarten students). The use of distinct types of vehicles for regular and special needs transportation also contributes to routing difficulties...Routing and scheduling are done independently for each district. This practice prevents the use of vehicles for routes in different districts when location and availability might justify it....The contractor's incentive is to schedule vehicles and drivers so as to give him the lowest cost per student. This may not be most effective, however, and since service is priced on a per student basis, cost savings are not passed along to the school committee.

> Insufficient Mechanisms Exist For Adequately Controlling the Quality and Cost.... No systematic approach to monitoring performance has been established, and other tasks have been given higher priority.

> The Bus Monitor System Needs Re-evaluation.... Bus monitors are expensive, with $900,000 budgeted for the current year. Their function is to ensure safety on buses. The need for monitors on an as extensive a basis as currently used, however, is questioned by school staff and by practices elsewhere.

> The Effectiveness of the Complaint Handling Function is Inadequate.... There appears to be widespread dissatisfaction among parents [concerning] the speed and effectiveness with which complaints about transporta-

tion services are handled. Parents are uncertain of the proper place to direct questions and complaints and dissatisfied with the responsiveness of those whom they reach.[4]

In a long concluding chapter, the analysts recommend remedies for every one of these problems and urge the school committee to begin to purchase its own fleet of vans and minibuses as a preliminary to later purchases of buses and the hiring of contractors to manage the operation. The criteria, the findings, and the recommendations are ones any set of informed observers would have been likely to develop as early as 1974. They are in hand at last, though, after massive disruptions and difficulties have been endured by the public. They demonstrate that busing cannot be listed among the intractable problems some urbanists say all cities are heir to. Quite to the contrary, the Cresap, McCormick and Paget report demonstrates that busing services can be planned in advance, managed rationally, and made very cost-effective. What was missing for six years, then, was not expertise—it was widely available from management consulting firms, transportation engineering faculties, and public management in the Boston area. What was missing was the political will to tackle the challenge.[5]

INTERPRETING THE SILENCE

What might account for the stunning contrast between evolving chaos in school busing services and silence within the councils of the concerned? Why was the court not barraged with complaints from parent councils, for instance? Why were the attorneys, most of them eager to watch for every angle of every developing issue, numb to the gigantic busing failures that were building up daily? The *Boston Globe* editorials that twice monthly instructed everyone about what should be done in the desegregation case did not lift the rock laid on the topic of transportation management until 1980, when the editors cheered for the advent of a school bus fleet.

One important explanation might lie in the social baseline of expectations. This was the era when Boston was gaining national notoriety as the car theft capital of America; when its commuter trains were breaking down or being discontinued; when the dozens of new light rail vehicles purchased as additions to the subway system went into early retirement due to breakdowns; when citizens were preoccupied with gasoline shortages and the energy crisis. This was the era when Boston, with its haphazard traffic patterns and continually erupting gas mains and water pipes, was nevertheless beginning to compare favorably in the public image with such cities as the bankrupt New York, where transportation nightmares were a constant plague.

Under these conditions, and because, despite all of its imperfections, the school transport system was measurably superior to anything that had been provided before 1975, the failures seemed to be of a piece with life in general.

They did not stand out as exceptional, and they occasioned less public confusion and irritability than did student assignment mistakes.

Thousands of students who before had no choice other than to travel to school by MBTA, with its historic record for delays, breakdowns, inconvenience, and dangers to safety, now waited for yellow school buses (that tended to show up and to return most children at predictable times each afternoon) at corners near their homes and apartments. The value attributed to busing by CDAC parents in 1975 did not change during the next six years. As the enrollments in the system declined, the number of buses remained constant. What is more, some parents achieved improvements in the buses by organizing inspection teams that visited the garages and parking lots and by relentlessly pressing the school department for safe and timely service.

Yet another explanation is that city hall, the school committee and its Department of Implementation, and the state Education Department were implicated in the generation of problems associated with busing.[6] None of the agents for these public agencies wanted to call attention to their failures. Within the confines of the court case, challenges would have to come from the plaintiffs, whose attorneys never joined the issue of busing failures, perhaps because there was no pressure from constituents to do so.

We have one other explanation for the silence, although it is speculative. Just as we have some reason to believe that school construction, renovation, and repair contracts in Boston have long been the stuff from which extra profits and complicated kickbacks are developed,[7] so do we think that the twelve million dollars a year expended on bus vending contracts have resulted in a number of complicated and semi-legal deals that benefit some politicians and their agents. As we have noted in our postscript at the close of Chapter Ten, Boston School Committee member Gerald O'Leary was indicted late in 1980, and later pleaded guilty, on charges of negotiating a kickback.

VALUABLE LESSONS FOR DOING IT RIGHT SOMEWHERE

There are several valuable lessons in the story of student transportation in Boston. Someone committed to properly planning and managing a transport system in another city might benefit from having the lessons spelled out plainly. Perhaps the most important one to be learned is that busing has no actual undesirable properties, contrary to popular opinion, and that most people opposed to busing are really opposed to school desegregation or related, involuntary changes in school assignments. Parents, students, and teachers benefit from timely, safe, and reliable bus service from home to school and back. Once the service gets going, in fact, its scale expands rather than contracts as a result of public demand, and the delivery of good service would probably generate votes and even tax support within many localities.

Cities from San Francisco to Denver to Baltimore learned the second lesson long before Boston began to botch its busing operations—that *fleet ownership* is the key to economy, control, and efficiency in maintenance and operations. There is no imaginable circumstance under which local vendors have the equipment, manpower, or organizational capability to expand suddenly far beyond their customary scale of enterprise in order to take up the challenge of busing a large student population. When vendors are invited to do so, they are likely to blame their failures in delivery on the riders and the public (see Table 5.2).

Taxicab company owners and managers lack the experience or expertise to undertake massive service operations. Small charter bus companies are often owned and managed by men who came out of trucking and taxi companies of the small-scale variety. Try as they may, they cannot rise to the challenges imposed by very large public contracting and bidding procedures. Those procedures often encourage leasing to the lowest bidders, who do not possess the competence or the resources for dealing with contingencies.

Based on evidence not only from Boston but also from New York City and other large urban districts, we think that a vending approach is bound to result in a snarl of failures, litigation, and excess expenditures. This outcome might be mitigated by competent public service agents skilled in public management and transportation engineering. But in most cities, incompetent vendors will be matched with incompetent and sometimes venal public officials. And in the case of school transportation, most of the public officials will be former classroom teachers rather than managers or engineers.

Where political resistance to school desegregation is very highly developed and widely demonstrated, the decision to purchase buses and vans will be most vigorously avoided. In Boston, the idea itself could not be raised, let alone considered, until the school committee had shed its most adamant antibusers, Louise Day Hicks, John J. Kerrigan, and Paul Ellison. Mayor Kevin White, whose lawyers controlled many aspects of busing, would never have risked considering the merits of bus fleets purchase in a period when the city was caught between rising property taxes and declining credit ratings among lenders and bond issuers (see Tables 5.3 and 5.4).

Our impression is that the court might have forced consideration of purchase in the course of systematic and demanding review of busing plans and implementation, *if* the judge and his advisors had understood more fully what was at stake. We had access to the facts. We discussed the implications of what might develop between the inept vendors and the inept school department transport managers in 1975. Based on our recommendations, in fact, Judge Garrity urged the defendant to use transportation engineering facilities at Northeastern University and MIT in 1975 and 1976, in an effort to gain an independent perspective and to inject superior planning. These promptings were brushed aside in spite of offers of help from those faculties.

Our own scarce resources were concentrated upon studying student assignments, facilities, and educational issues; we lacked standing as transportation planners. Late in 1977, we took encouragement from Superinten-

TABLE 5.2

Boston Public Students Transported per School Day, 1980

Grade Level	Total Whites	Transported Whites	Total Blacks	Transported Blacks	Total Other Minorities	Transported Other Minorities
$K_1 + K_2$	3,579	1,013	2,722	1,425	1,374	590
Elementary (1–5)	7,175	2,721	10,834	6,770	4,687	2,610
Middle (6–8)	5,617	2,737	7,461	3,662	2,468	1,325
High (9–12)	7,149	4,428	8,753	5,012	2,687	1,539
13 +	497	1	313	3	304	2
Total	24,017	10,900	30,083	16,872	11,520	6,066
Percentage	100	45	100	56	100	53

dent Marion Fahey's judgment, shared with us during conferences at the courthouse, that door-to-door busing for kindergartners was a waste of terribly scarce funds and should be stopped. There were few such moments of candor, however, and even this one, when acted upon in September 1978, resulted in severe if temporary dislocations and breakdowns. For example, many children were "marooned" on street corners while buses ran empty along other routes.

TABLE 5.3
Annual Per-Pupil Transportation Costs, 1977–80

Type of Service	1977–78	1978–79	1979–80
Regular, including monitors	$ 179.81	$ 199.05	$ 229.49
Special needs, including taxi aides	520.52	917.14	1,171.98
Kindergarten	493.19	586.77	560.80
Isolated	470.40	646.88	1,275.30
Additional, per trip (10,500 trips per year)	26.29	74.38	48.19
Massachusetts Bay Transportation Authority (public transportation)	44.33	37.08	47.21

SOURCE: Cresap, McCormack and Paget, 1979.

By the time Superintendent Fahey reached this judgment, incidentally, city hall had hired an outside accounting firm to monitor every busing schedule and expenditure, with the result that cautionary efforts were being stimulated across the system. These accountants and those from Cresap, McCormick and Paget, Inc., who were later put to work studying the vending operations, did introduce economies of scale. These improvements were reinforced by the computerization of student records and bus routings within the Department of Implementation. Nevertheless, even the ablest of outside accountants and management consultants could do little more than tinker with the operations until the policy decision was made in 1980. That school committee decision was grounded in recommendations made by Cresap, McCormick and Paget in their final report, dated October 31, 1979.

The same report stood shy of recommending that the school department take on the task of hiring and managing drivers. It emphasized the sound business practice of contracting for drivers, maintenance, and other services, including management operations. In our view, the soundness is abstract and hypothetical. The report avoided considering the dangerous ambiguities that

TABLE 5.4

Boston School System Transportation Costs, 1977–80
(in thousands)

Item	1977–78	1978–79	1979–80
Salaries			
Administration[a]	$ 503	$ 533	$ 384
Bus monitors	926	888	900
Taxi aides	98	123	100[b]
Subtotal	$ 1,527	$ 1,544	$ 1,384
Services and Other			
Regular	$ 3,749	$ 4,148	$ 4,849
Isolated	588	621	630
Kindergarten	1,159	1,819	1,720
Special needs	1,500	2,766	3,182
MBTA	266	241	288
Additional trips	276	781	506
Office expenses	14	—	1
Subtotal	$ 7,552	$10,376	$11,176
Total	$ 9,079	$11,920	$12,560

SOURCE: Salaries for 1977–78 through 1978–79 obtained from payroll ledgers; for 1979–80, from budget. Services and other costs for 1977–78 obtained from internal accounting records; for 1978–79 and 1979–80, from budgets.

[a]Salaries for 1977–78 through 1978–79 include salaries for safety and security personnel. Salaries for 1979–80 include only transportation and facilities unit salaries.

[b]Estimated.

result from relying on workers who are neither public nor truly private commercial operatives to provide public services. It does not explore the public harm that has already come from this practice but instead emphasizes the need for the school department to set high standards and specialize in monitoring performance. Dentler's impression from having been interviewed by two of the study directors is that Cresap was discouraged in advance from examining the problems contracting was causing, and was commissioned to find the apparently most economical means to transport students in the future.

NOTES

1. MARC Busing Task Force, *Fact Book on Pupil Transportation*, Metropolitan Applied Research Center, New York, 1972.

2. Andrew M. Greeley and Paul B. Sheatsley, "Attitudes Toward Racial Integration," *Scientific American*, Vol. 225, December 1971, pp. 13–19.

3. Some vehicles were vandalized while parked overnight and on weekends. Others were stoned and hit by other objects while in transit. Still others were damaged from the inside by riders. While the frequency of all three kinds of incidents has diminished sharply from 1975 to 1980, a bus was stoned and its windows shattered, injuring student riders, as recently as May 1980.

4. Cresap, McCormick, and Paget, Inc., *The Boston Public School Transportation System*, New York, October 31, 1979, pp. IV8–IV13.

5. Northeastern University and Massachusetts Institute of Technology transportation engineers offered their services on more than one occasion. They were never utilized, except in the sense that Torrado was an MIT doctoral student at the time he was hired.

6. The Massachusetts Education Department staff certainly never created the busing problems. This agency suffers because of a basic contradiction in the political economy of the commonwealth: It is charged with administering educationally progressive policies that come from the legislature and the state education board, but it has never been given the budget or the authority to execute those policies effectively. In the case of transportation management, for instance, the department does not begin to have a work force large enough to carefully inspect financial records on a regular basis and it lacks the authority to intervene very far in operations. One result of this generic paradox is a sort of half-embarrassed administrative style.

7. According to testimony before a special State Contracts Commission, architect William Masiello testified that he gave former Boston Deputy Mayor Robert Vey between $10,000 and $20,000 in illegal cash contributions for Mayor Kevin White from 1974 to 1976. Vey was then chairman of the Boston Public Facilities Commission. Masiello also explained how his firm and subcontractors stole $250,000 in extra public fees during eight years. (*The Boston Globe*, May 15, 1980, p. 1) One engineering expert estimated in testimony before the same commission that about 60 percent of the public buildings and works in the state were structurally or materially defective.

Courtesy of the Boston School Department

Steve Rosenthal Photo

Under court order, the old Quincy School, erected in 1847 as
the nation's first multiclassroom public school facility and
serving as the segregated school of Boston's Chinatown for
generations, was closed and replaced by the multiethnic,
multipurpose community facility, the new Quincy, in 1975.

After fifteen years of planning and political delays, the court ordered the construction of the $40 million Hubert H. Humphrey Occupational Resource Center. The center shares the campus site with Madison Park High School which was planned earlier and financed by the state but erected for city-wide use under court order.

After fourteen years of planning and prevarication, Boston City Hall, with state funding, finally acted on a 1975 court order and replaced the 100-year-old Jamaica Plain High School with this renovation of the Boston Gas Company plant. Courtesy of the Boston School Department

What was probably New England's most dilapidated and outmoded public high school, Charlestown High, was replaced in 1976 by a fine new facility with state funds and court authorization. Courtesy of the Boston School Department

English High, the first public school to be erected in Boston since 1934, opened in 1974 but was converted into a city-wide magnet by court order in 1975.

The nation's oldest public high school, Boston Latin, with entrance by examination, was desegregated by court order in 1975.

THE MAGNET SCHOOLS

6

THE PURPOSE OF MAGNET SCHOOLS

BOSTON AND CAMBRIDGE ARE THE SITES of the nation's two oldest magnet schools. Boston Latin School and Harvard University (or at least Harvard College) are well over 300 years old. This tells us something about the meaning of the term magnet school. It is intended to refer to a school that attracts students the way a magnet attracts iron filings. In order for a school to possess this magnetic property, it should have a reputation for success, and a reputation takes time to develop. It also suggests that, in Boston, in one of the nation's oldest and most education-conscious cities, the notion of an enduring and venerable school that has seemed to enhance the life chances of its graduates is powerfully attractive.

Most of the older cities of America contain magnet schools. Some of these are part of public systems. These include Boston, New York, Philadelphia, Washington, D.C., and Louisville, to name a few. In each city, the notion of maintaining long-standing schools that are renowned (at least locally) for their special programs or for their selectivity has been cherished for more than a century.

In the 1960s the magnet idea began to be expanded in Philadelphia to include newly developed alternative school programs. Within a few years, planners associated the magnet school with the principle of integration, for it was apparent that a school sought after by thousands of parents and students city-wide could act as a device for furthering ethnic integration.

By 1970 magnet school programs had become one of the tools in the tool box of public school reformers.[1] Magnets expressed the ideals of integration; they also embodied the ideal of consumer choice that had come to be expressed in the voucher experiments. And because a magnet school depends upon cultural diversity, big-city system resources, and high demand for its viability, it depends upon the merits of urban as opposed to rural and suburban community life for its survival. Here, then, was a tool for reversing the trend toward loss of public confidence in the city school system, increasing alienation between the professionals who manage the schools and the public that uses them, and the diminishing ability of city high schools to compete with suburban ones for funds, gifted teachers, and motivated students.

The same tool has a unique use in the case of desegregation: Both minority and white students can be admitted to a magnet school they choose voluntarily. Early in the 1970s many believed that the magnet represented a desirable alternative to forced assignments and forced busing.[2]

THE ORIGINS OF BOSTON'S MAGNETS

Judge Garrity issued his liability opinion on June 21, 1974. He adopted the state board temporary desegregation plan for implementation in September, but he obligated the Boston School Committee to plan a permanent remedy for submission to the court by December 16.

In the six-month interval, two members of the committee began looking for alternatives to forced busing. One of their quests led them on a trip to Minneapolis, Minnesota, where a federal court had just approved a magnet school plan submitted by the school board. Other committee members, most notably John J. Kerrigan, began agitating for a metropolitan area plan. His suggestion was not a serious one, though, because the suburban districts had not been included in the liability proceedings; Kerrigan's aim was to mobilize public grievances and to encourage antagonism toward the suburbs.

The December 16 plan, therefore, included both magnet school proposals and a few metropolitan exchange ingredients. It also included two-way forced busing within the city, however, and, as we have explained, the committee voted the plan down. Forced busing was excluded from the committee's second plan, submitted January 27 as a committee-endorsed remedy. In that plan, emphasis was placed on forming a network of some fifty-five magnet schools.

This and other elements of the committee plan were rejected by the Panel of Masters as unconstitutional. Magnet schools were not listed in the plan. There was no reason to believe that one in every three facilities in the system could be made magnetic, even with special efforts invested over a four-year period, as proposed. Admission and assignment proposals in the plan were not fleshed out; they sounded like those left over from the era of free choice and open enrollment schools, an era that had been rejected by the courts in southern districts years earlier as unworkable and inequitable because of the special burden imposed on blacks to take the initiatives to achieve desegregation.

Nonetheless, the masters agreed with the magnet concept. They thought it fit well with the educational history of Boston, where such schools had flourished for many years. They viewed the concept as one that gave them an opportunity to adopt features of the committee plan for inclusion in their own design. They believed that if these schools were fostered, they could become demonstration programs for other schools in the system and thus contribute tellingly to the upgrading of instruction.

In addition, their attention was captured by the example of Boston Technical High School. Located in the heart of Roxbury, this school had been successful in attracting white and Asian-American students who lived long distances from its site, while it hosted many black students from its immediate neighborhood. Chartered buses had transported thousands of students to Boston Technical High over the years, and this seemed to demonstrate the possibilities of magnet programs for achieving quality desegregated education.

The masters wanted to adopt the magnet school as a remedial tool but they did not have a list of schools to review or amend. In mid-March of 1975, three weeks before a final report was due, the masters asked us to devise a list of possible magnet schools. It was to include elementary, junior, and high schools throughout the city that had already achieved distinctive reputations as well as those that might do so readily, and those that might serve this purpose in view of other desegregative aims, such as drawing students to East Boston.

We developed the list in a few days, added to it a matching list of colleges and businesses that could be paired with the schools, and advised the masters of our view that the entire set should constitute a separate city-wide district. We expected this would orient the district administration, teachers, and parent advisory committees toward the task of building magnet programs, that it would prevent pitting the city-wide magnet schools within districts against the interests of the community schools within them, and that it would make for a more workable method of student assignments.

Masters Willie and Keppel were especially supportive of these suggestions. With them, we devised the notion of encouraging some relation between neighborhood communities and the city-wide schools by enabling residents of a district in which a magnet school was sited to have first preference in a lottery selection among applicants—up to the first 20 percent of the seats. (Judge Garrity later increased this to 25 percent.) This was reminiscent of the New England preparatory school tradition of reserving seats for "townies," so that a school might preserve its connections with its host town.

Willie and Keppel also helped us develop the idea of requiring the school committee to prepare a multilanguage, comprehensive catalog of the schools, including pictures and descriptions of magnet schools, to accompany an application form. Again, the aim was to improve access to educational programs by disseminating information widely and by using a college admissions application procedure.

THE LIST OF MAGNET SCHOOLS

Our list, adopted and then recommended by the masters to the court, contained thirty-two schools. Eleven of these were schools that already had distinctive and magnetic programs. Three were the examination high schools, Boston Latin School, the Boston Latin Academy (formerly Girl's Latin), and Boston Technical High. About 4,000 students a year took the Secondary School Aptitude Test (SSAT) prepared by the Educational Testing Service (ETS) and used by many private prep schools in an effort to qualify for admission to these schools. It is this quality of selectivity that most Bostonians understood to be the meaning of magnet. Other high schools in this category included Copley Square High School, with its alternative program that grew up out of the innovative 1960s. As stated previously, the school, housed in two old brownstones, emphasized vigorous academic courses and exploratory "externships" for career experience.

English High was included in our list because it had once operated as a popular city-wide school and because it had the newest, finest, and most centrally located facility in the system.[3] Besides, after constructing it with state funds under a state–school committee agreement that it would be desegregated, the committee had tried in 1972 to convert it for use as the Girl's Latin School. This trick became one of the features of the liability decision. Designating it as a magnet would settle questions about its future use, the masters believed.

We did not know what to do with Boston Trade High. It was an old and dilapidated leftover from the era when vocational high schools stood apart from academic schools and prepared boys for apprenticeships in the blue collar trades. We probably should have recommended it for closing in view of its substandard plant and outmoded curriculum, but the state had recently pumped a quarter of a million dollars' worth of new hardware into its sclerotic arteries and the other high schools offered feeble vocational training resources. Thus, we settled for a magnet designation.

Temporary Madison Park High School became a magnet as a result of one of the few proposals submitted by Mayor White. He urged development of a downtown high school that would be located virtually next door to police headquarters as an alternative to some of the Phase I plans that had been enveloped in violence late in 1974. We adopted his recommendation, which included backdoor suggestions about which downtown building to rent for the purpose, but we linked it with provisions that would make this site temporary and would relocate the emerging programs to the Madison Park Campus that had been planned since 1953 and been under construction by the city since 1973.

The list of secondary programs also served as a convenient place for the Boston Business School, a two-year secretarial school that drew on graduates from all of the city's high schools. Similarly, the city-wide magnet list included the English Language Center, where newly arrived immigrants and other students with extremely limited proficiency in English could receive instruction in English as a second language.

Our decisions about these magnets were fairly well thought out, but our planning for middle and elementary schools was exceptionally shallow. We never took up the issue of whether the lower schools should have been included in a magnet system. We had no intention, for instance, of devising a separate district that would enable passage of a student through magnet schools without recourse to community districts. We had little evidence about schools already in operation that had achieved any programmatic distinction at these levels, with two exceptions: William A. Trotter Elementary and the Rafael Hernandez Elementary, which featured effective Hispanic bilingual instruction.

Our list therefore began with these two and expanded, the way hastily drawn policies and plans tend to do, as if there were a vacuum that needed to be filled. We included the Mackey Middle School because it was in Roxbury and because civic groups had been working there for two years to achieve integration. We chose the Martin Luther King Middle School because of its name, because it was not needed for local district seats, and because it was large enough to serve a variety of educational purposes. The old Horace Mann School for the Deaf was scheduled for replacement by a new facility and it was located in the heart of Roxbury. We therefore exploited its availability. A shortage of other middle school facilities limited our list to these three, together with a new facility under construction in East Boston. Combined, the four would have far fewer seats than needed if they were construed as feeder schools for the magnet highs. We did not conceive of them as such, but thousands of parents and students did and this created many strains within the three-year period after implementation.

We identified nine elementary magnet schools in the same fashion. Two were authentic magnet schools already. Two others were selected as part of a strategy for desegregating some facilities in East Boston. The Haley went on

TABLE 6.1

**Massachusetts Board of Education Expenditures
on Magnet Schools and Other Boston Public Schools, 1977**

Magnet Schools	Amount	Other Public Schools	Amount
M. L. King Middle	$ 95,000	District 1	$ 226,842
Jackson-Mann Elementary	16,000	District 2	13,000
English High	221,000	Roosevelt Middle	13,950
Copley Square High	129,057	Jamaica Plain High	93,000
Charles E. Mackey Middle	91,000	District 3	205,000
Mario Umana High	144,997	District 4	28,108
Wm. H. Ohrenberger Elementary	57,000	Hyde Park High	107,000
James Hennigan Elementary	59,301	District 5	87,364
Curtis Guild Elementary	19,936	J. Burke High	46,249
Madison Park High	130,000	District 6	85,106
Latin Academy	41,962	District 7	125,000
Wm. M. Trotter Elementary	27,862	Charlestown High	89,000
Phyllis Wheatley Middle	32,990	Roxbury High	79,000
Trade High	11,100	District 8	0
Technical High	49,999		
Boston Latin School	53,000		
Dennis C. Haley Elementary	32,450		
James Curley Elementary	47,825		
Total	$1,260,489	Total	$1,198,619
Total students served	18,147	Total students served	47,446
Per-pupil cost	$ 69.45	Per-pupil cost	$ 25.26

EXPLANATORY NOTE: Amounts shown are called 636 Funds and are mandated for use in assisting schools undergoing desegregation. These do not include other state funds for capital construction; vocational, bilingual, or special education; or transportation. Not all Boston public school students are served by the schools listed. The purpose of the comparison is to show how *magnet school pairings* have attracted more than twice the per-pupil support of nonmagnets, although under court order allocations were to be equal.

the list because parents there had been building a voluntary integration program for several years. Several others occupied well-designed, large, and attractive buildings and were well-sited for city-wide use.

For the masters' plan, we invented program themes for those schools that did not already have them, attempting to get a wide-ranging diversity of options going in the arts and sciences and in special services. Later, Judge Garrity asked us to arrange with the office of implementation to have themes revised and written by the faculties of the magnet schools, and their aspirations were incorporated in the court plan.

The magnet list thus included 32 schools with 26,760 seats, almost one-third of the seats scheduled to be available in the public system. No other system in the country had been asked to attempt magnet programs on this scale before, and few systems were, on the face of it, less qualified to accomplish significant improvements in even a few schools at this time than was Boston. The contradiction grew out of the combined effects of three considerations. First, the school committee plan had called for fifty-five magnets and the masters were, after all, cutting that number in half. But even with the closing of thirty-two facilities, the system was overbuilt, and the masters asked us to begin planning by devising the scale of the community districts; thus, we projected the number of seats that would be needed in them in order to guarantee places for residents and then treated the remainder as residuals. The masters were also straining to maximize the scale of zone set apart for voluntary desegregation, in the belief that this would offset the sting of forced busing.

Hindsight leads us to the conviction that the city-wide magnet remedy should have been limited to high schools and the English Language Center. Although the others have grown in popularity with parents each year, their separation from the community districts has compounded severely the difficulties of desegregating schools in the various neighborhoods, as we shall show.

In any case, the masters recommended formation of 32 magnet schools with a total of 26,760 seats, and Judge Garrity reduced their list to twenty-two, suggesting that the contradictions were already apparent in April 1975. The wishful quality of the plan is suggested in the last paragraph of the masters' report:

> The Citywide District should constitute the source of dynamism toward quality desegregated education for the total system. With half of its schools within ready reach of exerting magnet potential in the Fall of 1975, and with most of the remaining half within reach through planning and effort by September, 1976, this District can revive the educational vitality of the city, enable the exercise of preferences by citizens, and contribute fundamentally to the system. This cannot be fully accomplished without a two year timeline, however. The Court... should maintain special vigilance over (this) District for this reason.[4]

THE EXAMINATION SCHOOLS

The masters not only recommended phasing out grades seven and eight in the Latin Schools, but also called for desegregating the three examination schools by requiring that their student populations be in line with city-wide racial/ethnic composition, as in all other magnet schools. They also recommended that SSAT scores be used in combination with cumulative grade point averages or percentiles on grade point standings as a method of academic selectivity. They wrote, "For example, these selection criteria may be combined in such a way as to select for admission those who fall above the *median* of all students who apply in any given year," adding that, "Not less than 20 percent of the students accepted at examination and all other city-wide schools shall live within the community district in which each such school is geographically located (if such number of students have applied and are qualified)."

In the month after the masters retired from the case, no other feature of their report was more hotly debated than that of selection criteria. Letters poured into the court from alumni of the Latin schools objecting to this proposed demise of the principle of selectivity. Attorney after attorney testified to the heresy of changing the grade structures and violating the principle of competitive selection. Attorneys for the plaintiffs joined in the chorus, revealing their belief and that of at least some black parents in the desirability of strictly academic selectivity. It became evident within a few weeks that many Bostonians believed devoutly in the efficacy of elite schools.

Backstage, we mounted a case with Judge Garrity in support of the masters. We showed that four-year high schools had become increasingly commonplace among the private academies of New England. We showed that selection for high school should begin after the middle school years and that other arrangements were designed to give preference to those who got admitted earlier and were thus sheltered from the regular middle school programs. We also argued vigorously against the appropriateness of the SSAT. Its creators at ETS made no claims about its predictive validity and the instrument had never been formally evaluated. It had not been in use at the examination schools for more than a few years, and in 1973 the Harvard Law and Education Center protested its use as racially biased and unvalidated to the Massachusetts Commission Against Discrimination.

Our deeper conviction as educators was that selectivity for the examination schools constituted a false arrangement. Although the schools' selection process allowed parents to think of these high schools as elite and to denigrate other offerings of the system, their curricula were outdated and the instruction mediocre. We did not think these conditions could be reconciled with the quest for superior quality, desegregated (and hence equalized and upgraded) public instruction. Both of us had begun as secondary school teachers, and we doubted the claims to prestige voiced by Boston Latin School, Latin Academy, and Boston Technical High School.[5]

We were overruled on every point, and Judge Garrity, responding to the consensus arrived at by all parties to the case, revised the masters' recommendations. He adopted a compromise designed by clerk Terry Seligman,[6] who proposed that the sixth grades be phased out at the Latins after one year but that the seventh and eighth grades be preserved. Seligman's compromise also recommended that

> at least 35 percent of each of the entering classes at Boston Latin School, Boston Latin Academy and Boston Technical High . . . be composed of black and Hispanic students. The School Department may utilize the scores of applicants on the SSAT, alone or combined with students' grade point averages or standings as criteria for admission, . . . so long as the criteria chosen result in entering 7th and 9th grade classes at least 35 percent black and Hispanic.

This stipulation, as well as other features of the plan adopted by the court, was appealed by the school committee and reaffirmed in 1976 by the U.S. Court of Appeals. The appeals court opinion gave extra force to the compromise by instructing the district court to take special care "to safeguard the elite character of the examination schools" in future. With this instruction, the stakes of our tent of opposition were pulled and we fell into compliance. Six years later, however, we could hear educators in the system stating that Scott and Dentler were opposed to the examination schools and our assertions of this fact revealed to them our bizarre values.

We did have the satisfaction of helping the court adopt an explicit stricture against the remanding of students out of the magnet high schools. This had long been the preferred method of control in the Latin schools, with the headmasters threatening to send misbehavers and reluctant learners back to one of the district high schools. Within one term after the opening of the schools in 1975, this stricture caused havoc at Boston Latin School. Teachers and headmasters were unable to imagine what to do with those who did not conform to their prescriptions. It took them a year to learn that students could transfer out if their parents made application to the office of implementation.

Boston Technical High, housed in what had been built as Roxbury Memorial High School, achieved rapid compliance with court desegregation guidelines and maintained its previous reputation for hospitality to all ethnic groups. It really should not be equated with the elitist Latin schools, and in the main, the examination feature operates there simply to ensure that students are numerate enough on entry to benefit from a scientific and technical education.

The Latins, on the other hand, continued to resist change at every turn. We renewed our challenge of the validity of the SSAT in 1976, after having supervised its use in assigning students. Scott arranged for expert reviews of the instrument by educational psychologist Dr. William Cooley and a measurement analyst at ETS. Their comments supported our contention that the instrument had not been devised to serve the purpose for which it was being used in Boston.

Judge Garrity responded to instrument review findings by ordering the school department to conduct a study of test validity through a subcontractor. The department turned to ETS, the test producer, and filed a perfunctory justification early in 1978. No one at the Latin schools or in the Department of Implementation ever moved to devise a better selection procedure. Latin Academy did not achieve compliance with the guidelines until 1979, and Latin School was in violation every year for five years. Although in 1979 the city's public school student population was 13 percent Hispanic and 46 percent black, Boston Latin School enrolled only 2 percent and 16 percent, respectively. Of the forty black ninth graders who were admitted to its classrooms in 1976, eighteen survived as twelfth graders in 1979. Many students transferred out when they realized the curriculum did not speak to their interests and when they found an absence of support services. In most years, more than a third were failed for the year and the rate of nonpromotion was twice as high for black and Hispanic students.

Even Boston Latin School changed a bit over these years, however. A new headmaster was appointed who was not a gusty segregationist and who was open to minority parent advisory pressures that led to the advent of guidance counseling, as well as remedial and tutorial services. Some new teachers were appointed who brought youth and progressivism to the school. An integrated parent advisory committee and support from Freedom House, a Roxbury-based center for civil rights advocacy, contributed to a positive change in climate. Faculty and students from the school's partner, Wellesley College, helped to bring the school and its faculty out of isolation and into the post-Vietnam era.

When Scott visited Boston Latin School in 1980, he observed at least one minority-segregated classroom. He also noted that the facilities of the school continued to be inferior to those common to most suburban public high schools. The student track team practiced by running in the corridors, for want of a real track, for example. A highly controlled and conformity-based social climate also continued to characterize the setting.

At the same time, Latin School, which had been losing in its competition for students with suburban schools each year from 1968 to 1974, was now full. There was ample evidence to support the conclusion that this hoary institution would continue as the bastion of selectivity that made it famous. Scott could testify, however, that admissions were no longer subject to a series of special arrangements requested by school committee members, administrators, and influential alumni, as had been the case before court intervention.

BOSTON TRADE HIGH

All of the magnet high schools except Boston Trade flourished under the court plan. All were oversubscribed for seats, all except Boston Latin achieved desegregation swiftly and peacefully, and all benefitted from pairings with colleges and businesses. Boston Trade was on a downward course when we intervened, as we noted earlier, and this trend persisted until we decided to phase it out beginning in 1978.

Boston Trade could not attract sufficient white applicants in any year and most of those who enrolled withdrew or secured transfers to other high schools within one term. The court had to force the system to repair the plant in 1975, but the repairs did not hold. Scott visited the school one day in 1976 when water was pouring through the walls and ceilings as a result of a rooftop water pump that had broken days earlier. Some of the equipment funded by the state Board of Education never got installed completely and some pieces of machinery rested on floors weakened by the effects of flooding and could never be used.

The court had to insist upon the addition of academic faculty in order to ensure that instruction would be comprehensive rather than merely vocational, but the new teachers were left isolated by the angry veterans of the trade faculty who thought that precious time in their important courses was being sacrificed. Efforts to introduce special programs for handicapped and mildly retarded students were undertaken by headquarters, but these failed to become part of the school's curriculum.

Judge Garrity was particularly sentimental about Boston Trade High because in 1942 he had taken a course there in radio repair that had helped him during his military service with the U.S. Navy. He also believed that job skills training was a boon for those seeking a path out of urban poverty.

The judge's sentiments and the hopes of the state Board of Education gave way to reality in 1978, however. Boston Trade was segregated still, its curriculum was not authentically comprehensive, it did not offer vocational programs in occupations that were fitted to the future labor force requirements of Greater Boston, and few parents wanted their sons and daughters to enroll. On our suggestion, and in part because the Occupational Resource Center was under construction for use in job skill training for all secondary students in Boston, the court ordered that no ninth graders be assigned to the school for September 1978. A few months later the school department recommended that Boston Trade be phased out of existence, and the court approved.

MADISON PARK HIGH SCHOOL

A campus park for public school facilities was on the city drawing boards as early as 1956. The area chosen was related to mammoth schemes for massive demolition of housing and commercial buildings in Roxbury in order to build an interstate highway with federal funding and to redevelop land that was depreciating in dollar value each year. The demolition was accomplished on hundreds of acres of land but very little renewal got underway. The highway plans were successfully blocked by local opposition, and private developers lost interest in the remainder of the projected plans. But the redevelopment efforts left a vast swath of Roxbury that to this day looks like a carpet bombing run over North Vietnam.

Mayor White revived some of the renewal plans of his predecessors at the close of the 1960s, and the Madison Park Campus plan was among the elements he chose to revive. Architect Marcel Breuer was retained to design the campus. At one time, the city projected plans to erect a 5,000-seat high school with 5 buildings on the Roxbury site. No new high school had been built since 1934 and the postwar baby boom had pressed the aging district high schools into double shifts and extreme overcrowding by 1967. Madison Park was intended to remedy that problem, and the state Board of Education pledged to fund nearly four-fifths of its construction.

This major project proceeded with astonishing slowness. Preparations for the site dragged on for years and by 1975, construction had been halted many times by faulty execution, labor disputes, and funding controversies. By that date, the scale of the high school had diminished to 2,500 seats. The foundation had been improperly set at one juncture and had to be taken out and begun anew. Other facilities planned for the site were not even begun, including the Occupational Resource Center, which was later ordered into construction by the court. In 1975, the court was informed that the new high school would be completed in time for use in September 1976, but it did not open until September 1977.

Madison Park High is an excellent example of the sociological principles of urban school desegregation in operation. Both the economy and the polity of Boston impeded the school's emergence. The superior architectural design features were constrained by unimaginative and inappropriate educational specifications that called for separate buildings and for floors given over mechanistically to use for separate grades within buildings. When the building was finally completed, it had to be modified in the extreme to be fitted to its actual projected uses. Much of the value of the original architectural vision was damaged permanently. The swimming pool, for instance, was constructed with a large supporting pillar jutting up perpendicularly from underneath the water near the middle of the pool.

The operation of Temporary Madison Park for two years enabled formation of a school program, an experienced administration, and a student body with reasonably good morale. Thus, the new school could have begun with an educational head start. This prospect was stymied by the school department, however, whose senior officers avoided providing the planning support that would have made the opening year a triumph.

Madison Park High School opened in a climate of gloom. Voluntary applications were less than sufficient to produce a desegregated student population. The faculty assignments were delayed and program schedules could not be planned in advance under these conditions.

We were still actively supervising student assignments when Madison Park opened. Judge Garrity instructed us to take every step we could to ensure that the school opened as full as possible and was in compliance with racial/ethnic guidelines.

There were not enough seats available in several of the district high schools, especially since there were many students seeking readmission to public high school in that year. Therefore, we filled the school with the spillover of approximately 1,500 unassigned students and with voluntary applicants, having set aside 400 seats for a second-year filling at the request of the headmaster.

Madison Park High opened with a full house and with complete desegregation. But within months, many students withdrew and many others managed to obtain transfers to other schools. By 1978, the school was verging on becoming minority segregated.

During that first year, however, word-of-mouth messages between parents worked a change. The comparative superiority of the plant, its central location, the energetic efforts of its youthful administrators, the support of Northeastern University as its paired university, and strong parent advisory investments combined with strong business pairings to turn the climate of gloom into a climate of enthusiasm.[7]

By the winter of 1979, Madison Park was featured in full-page advertisements in national weekly newsmagazines as representative of the new partnerships being created in Boston. By May, student applications for admission began to soar, and by January 1980, Madison Park High could boast a student body of 2,434 (with a court ceiling of 2,400)—37 percent white, 48 percent black, and 15 percent other minority, a ratio nearly identical to that of all students enrolled in the system. The curriculum was genuinely comprehensive. Special service bilingual instruction was available for 133 French Haitians and 112 Hispanic students.

Madison Park High, a school that for several years trembled on the brink of failure, emerged triumphant after enduring conditions that would have flattened a more genteel administration and faculty in any of the surrounding suburbs. When it was finally ready for use, the school nearly succumbed to the patterns of racial/ethnic avoidance basic to the subcultures of Boston. Still, the same subcultures contained resources of ingenuity and vitality in proportions equal to the challenge and the new plant finally sprung to life, took root, and grew. It will withstand the forces of change in the future and it will come to compete in New England for top billing as a great high school. Central to its achievement will be the record of leadership established by Headmaster Tom Hennessy, former star halfback at Holy Cross, and black Assistant Headmaster William Lawrence.

OCCUPATIONAL RESOURCE CENTER

In the preliminary designs for the Madison Park Campus, space was set aside for erection of a large plant to be called the Occupational Resource Center (ORC). In August 1975, responding to a court order recommended by the masters and the two of us, the school committee, the state Board of Education, and the city submitted a "Long-Range Plan for Occupational and Vocational Education."

This plan, endorsed from the witness stand by such chief officers as Massachusetts Education Commissioner Gregory R. Anrig, pledged resources to construct the ORC. The center was to become the giant hub in a wheel of career exploration, technical and vocational instruction, and job skills training. The spokes were to extend from the hub to smaller programs sited at various high schools, and the wheel was to rotate in such a way that students could move about to participate in different programs while retaining a base enrollment at a particular high school. The court heard the plan debated and then approved it, incorporating it into part of the permanent remedy.

Bringing the ORC into being proved as difficult a task as erecting Madison Park High, and bringing a set of vocational and educational program plans into being proved even harder. The state had just appointed a new associate commissioner of occupational education, Dr. Patrick Weagraff, and he and Commissioner Anrig pressed hard for the appointment of an associate superintendent of vocational education for Boston, arguing that progress in executing the plan depended upon the presence of qualified leadership.

After months of school committee wrangling and dispute, Boston Superintendent Fahey agreed with Weagraff and Anrig and attempted to appoint the associate superintendent for vocational education from nearby Worcester to the post. He took a leave of absence from his Worcester job and tried the new position for about sixty days. He then fled Boston for a life of comparative calm in his native Worcester. We talked with him and he stated that he'd found the prospects of properly supervising the system's vocational education programs dismal beyond description. He also said that authority could not be concentrated, that programs were in the hands of political hacks, and that no one in the upper echelons of the Boston system, with the possible exception of Miss Fahey, was committed to the building of a sound vocational program.

As the search for a new officer got underway, city hall began to argue that there was no need to build the ORC. In some weeks, they suggested cutting back the scale drastically; in others, they wondered aloud about the wisdom of building anything. After some months, Fahey came forward with a new nominee for the associate superintendent position—Dr. Bertran Wallace. An experienced black vocational educator from the Yonkers, New York, public schools, he was appointed by the school committee.

The conditions facing Dr. Wallace did not differ from those encountered by his Worcester predecessor, except that he moved to Boston (leaving his wife temporarily ensconced in New York) and quit his old job. Thus, he had greater motivation to succeed.

Not long after Dr. Wallace's appointment, scandal broke across New England as the state indicted Patrick Weagraff and a string of vocational education associates on a variety of felony counts. He admitted guilt and was sentenced to prison on conviction of graft and variations on the theme of cashing in on the allocation of federal and state vocational education funds. For a year, a twilight of silence fell across the Massachusetts Education Department's initiatives in implementing the long-range vocational education plan in Boston.

The court forced construction of the ORC on its originally projected scale—a project estimated in 1976 to cost $23 million—but efforts to prepare Boston for a positive transformation of its programs foundered. Early in 1978, Dr. Wallace was dismissed by the school committee. Planning and preparations returned to their steady state of diffuse chaos.

By then, Judge Garrity had appointed architect Earl R. Flansburgh as a special master to monitor construction of the ORC. As the seasons rolled by, however, his reports to the court became shorter and dimmer, communicating little more than setbacks and revisions in the expected date for opening of the new center.

When Robert Wood became superintendent of schools in September 1978, he supported program planning for the ORC. He broadcast his conviction as an urban policy planner that occupational instruction was central to the well-being of students and to the economic viability of Boston's future. Staff, most of them drawn from inside headquarters and few of them qualified professionally as vocational educators, formed a task force and began to give new definiteness to plans and schedules.

The ORC opened for use in September 1980, nearly five years after construction began. When it did open, half of its equipment and materials—selected but not even ordered by February 1980—were not yet available to contribute to the introduction of city-wide magnet programs in job skills training and trade apprenticeship instruction on a scale and of a quality that can someday become the envy of all of New England.

The potential of such programs is vast. The most exciting prospect is that students of the future will not have to choose between life as a blue-collar or a white-collar worker but will be able to complete an academic program in a comprehensive high school and travel to the ORC for skills training at the same time. The ORC *may* help to break the barrier between general and vocational education, a barrier erected in the 1920s in most eastern seaboard schools and then strengthened for decades by the infusion of hundreds of millions of dollars from the federal government in support of blue-collar separatism.

As with other magnet schools, the details of governance and operation will doubtless dictate the general policy outcomes of the ORC experiment. As of 1980, those details did not exist and the court was hampered in withdrawing from the case by the uncertainty of the results. How students would be assigned, who would in fact attend, what the array of actual, in contrast to paper, curricula would come to be, and how the hub would turn the spokes in the several high schools, were among the unknowns in the story. Thomas Hennessey from Madison Park became the ORC headmaster, however, and we believe he will make it a successful desegregated magnet.

EAST BOSTON AND MARIO UMANA HARBOR SCHOOL OF SCIENCE AND TECHNOLOGY

We had instructions from the masters to demonstrate that the remedial order should impinge significantly on East Boston, even though eleven schools in that part of the city were destined to remain 95 percent white. Later, Judge Garrity adopted our plan, which entailed sequestering four facilities on that island for use as city-wide magnets.

Two of these facilities were elementary schools. One of them, Donald McKay, was designated to be a kind of feeder to the middle and then the high school in a small network of scientifically and technically oriented magnet programs. Our most intrusive act, however, was to take the newly constructed middle school in East Boston out of use for all but a fraction of the local residents. They had eagerly looked forward to the completion of the very costly new facility. It boasted a magnificent plant, a large swimming pool and gymnasium complex, and a marina, and we made the school open to all students for these very reasons. The marina, the science labs, and the closed TV circuitry all made the new plant ideal for a scientific program.

We paired this facility, McKay, and East Boston High (renamed the Citywide East Boston Technical High School) with the Massachusetts Institute of Technology, Wentworth Institute of Technology, and the Massachusetts Port Authority. As the new plant would not be ready to open until 1976, we delayed the changeover for East Boston High to coincide with this date.

During 1975 and 1976, then, a great protest began to swell inside East Boston. Its residents stated, quite correctly, that the district would be the only one in the city to be deprived of a district high school. We had intended this deprivation because we needed ways in which to desegregate schools in East Boston, and because some trade-offs were required in the scales of equity since other district schools remained unaffected.

The paired institutions were anxious to avoid getting caught in the middle of the dispute. The district superintendent wanted to deliver a high school to "his" parents above all else, as did East Boston High Headmaster Carmen Scarpa. Within half a year a large coalition had formed to propose a modification in the court plan—the first substantial one to come before the court during 1976. The group recommended preserving East Boston High as a district school because it was needed as such and because it was not suitable for use as a scientific and technical facility, and converting the new middle facility into a substitute that would also serve seventh graders so that no city-wide middle school would be needed.

Judge Garrity approved of the proposal but added to his Phase III order the requirement that East Boston High develop a city-wide magnet program in legal secretarial preparation modeled along the lines of the one proposed by the headmaster. A detailed plan was put forward by the school committee for this and was modified slightly and approved by the court. That program has flourished, thanks to strong interest among parents and students and to sound leadership from Headmaster Scarpa, who took enormous pains to demonstrate that minorities were welcome in his school.

East Boston High today is a successfully desegregated, peaceful, educationally improved school. More than 200 minority students travel long distances to enroll there in 2 excellent vocational programs. The transition from a white segregated to a multiethnic school has been guided by a special monitoring committee appointed by the court.

Events did not go as well initially at the new high school, named Mario Umana Harbor School of Science and Technology in 1976 by the school committee. Overseeing the operation of the paired institutions was Dr. Stanley Russell, a former suburban superintendent hired by MIT. Dr. Russell helped form a very effective task force that planned intensively for the school opening and the first years of operations. Under the administrative desegregation orders of the court, the first headmaster to be appointed was Gustave Anglin, a black educator. While he was not welcomed by East Bostonians, he got down to business immediately and joined the task force as a prime mover.

The planning was excellent but city hall managed to botch the implementation at Umana as it had at the ORC and Madison Park High. The new facility was not at all equipped for its purposes. Construction features were faulty. Lighting was poor in the swimming pool room, for instance, and a student, unnoticed by both teacher and classmates, drowned during a class. According to the teacher, no one could see the bottom of the new pool. Defects and insufficiencies were pervasive. The planners spent a year trying to get it renovated and equipped without success until the court again intervened. Altogether, more than $4 million was spent preparing the buildings—after they had been declared ready for use—to make them usable.

137

In fairness, some of the difficulties arose from the changes in planned use for the new facility, such as the need for instructional hardware, appropriate only for a technical high school. Some of the other defects led us to suspect that construction modifications were a part of routinely corrupt practices in public facility construction in Boston—a suspicion fueled by sources in the employ of city hall. We have never verified this suspicion, however.

For the first year and a half classes at Umana were conducted in the midst of construction activities of all kinds. In addition, the school department was not supportive in enabling the appointment of a faculty equipped by training to implement the new curriculum. Student discouragement, faculty anger, and parent confusion were commonplace.

Yet, by late 1978, careful program planning initiated in 1975 began to bear fruit. A genuinely magnetic, unique, and enlightened core curriculum had come into being, and a visitor could witness quality teaching and learning going on in most classrooms.

The quality of instruction at McKay Elementary, which was designated as a magnet feeder, was not equal to that of Umana. What is more, the citywide student assignment system publicized the nature of Umana's program but did not allow screening of students to take place. Hundreds of parents applied to send their scientifically and mathematically unprepared and disoriented children to Umana; by 1978, hundreds of them were being failed by the faculty.

Unlike most of the comprehensive high schools throughout the United States, which allow students to participate in a chosen course for a few days and then drop out, with advisor or counselor approval, if they feel the class does not suit their abilities or interests, students at Umana were obligated to take mathematics and science courses in every term from seventh through twelfth grade. The core program had *no* escape hatches. In June 1979, nonpromotion rates for seventh graders ran as high as 40 percent for whites and 65 percent for blacks.

Some of the failure stemmed from elitist assumptions built into the curriculum plans by the paired institutions. For decades, the tradition in the "best" engineering colleges of the nation has been to cut each year's freshman class in half by overloading the course requirements list. This tradition eroded at the close of the 1960s and in the early 1970s, when the national demand for engineers sagged considerably, but was revived after 1975.

One hypothesis for student failure is that many of the school's high school science and mathematics teachers had not mastered the pedagogy. This theory grew out of education studies conducted during the 1960s. Teachers in these disciplines are traditionally subject and method centered, not student centered, although there are exceptions, of course.

Another source of the failure comes from the poor fit between the program and its participants. It was this improper fit that Headmaster Anglin and his associates labored to revise. In studies they undertook in 1979 the group showed that students with grade point averages of B and above in grades below seven were much more likely to survive and even flourish at Umana than were students with lower grade point averages.

In 1980, they proposed assigning to Umana those students with B – or better averages and a small fraction of other students, chosen on a random basis, for purposes of equity and educational experimentation. Their proposal gave full attention to racial/ethnic guidelines in student composition, but their study demonstrated that some form of academic eligibility criterion was needed in order to reduce the appalling rates of failure and withdrawal.[8] Their proposal was ignored or rejected by the school department.

NATHAN HALE AND WILLIAM McKINLEY SCHOOLS

Only two schools have been added to the city-wide magnet list since the Umana. Their stories suggest the variety of uses to which the magnet idea can be put.

Nathan Hale Elementary is an old building located in Roxbury. It was included in Community District 7 and was assigned white students from the South End and Charlestown. Children from Charlestown never got on the buses and Hale was in violation of the court guidelines from September 1975 to 1977. Judge Garrity directed the school department to take what he called "special measures" to ensure that Hale and several other such schools met the court's guidelines, although he left the particulars up to the department. John Coakley, the chief exponent of magnets since the summer of 1975, was assigned by Superintendent Marion Fahey to decide what special measures should be taken. Within six months he proposed that Hale be added to the city-wide list of magnets as a "traditional program emphasizing the basics."

In the first year, Hale's magnet concept did not work. But by 1979, after a year of success in introducing an extended-day kindergarten program for four- as well as five-year-olds, Hale began to attract and hold white as well as minority students. The school's programmatic emphasis, while authentic, did not appear to be the reason for its popularity. Word of mouth among parents disseminated the view that Hale was a friendly, quiet, safe, and small elementary school worth attending. Early in 1980, Hale enrolled ninety-four black students, seventy-two white, twenty-nine Hispanic, two Chinese-American, and two American Indian.

McKinley opened more than half empty in 1975. Its geocodes contained fewer students than had been estimated, the location of the school was not attractive, and there were ample elementary seats in district without McKinley, It appeared to have no future save as a half-empty, black-segregated building tucked out of reach of the remainder of Community District 1. With the support of the district superintendent and others, the court ordered it closed for school use.

One of the reasons for the failure of McKinley may have been that before court intervention, it had served as a separate facility for mentally retarded students of middle and high school age. The masters found this to be a violation of the state law for mainstreaming and otherwise integrating students with special needs into the regular public school system. (The so-called vocational training program for retardates at McKinley had featured a basement room where students were taught to pour plaster into molds to make statues of saints.) Our effort to return the facility to its designated design as a neighborhood elementary school failed, but in 1977 the school committee returned to court with a proposal to use McKinley as a special school for severely disturbed adolescents, and this plan was endorsed by the Massachusetts Division of Special Education.

After two hearings and much debate, the court approved the new proposal. McKinley is now part of city-wide District 9 and is in active use for this special purpose today.

INTERPRETATIONS AND CONCLUSIONS

With few exceptions, the magnet schools in Boston have achieved substantial successes. They are desegregated, they have an overabundance of applicants, they are peaceful and safe, and some of them have educational programs that distinguish them from other schools.

The school reforms and program achievements made despite unfavorable odds are the results of strong leadership, teacher commitment, and strong parent support. The Martin Luther King Middle School illustrates this power of transformation. One of its faculty leaders, Kim Marshall, has published a memorable account of how it was done.[9]

The court plan provided an essential framework within which the magnet schools could take shape. The plan prescribed enduring rules for their operation and for the equitable assignment of students. The court also intervened actively during a period of six years to ensure that its plan was implemented. This intervention made the difference between evolution and death for many of the programs.

One feature of the court plan has been violated each year. That is the prescription that magnet schools be equal to community district schools in every way, including funding and staffing. There is evidence that the school committee and the Massachusetts Education Department have pumped more resources into magnets than into community schools. The disparities are not great and some of them are the result of peculiar facility and equipment requirements called for in magnet programs. Still, the view that magnet schools receive favored treatment is held by more parents each year.

In addition, one intention of the court—to prevent the magnet schools from contributing in any way to the segregation of community district schools

—has been difficult to accomplish as a result of the withdrawal of thousands of white students from the public schools. As the total white student population has dropped from 52 to 37 percent from 1975 to 1980, the percentage of whites in the magnet schools has declined too, but to 43 percent. Even this small difference represents a strain on some elementary facilities in a few community districts that the court rules governing assignments have not reduced. And as the system becomes one that is close to one-third white, some of the magnet elementaries draw off white students from district elementaries where their absence generates a severe violation of district guidelines. Attorneys for the plaintiffs and the state warned of this possibility when the masters' plan was argued in 1975, but no one in the case has ever seriously opposed the use of the magnet as a tool.[10]

In 1978 we made an analysis for Judge Garrity that showed that some elementary magnets were not genuinely city-wide in their drawing power. In District 1, for instance, James Hennigan School was based in a black and Hispanic neighborhood; its applicants poured in from within a six-block radius. Jackson-Mann School, based in a white neighborhood, was heavily overpopulated by nearby whites. Neither school was in violation of city-wide guidelines, but both radically affected the composition of some surrounding community district schools and both were failing to demonstrate a city-wide magnetism. Judge Garrity added new rules, limiting within-district admissions, and this improved the situation. Still, the assignment gears for magnet elementaries continue to mesh poorly with those of the other districts because of Boston's shortage of white students.

We have permanent doubts about the wisdom of having designated elementary and middle school magnet programs. Thousands of parents now behave as if these programs are feeders to the high schools. In two instances, this impression has been fostered by the court—one with the science programs at the Umana High School and one where three magnet schools were designated as a special subsystem for some Title I students. More significantly, perhaps, none of the elementary and middle school magnets is truly innovative or experimental.

These doubts were strengthened for us by a survey conducted in 1978 by the Citywide Education Coalition, an organization of public school parents. The large sample of parents surveyed approved heartily of magnet schools but indicated that they choose them not because of their distinctive educational programs, but because they had heard from friends and kin that school X or Y was a "good school" [a generic attribution that does not pertain to particular program elements) and because they had heard their children had a good chance of being assigned if they applied.

If the envelope of public support for public education were vast enough to contain a concern for the entire city system, the distinction between magnets and other schools would be unimportant. The envelope is much smaller than that, however, and the most avid supporters of public education are those who support the city-wide magnet sector.

By 1979, some observers were speculating that students attending magnet schools were more socioeconomically advantaged than those attending district schools. There is no evidence to substantiate this speculation, except at the Latin schools, but it may grow up out of the fact that the more upwardly mobile parents in every ethnic group are more likely to evaluate their options each year and to search out spots for their children in the city-wide magnet sector. Over time, then, this dynamic will produce a socioeconomic disparity of the sort that fostered the Latin schools generations ago.

The parents of students attending city-wide magnet schools can also exert more political leverage than can "community district" parents, for school committee members are all elected at large. When the school department proposed converting the Hennigan magnet to a middle school in 1979, for example, parental and faculty pressure on the committee and the superintendent to preserve it as an elementary magnet was extremely intense and effective.

As the community districts shrink in size through continuing declines in births and through the continuing migration from New England to the Sunbelt region, the city-wide district has maintained its size. Judge Garrity included 18,590 seats for it in 1975 and added 310 at Hale and McKinley later on, for a total of 18,900. In 1980, those magnet schools enrolled 18,955 students, while the total enrollment for the 8 community districts had shrunk from 69,400 in 1975 to 48,900. Facilities continued to close each year in the eight districts while nothing changed in the magnets. By 1985, if population projections hold, the magnet schools which once served nearly one-third of the students will serve closer to half of them.

Our fears concerning school enrollments may be unimportant in the long term. What is more likely to endure is the American consumer's response to product differentiation and that is what magnets appear to offer. The sameness that pervaded public schools when Coleman and his associates surveyed thousands of them in 1966 is a characteristic that has been modified by the advent of city-wide magnet schools in Boston. Although some magnets may revert to this sameness over time, many of them, particularly those that have achieved distinctiveness (and often against great odds) are likely to grow along with the expectations of parents.

NOTES

1. Eugene Royster et al., *Magnet Schools and Desegregation: Study of the Emergency School Aid Act Magnet School Program*, Abt Associates Inc., Cambridge, Mass., July 1979.
2. Daniel U. Levine and Robert J. Havighurst, *The Future of Big-City Schools: Desegregation Policies and Magnet Alternatives*, McCutcheon, Berkeley, Calif., 1977.

3. Indicative of the extent to which attorneys for the plaintiffs avoided touching upon educational matters was their proposal to use English High as a catchall for students who did not get assigned to other high schools. The masters rejected this emphatically.

4. P. 17.

5. Dentler gained insights into the relative academic mediocrity of the Boston Latin School during two years of active study of it and other high schools as a member of the Boston Secondary Education Commission, formed in 1973 and funded by the Ford Foundation.

6. We are not certain, but some evidence suggests this compromise was proposed to the court in correspondence from a Latin School alumni group.

7. Northeastern University's pairing efforts flourished under the leadership of Professor Gregory Coffin, who had integrated the public schools of Evanston, Illinois, as superintendent in the late 1960s. Coffin's leadership was not impaired by Asa Knowles, an early opponent of pairing, because he retired in 1976.

8. Umana's request for student selectivity fell on deaf ears inside the school department. Robert Wood, long-time director of the Harvard-MIT Joint Center for Urban Studies, would not consider the proposal. John Coakley, for a short time the city-wide magnet district superintendent, concerned with school system stability, resented the rising competition Umana was giving Boston Technical High, and he gave the proposal no advocacy. In May 1980, Coakley designed and implemented an application procedure that invited Umana students and others, except those at the Latins and Boston High, to apply for half-day programs at the ORC, thus undercutting Umana's core curriculum.

9. Kim Marshall, "The Making of a Magnet School: A Personal Account of the Journey from Chaos to Quality," *Journal of Education*, Vol. 160, No. 2, May 1978.

10. Attorney Larry Johnson raised objections to the inequities in April 1980, but he did not move to terminate any magnet programs. Instead, he sought to upgrade the community district facilities to magnet-facility levels.

SPECIAL PROGRAMS: 7
Special Needs, Bilingual, and Other Instructional Groupings

BOSTON'S POSITION AS AN EDUCATOR

SINCE 1880, GREATER BOSTON HAS BEEN A PRIME WORLD CENTER for education, medicine, and the allied health professions. Schools, hospitals, and human service treatment centers of every kind had their earliest origins in Boston. These included services for the deaf, blind, speech impaired, mentally ill, and otherwise handicapped persons of all ages. The Boston public schools established the Horace Mann School for the Deaf before the turn of the century, just as they pioneered in programs in school nursing and other health care services.

This legacy fell into neglect during the decade of the Great Depression. The Massachusetts Board of Education and Education Department continued the tradition of providing for outstanding special services elsewhere in the commonwealth. They influenced the legislature's passage of Chapter 766, concerned with the education of special needs children, in 1973. This statute laid the groundwork for federal passage of Public Law 94–142, the Education for All Handicapped Children Act, in 1975, but 766 and the State Transitional Bilingual Education Act of 1971 had barely begun to be implemented in Boston when Judge Garrity issued his Phase II order in 1975. This chapter traces the impact of court orders upon both special and bilingual education, examines problems in their implementation, and outlines some other special programs such as advanced work classes and extended day kindergartens.

CHAPTER 766 AND SPECIAL NEEDS STUDENTS

According to the National Center for Education Statistics, in 1970 there were 4.752 million school-age children and youth with handicaps in the U.S. population—10.7 percent of all those enrolled in schools.[1] In the studies leading to passage of Public Law 94–142, some experts expanded this estimate to 8 million in 1974. A 1980 Carnegie Council report gave an estimate of 10 million.[2]

There is uncertainty about, and thus elasticity in, the accuracy of some of the categories and diagnostic interpretations presented in these studies. Only a few groups have handicaps that are subject to exact measurement: the deaf, hard of hearing, blind, partially sighted, crippled, for example. Others, including the learning disabled, speech impaired, functionally retarded, and emotionally disturbed, depend heavily upon clinical judgments for estimates of incidence, and the mesaurements used vary from region to region and across diverse professions. We estimate that somewhere between 11 and 17 percent of all school-age children in the nation have handicaps that warrant special educational as well as health care treatment.

Within this range, big, old central cities have child populations whose incidence of handicaps lies at the high end of the spectrum, for many disabilities are the products of economic deprivation and subcultural isolation. When we began digging up facts for the masters, therefore, we were astonished to find that by 1974 only 3.5 percent of Boston's public students were receiving special educational services. Implementation of Chapter 766 had barely begun in Boston, the state capital. The diagnosis of handicaps and the delivery of special services had been delayed where they had not been totally neglected. And most of those receiving special educational services were clustered in separate facilities or programs that were racially and ethnically segregated.

The masters noted in one of their reports to the court that, under Chapter 766,

> special needs children should be assigned to a specific school or to a specific program where such placements are recommended by the Core Evaluation Team (CET) and approved by the parent as the most appropriate to meet those needs.

They urged Judge Garrity to require the system to comply with Chapter 766, including the statute's demand that states take steps to ensure that every school be equipped with faculty and rooms to service mildly and moderately handicapped students who were to be mainstreamed (included in regular classes) for most of every school day. As part of this recommendation, the masters noted that

> special needs transcend ethnic definitions. Assignment on the primary basis of special needs should have no adverse effect upon desegregation. Assignments to specific schools and programs will inevitably involve children of diverse ethnic backgrounds and should in most instances result in special programs which are themselves desegregated.

With our active assistance in planning, Judge Garrity included these recommendations. In May 1975 he ordered the following:

> Every school facility shall receive and educate mild and moderate special needs students, who will be assigned to schools in accordance with regular assignment procedure by geocode. No less than one resource room and one special needs services space shall be set aside in each school. Each school shall have special educators and materials. Some moderately and severely handicapped students will be assigned directly to schools with special facilities and staff, apart from the geocode procedure. To support special education both in regular schools and in special resource schools, at least three such special schools in each community district shall be identified and planned by the school department, for review by representatives of the court, not later than July 15, 1975. No special school shall consist wholly or primarily of special needs students . . . . Certain students will be assigned without the use of geocodes. Students in need of bilingual education or special education will be assigned individually to appropriate programs within the district of residence.

Judge Garrity also directed that special needs students be the second persons assigned to each school each year, and bilingual students the first, so that their relatively preferential status would be protected. He made sure not only that they would have seats but also that they could cross district boundaries, be assigned outside residential attendance areas, transcend grade structures, and obtain special transportation services.

The court plan provided for an expansion of services and school sites, estimating the special needs student population to grow from about 3,000 to about 6,000 within a period of two years and anticipating a leveling off after that. Actually, more than 6,400 students had already been diagnosed and evaluated by a core team as of May 1975, but had not been assigned to schools or given education plans.

By the time schools opened in September 1975, then, the number of special needs students had swelled to 6,980, or to 9.4 percent of all students, while the number of students assigned to separate facilities was cut nearly in half. The school department had begun to deal with the educational requirements of these special needs students when the court intervened, pressing for full execution of its orders.

The harshness of the court's demands became clear to us for the first time during the 1975 round of assigning students. All student records were in poor condition, but the record system in use for special needs children was primitive. The schedule for regular assignments was bottlenecked for two weeks while we tried to supervise the one-at-a-time process for assigning handicapped children and youth.

Chapter 766 and state agency regulations attached to it obligated school districts to generate absolute tons of paper in the process of assessing, evaluating, planning, and then placing those who came to be called "766 students." The process was intended to ensure that great care was taken in providing for due process, close parental involvement, and documentation so that the adjudication of complaints by hearing examiners could be conducted easily. Some wealthy suburban districts were staggering under these new procedural burdens of the law, including some with a proud history of effectiveness in serving children with handicaps, and Boston was virtually prostrate under the burden.

The record-keeping and assignment procedures were not adequate until 1978. In 1977, for example, 1,100 out of 1,800 severely handicapped students, including blind children who had spent months learning their way around specific buildings, were assigned to the wrong schools as a result of mistakes in the school department's special education classification numbering system, mistakes that were not spotted until two weeks before schools opened.

Transportation arrangements were unsatisfactory from 1975 through 1980, when a state court was still hearing complaints against a chartered taxi and bus corporation. Month after month for six years handicapped students were left waiting for taxis that never came, or they were delivered to school late and returned to their homes after dark. Defending the transportation company against attacks, the company's managers stated that more than 100 changes in pickups and routings were sent them each week in 1979. There was some truth in their claim because of ever-changing classifications, educational plans, and school assignments.

Each year, the system strengthened its ability to locate, place, and serve students with special needs; but the dynamic set in motion by state law and then by court intervention was so enormous as to create a mystifying scene much like that conjured up by the sorcerer's apprentice. In 1974, 3.5 percent of the student population was receiving special services; in 1975 the proportion rose to 9.4 percent; and in 1980 it soared to 15.5 percent. During this period total student enrollment declined by 9 percent, but the number of mainstreamed special needs students increased by 53 percent and the number of students classified as severely disabled grew by 46 percent (see Table 7.1).

As the number of special needs students grew exponentially, the system required far more special educators than were available from within the ranks. The number of special education teachers leaped from about 500 in 1974 to 983 in 1980, a period when the total teaching force declined slightly in size.

TABLE 7.1

Mainstreamed Boston Special Needs Students
by Racial/Ethnic Group, 1975-80

Year	White	Black	Asian	Hispanic	American Indian	Total
			Mainstream			
1975	2,104	2,939	41	400	15	5,499
1976	1,972	2,760	36	325	20	5,113
1977	2,658	3,834	34	647	28	7,201
1978	2,658	4,287	72	842	40	7,899
1979	2,709	4,647	80	924	43	8,403
1980	2,552	4,670	80	972	37	8,311
			Substantially Separate			
1975	663	665	6	146	1	1,481
1976	665	660	6	156	2	1,489
1977	785	833	10	184	3	1,815
1978	790	924	16	215	13	1,958
1979	872	1,021	10	248	10	2,161
1980	904	1,221	12	285	12	2,434
			Total Student Enrollments			
1975	32,538	31,262	2,296	7,242	255	73,593
1976	33,713	32,016	2,323	7,486	283	75,821
1977	30,776	31,300	2,214	7,752	296	72,338
1978	27,409	31,713	2,485	8,566	370	70,543
1979	26,254	29,838	2,473	8,263	344	67,172
1980	24,017	30,083	2,864	8,363	293	65,620

SOURCE: Data from Boston School Department, 26 Court Street, Boston, Massachusetts.

In keeping with the expectations of the masters, the provision of special services has transcended ethnicity. Our estimate is that by 1979, 78 percent of the classrooms serving special needs students (whether mainstreamed or separated from the regular student body) were in compliance with the court's desegregation guidelines. The major source of segregation was due, moreover, to a dearth of white students in a school as a whole and not to a special needs placement pattern that was in itself racially segregative.

Boston has been evenhanded in classifying students as severely handicapped and placing them in programs that are substantially separate. Two percent of all students were classified as handicapped in 1975; the figure rose to 3 percent by 1977 and has remained constant. This percentage holds for white, black, and Hispanic students. For reasons we do not understand, no Asian-American students were so classified in four out of five years.

The percentage of black students classified as mildly and moderately handicapped has increased from 9 to 16 percent from 1975 to 1980. The percentage of whites has gone from 6 to 10 percent, and the percentage of Hispanics has increased from 1 to 11. Again, mysteriously enough, Asian-Americans have changed from 2 to 3 percent over this period. In 1980 the state board cited Boston, along with a few smaller cities, for relatively excessive classifying of black students.

Scott has supervised the assignment of special needs students one by one for four years. The disparity between white and black rates cannot be due to economic deprivation differentials because the rates for Hispanics and American Indians are very similar to white rates. It may be that a disproportionately greater number of black students tend to be classified as having special needs because of teacher attitudes, with black students more likely to be diagnosed as *behaviorally* disturbed or as socially maladjusted when first identified by white educators.[3]

There is much about the diagnostic and evaluative quality of the classification and placement process that creates uneasiness in us. Many of these evaluations are not conducted by school psychologists. This work is farmed out to psychologists who are not in direct daily contact with the students. Some of the records we have examined—although they have begun to improve over the last two years—seem sketchy and indifferently developed. In addition, regular teachers were often appointed to serve as acting school psychologists and others were made temporary or acting special educators as the volume of special needs students increased, although most were not educated or trained to perform these sensitive tasks. Extra training arrangements were introduced in 1980.

Nevertheless, the Massachusetts Education Department has invested millions of extra dollars to provide better services to Boston's population of special needs students. The department's officers have worked closely with the school department, and several able state specialists have worked full time inside the Boston school headquarters. In 1979 the state conducted a systematic audit of Chapter 766 programs. It pressed vigorously for reforms, including surveillance of special services desegregation. This effort is now buttressed by federal policies, and some federal funds have begun to reach the state, and thus Boston. Thousands of students are being better educated today than they were in 1974 as a result of this massive and progressive reform.[4]

One remains concerned about the sorcerer's apprentice, however. Will the rate of special placements in Boston level off? In order to make a comparison Dentler obtained data from the state's education division for 1978 on the state's second largest city, Springfield. Rates for substantially separate students were similar for Boston and Springfield, but Springfield had mainstreamed 5.2 percent of its students, compared to Boston's 10.5 percent. An estimated 12.8 percent of all black students in Boston were mainstreamed in that year, compared with 5.3 in Springfield, but the rate for Hispanics in Springfield was 17.6 percent, compared with 9.1 for Boston (see Tables 7.2 and 7.3).

TABLE 7.2

Special Needs Students in Boston and in Springfield, Massachusetts, Public Schools by Ethnicity, 1978

Students	White	Black	Hispanic	Asian	Indian American	Total
Mainstream						
Boston	2,597	4,071	789	67	35	7,559
Springfield	784	382	215	4	0	1,385
Separate						
Boston	1,367	1,415	280	24	13	3,099
Springfield	477	314	139	0	0	930

SOURCE: Massachusetts Board of Education data for October 1, 1978.

TABLE 7.3

Special Needs Students in Boston and Springfield, Massachusetts, Public Schools by Percentage of Total Enrollment, 1978

	White	Black	Hispanic	Asian	American Indian	Total
Total Enrollment						
Boston	28,716	31,798	8,715	2,490	386	72,105
Springfield	14,590	7,627	4,480	62	16	26,775
Mainstream						
Boston	9.0	12.8	9.1	2.6	9.1	10.5
Springfield	5.4	5.3	17.6	6.4	0	5.2
Separate						
Boston	4.8	4.4	3.2	1.0	3.4	4.3
Springfield	3.3	4.1	3.1	0	0	3.5

SOURCE: Massachusetts Board of Education data for October 1, 1978.

Something sociological is needed to interpret these comparisons, but we do not know what the explanation might be. National studies suggest that the concept of special needs may be stretched beyond credibility when it embraces more than about 17 percent of the school-age population. In 1980 Boston had classified 10,486, or 15.5 percent, of its total enrollment as handicapped, and the core evaluation teams were still hard at work evaluating others. Inasmuch as 8,188 of these special needs students were enrolled in regular classes, with considerable vitality in movement out of the classification as well as in, this seems superior to the dearth of services in 1974 (see Table 7.4).

TABLE 7.4

Boston Special Needs Classes by Desegregation Status, 1979

School Type	In Compliance (%)	In Noncompliance (%)	Total (N)
Elementary (K–5)			
Mainstream	80	20	103
Separate	84	16	68
Middle (6–8)			
Mainstream	58	42	26
Separate	91	9	22
High (9–12)			
Mainstream	90	10	21
Separate	82	18	17
Total	81	19	257
All Schools	78	22	153

SOURCE: Analysis by Dentler for the court, September 1979.

BILINGUAL PROGRAMS*

Just as programs for special needs students resulted from state-wide and then national policy transformations—the latter to extend to all children and youth with handicaps equalized and individualized educational services, and

*This section draws on the work of Sarah Nieves-Squires et al., *A Bibliography of Significant Features in Bilingual Education Programs*, Abt Associates Inc. Report No. 80–12, U.S. Government Printing Office, Washington, D.C., January 1980.

the former to integrate these students with regular program students wherever possible—so bilingual programs stem from two parallel policy transformations. One provides strong support for the process of linguistic transition from minority language to English, the dominant North American language. This policy is backed by the Title VII amendment to the revised Elementary and Secondary Education Act of 1968, which was supported by an initial allocation of 7.5 million dollars, an amount that has been increased annually until it will reach 400 million dollars in 1983.

In Massachusetts, moreover, the Transitional Bilingual Education law supports this policy of linguistic transition while also giving implicit support to the idea of assisting with the maintenance of the minority language.

Much more political tension surrounds bilingualism than special education. Although at least ten states still have laws that enable them to sterilize retarded persons, for example, those laws have gone out of fashion, and nowhere are they implemented without judicial review.

In upholding the Virginia Supreme Court view that sterilization "was not meant to punish but to protect the class of socially inadequate citizens from themselves and to promote the welfare of society by mitigating race degeneracy and raising the average intelligence of the people of the state," U.S. Supreme Court Justice Oliver Wendell Holmes, a Bostonian, wrote in 1927 that "three generations of idiots are enough."

By the 1970s, social policies had changed. The policy of providing special education, while still resisted as costly and inconvenient, was widely shared. Mainstreaming grew up out of the twin influences of educational research evidence that illustrated the negative effects of segregation of the handicapped and out of the civil rights demands of advocates and affected parties.

Transitional instruction for bilingual minorities similarly stirs few controversies. In the nineteenth century and at least until World War I, many big cities and some remote rural schools sustained bilingual programs in many languages, but by 1920 the pressures toward cultural assimilation had become fierce and whole states maintained laws prohibiting minority languages from being spoken, written, or read in public schools or on their playgrounds. After World War II, however, programs in the teaching of English as a second language cropped up everywhere and there was some public acceptance of the notion that every child ought to have a chance to become proficient in the English language.

What upsets the melting pot, however, is the view that minority language proficiencies and cultural heritages ought to be nurtured at public expense. Critics of bilingual schooling, drawing on the arguments advanced by English-speaking policymakers in Canada, regard language maintenance as a form of cultural imperialism that threatens to fragment a nation into divisive pluralism. They are supported by some liberals who see maintenance as a danger to the furtherance of social integration. Advocates have argued to the contrary that lingual and cultural parity are essential preconditions of equal opportunity.

The place of nonblack minorities in federal desegregation cases was contested repeatedly until the *Keyes* decision in Denver. There, the Supreme Court extended the principles of *Brown* to include other minorities, most notably Mexican-Americans. At this juncture, the fate of bilingualism and desegregation became intertwined. In Boston, in the first major federal case to come after *Keyes*, the intertwining had to be worked through in novel ways.

The Boston plaintiffs were the parents of black Americans. Their attorneys defined their cause as a "race case," intending to pursue it with strategies that had been worked out in South Carolina and elsewhere in the Deep South even before *Brown* in 1954. When Judge Garrity came to the remedial phase in Boston, however, he attached the Hispanic parents' organization, El Comite, to the case as intervenors and solicited their active participation in planning and implementing a remedy that would address the needs of nonblack or other ethnic minorities.

El Comite's range fell far short of representing the city's diverse ethnic minority populations. The group did not speak for the Chinese Education Association, for American Indians, for Cape Verdian Islanders, or for other minority groups whose children were enrolled in segregated schools; and El Comite represented only a small portion of the Hispanic community. It was not surprising, then, that the group's role in the case became coterminous with bilingual programs, especially those aimed at Hispanic students. As Judge Garrity put it in his May 1975 memorandum:

> The assignment guidelines are intended to assure that "other minority" students will also be afforded "equally desegregated education," as stated in this court's order of October 31, 1974. They therefore provide for assignments that neither isolate nor excessively concentrate "other minority" students. This policy is adopted in the interests of all, not only for the sake of the "other minority" students. Taking advantage of Boston's ethnic variety, then, the guidelines provide that in the districts with substantial numbers of "other minority" students [about half of the eight community districts], students from that group will be enrolled at each school. . . .
>
> The plan's assignment guidelines thus take account of "other minority" students, but do not simply aggregate them with black students, in prescribing school composition limits. Plaintiffs-intervenors, El Comite de Padres Pro Defensa de la Educacion Bilingue, representing the class of Spanish-speaking students and their parents, have stressed their right to adequate bilingual education. The remedy accordingly concentrates on providing bilingual schooling for Hispanic students and for others in need of this service.

Assignment of bilingual students before others will prevent excessive dispersal. Thus the "clustering" of bilingual classes will be possible and Boston's schools will be enabled to fulfill the promise of this state's exemplary bilingual education law . . . as well as to meet the requirements of the federal Civil Rights Act of 1964.[5]

These were also among the points advanced to the masters by attorneys for El Comite and by experts who testified for them. Central to the fashioning of the remedy, for instance, was the testimony of Dr. Maria Brisk, an associate professor of education at Boston University. Brisk was influential in advocating the value of bilingual education and the special importance of clustering bilingual students in large enough numbers, but in small enough classes, to achieve an effective critical mass for both language and social learning. Her testimony helped the masters work through the contradictions several of them sensed between the methods of bilingual instruction and the aims of complete desegregation.

There had been a handful of bilingual classes started in Boston between 1972 and 1974, but these were too few in number to offer guidance on where the greatly enlarged number of court-mandated programs should be located. By the spring of 1975 no one knew how many bilingual students might materialize or where they should be assigned. El Comite kept emphasizing in court the importance of a school-age population census, which the court had directed the system to conduct (see Table 7.5). In the group's view, based on some efforts by experts to estimate the population, thousands of Hispanic and Asian-American children had never been enrolled in school. The census was never taken, however, and by the time the court plan was issued, no knowledge base other than the enrollment printouts filed on April 8, 1975, was available.

TABLE 7.5
Estimates of Hispanic Population of Boston, Selected Years

Date	Hispanic Population	Source[a]
1960	2,104	U.S Bureau of the Census: 1960 Census
1969	32,000	Mayor's Office of Human Rights
1970	17,984	U.S. Bureau of the Census: 1970 Census
1974	45,000	Bilingual Information Center, Secretary of State's Office
1977	45,000–60,000	Hispanic Office of Planning & Evaluation, Council of Administrators of Hispanic Agencies
1978	60,000–75,000	Alianza Hispana, Public Education Office

[a]Data originally published in The Puerto Rican Community of Boston, Hispanic Office of Planning and Evaluation, December 1978.

At the prompting of the masters, Dentler met several times with attorneys for El Comite, getting their suggestions on who might be assigned where. The upshot of these meetings became the basis for the court plan, which called for the following:

> Schools where bilingual programs shall be provided are shown in the school tables which are part of this plan. Where 20 or more kindergarten students attend a school and are found to be in need of bilingual instruction, the school department shall provide it. Parents who seek bilingual instruction for their children at any grade level shall note this on the enrollment application form which the school department shall mail to them. However, the School bilingual department staff shall make the decision to *assign* students to programs, but not to specific schools within Community Districts. Bilingual program assignments will be the first made by the Assignment Unit.

The court plan listed the schools within each district that should host bilingual programs in each of six languages. In composing the list, we drew on a list of then-current sites from the school department and on data from the printouts. Our relations with school officials were not friendly, however, for they were adversaries by definition, and the El Comite attorneys were as unfamiliar with particulars as those of us working for the court. They did test out our lists on El Comite leaders, however, and we took most of their suggestions.

After a time, it became apparent that some of the leaders were determined to have the programs located in schools closest to their homes and apartments. This was a direct, practical expression of the tension between desegregation imperatives and the actual process of desegregation. We could see that we would have to strain for "equitable consistency," lest the bilingual programs became a kind of haven of convenience that exempted this set of students from the otherwise equally shared burdens of redistributive assignments.

Using estimates offered by Associate School Superintendent Charles Leftwich and obtained from bilingual administrators in the department, we set aside 3,870 seats for bilingual Hispanic students—55 percent of those Hispanics projected to enroll in the schools in September 1975. We tried to keep them in schools where they were already functioning well, in schools within walking distance of their homes, and in schools where different distances of busing would be required for transportation from home to school.

When the parent applications were mailed in June 1975, many parents assumed that bilingual programs offered a special opportunity for their children to learn a second language. The demand for this service was immense. In fact, more than 5,000 parents applied for bilingual program assignments, including thousands who did not qualify.[6] Our aim had been to look beyond the lists available to the bilingual department of the school system to ensure equal access and to encourage unenrolled students to come in off the streets. But what we achieved instead was a bureaucratic snarl and no means of solving the mystery of who was eligible. Therefore, we fell back on the department lists, which had not been shared prior to casting the order, and arranged to allow applications to be accepted throughout the summer and early fall.

Before the first round of student assignments was even reviewed by Judge Garrity, the premises of the court plan for bilingual assignments had been fractured. Fewer than 2,000 bilingual Hispanic students had been identified. If the schools listed by the court were used, these students would be dispersed across 26 schools and would occupy half-empty classrooms because of the 3,870 seats that had been set aside. Dispersal rather than clustering would be the outcome. We conferred with the El Comite attorneys and drew them into efforts within the assignment unit to remedy the snarled situation, but no one could repair the damage.

With Judge Garrity's permission, therefore, the assignment unit began to revise the program location lists and to exploit the plan's authorization to assign students across district boundaries. Matters were patched up provisionally by the opening of school, but in the course of both planning and implementation, everyone could sense that the difficulties of incorporating bilingual programs were far from resolved in 1975.

For example, some 400 students were transferred into the Hispanic programs between September and January, but in the course of this change, we realized that the headquarters bilingual staff was severely undermanned and lacked the means to screen and identify English-language-deficient students quickly and accurately. By the close of the year, hundreds of others were withdrawn by parents who became disenchanted with the quality of instruction or who decided to try for a different school assignment. These were among the continually increasing clues that the system was far from ready to mount and maintain effective bilingual instruction.

Another clue came earlier when the little Office of Implementation attempted to translate the first parent orientation and application booklet into six languages. Hundreds of errors were made in the process. Some of these were fundamental enough to mislead or discourage parents from pursuing their best interests. It took the system three years to bring translation, editing, and printing up to a level of adequacy.

During 1976 parent advisory groups conducted public hearings about the quality of bilingual programs. Days and nights of complaints were stenographed and transcribed. Some program locations were deemed to have caused the isolation and dispersal of students and to be physically inadequate. Some were half empty or, in contrast, in violation of the state standard that called for no more than twenty students per classroom. Still others were staffed by teachers who were said to be monolingual; others had teachers who were certified but regarded by parents as incompetent or prejudiced, and others had teachers who were uncertified. To read the record of the public hearings was to conclude that the system's response to state law and court orders was deserving of a grade of D – , at best.

Few of these deficiencies were attacked assiduously by the court. Attorneys for El Comite filed many motions and briefs and attended hearings faithfully, but the group's resources were very limited and its concerns did not seem to compare in urgency with those of the plaintiffs, the school defendant, and the board of education. The board attorney and the assistant attorney general seldom joined forces with attorneys for El Comite, and generally the hearings held from 1975 through 1978 proceeded as if the bilingual programs were an afterthought.

Part of this lack of attention to bilingual education and its relative low standing in the case was the result of El Comite's avoidance of a union with the black plaintiffs to fight for a common cause, at least up until 1979. El Comite's attorneys seldom joined in the struggle for desegregation. Their advocacy of bilingual instruction amounted with few exceptions to the one note they struck in the case, often with support from the attorneys for the black plaintiffs. Whatever issue came up—facilities, assignments, finances, teacher desegregation, or other programs—tended to be converted into the theme of bilingual program needs.

In part, this was due to the conditions under which they entered the case, conditions which neglected the needs and interests of *each* of the ethnic minorities. In part, it was due to the abysmal performance of the system in rising to the task of implementing state law. In a deeper multicultural sense, it was due to a mutual absence of resonance between white, black, and Hispanic constituencies. The case was truly multiethnic, but neither federal law and civil procedure nor bilingual concerns were extensive enough to take the full scope of multiethnic needs into consideration.

There were 7,000 Hispanic students in the system in 1975 (see Table 7.6), but there were 2,800 Chinese-Americans, other Asians, and American Indians as well. About 34 percent of the Hispanic and other minorities were enrolled in bilingual programs, and those extended to Greek and Italian-American students and to black French Haitian students. Thus, bilingual programs did not begin to encompass the range of multiethnic interests, and at least two bilingual programs—those for Italian and Greek nationals—had nothing to do with racial/ethnic minorities.

If it had not been for demographic changes and for corresponding increases in parental involvement by other minorities in the public schools, it seems in retrospect that bilingual programs could have continued to play the part of the half-starved flea on the leg of the system elephant.

Hundreds of new immigrants from Taiwan and Hong Kong entered the system from 1975 to 1979, and the number of Puerto Rican, other Caribbean, Latino, and Chicano students swelled from 7,000 to 8,670. The number of other minority students increased over six years from 9,800 to 11,343, while the

TABLE 7.6

Bilingual and Hispanic Students in Boston Public School System, 1973-79[a]

Date	Hispanic Students	Hispanics in Bilingual Programs	Total Students in Bilingual Programs
1973-74	6,052	—	—
1974-75	6,904	—	—
May 1976	7,071	2,407	3,758
December 1976	7,331	2,358	3,662
December 1977	7,708	3,029	4,647
December 1978	8,134	3,387	5,111
October 20, 1979	8,670	3,775[b]	5,890

[a]The 1973-74 and 1974-75 Hispanic student population figures are from *The Puerto Rican Community in Boston*, Hispanic Office of Planning and Evaluation, December 1978. All other figures are from the bilingual implementation team's 1979 report to the Boston School Department. These are actual figures, except those for October 20, 1979 (bilingual programs), which are assigned figures. However, assigned and actual bilingual numbers are comparatively the same.

[b]This figure was obtained from the School Department Data Processing Department.

number of white students declined by half and the number of black students remained constant. The public schools were 12 percent other minority in May 1975, and 17 percent in 1980.

As the numbers increased, El Comite pressed more successfully for bilingual programs in every category; they sought and obtained bilingual kindergartens, advanced work classes, extended-day kindergartens, and vocational classes, as well as bilingual classes for most categories of students with special needs. In these efforts, El Comite's attorneys enjoyed success before the federal bar. And although the school committee complied slowly and reluctantly at first, it eventually supplied the programs with more and more resources. The number of bilingual teachers hired by the system grew from just under 100 in 1974 to 300 in 1980. As this change took place, some committee members began to see the rich possibilities of new constituencies the bilingual programs could bring them.

In February of 1977, at our request, Albert Tutella of the school department's DP center conducted an analysis of the numbers of students who were attending schools out of districts they were originally to attend. Small studies over the preceding months had led us to suspect that the constant flood of transfers and reassignments, the extraordinarily high turnovers in special needs and bilingual assignments, and the extreme underutilization of some schools were all contributing to resegregation of parts of the system. By that time, Tutella had the student records computerized well enough to make such an analysis. With our prompting, he coupled the data with a table showing the number of years students had remained enrolled in bilingual programs. Our objective was to prepare for a late spring season of making all student assignments in a systematic manner—after two years of tinkering and improvising.

Tutella found about 2,000 students who were enrolled in and attending schools in violation of court assignment rules. He found students who had been enrolled by fiat of principals and district superintendents; others who had devised schemes for withdrawing and then re-entering under false addresses, and so forth. We immediately began to correct these violations. Public reactions were stimulated even before new assignments were so much as outlined in the data processing center.

Among the bilingual students, Tutella identified approximately 400 who were enrolled out of their residential districts when there was space available for them in classes sited in the appropriate districts. Examination of his tables and the system maps suggested that the rule enabling out-of-district assignments for bilingual students had been abused on a fairly massive scope, that parents were choosing schools for convenience and safety, and that a few lingual minorities were treating the bilingual classes as a haven.

Chinese bilingual students displayed compliance with the rules and prompt movement out of bilingual programs as their English language skills reached adequacy, but some Italian, Greek, and Hispanic students, in that order, were tending to use the programs for purposes of language and cultural maintenance and separation.

Because program locations had never been worked out rationally, Leftwich and Tutella proposed to devise sites that would meet the numbers and needs of bilingual students within each community district and in selected magnet schools. We discussed this with Judge Garrity in terms of developing a durable "space/program matrix," as Tutella labeled it, and he encouraged our planning efforts. In the 1977 student assignment operation, then, we relocated some bilingual programs—about ten of them altogether—and changed assignments in order to fit students into suitable clusters within their residential districts.

Public reactions to the changes were so hostile and widespread that we knew bilingualism had helped establish a vocal minority constituency. Most of the program sites had become immovable objects in the path of the court. After two hearings, Judge Garrity directed us to "fine tune" the assignments and, in particular, to provide relief for disgruntled and alarmed bilingual parents.

The Massachusetts Board of Education argued that state law did not prevent students from continuing to attend bilingual classes on a rather indefinite basis. All of the parties urged a return of students to their previous sites.

159

Some of our new locations were in physically superior, safer, and better-sited schools, but as with other program-based constituencies in Boston, such as vocational education, business education, and kindergartens, those that had operated for two to three years were regarded as the best ones. Changes in locations were viewed as disruptions of the stability owed to students. That hundreds of students moved in and out of schools and programs through the revolving doors of transfers and corrective assignments their parents sought did not detract from the force of the pleas.

By 1977, one year after the public hearings had recorded a tidal wave of grievances against bilingual programs, parents rallied in support of their *status quo ante* as if it had been in place for a generation. Parental participation itself had come of age.

THE HERNANDEZ MAGNET

As noted in Chapter Six, the masters handled the question of what to do with the Rafael Hernandez Elementary School, one of the few pre-1975 sites for bilingual instruction in Boston, in an imaginative way. Following Master Charles Willie's dictum that social integration entails composing a school so that the majority group may be comprised of whites, blacks, or other minority group members, so long as the minority is from one-third to one-fifth of the total student body, they recommended that the Hernandez be designated a magnet for Hispanic bilingual students.[7] Judge Garrity endorsed this idea and Hernandez emerged as a fully bilingual, multicultural school that acquired a reputation as a model of the best in bilingual education.

At our suggestion, Hernandez and other Hispanic bilingual programs throughout the city were paired with Boston University, which had the strongest and best-staffed faculty in that field in the northeast quarter of the United States.

The first two years were frustrating and tumultuous for the Hernandez faculty. The school was heavily oversubscribed by Hispanic parents. Many of them lived nearby and had come to expect that they could avail themselves of the school's benefits. There were only 200 seats in the little school, however, and with 66 of these reserved for non-Hispanics, the struggle for entry became intense.

Assignment unit staff thought the matter would be simple to treat compared with schools with enrollments of 2,400 students, but they were wrong. For two years, jockeying occurred for the most part around the number of seats available for kindergartners because this was the least prescribed feature in the court plan for all schools. The Hernandez principal would state that space was available and then, when school opened, it would become apparent that Hernandez was overcrowded because room space was being taken away from upper grades.

The pressure always seemed to move in the direction of adding to the number of assigned Hispanic students. The control valve on proportions would erupt when some non-Hispanic students would obtain transfers early each fall after their parents concluded that a bicultural experience was not what they sought. Personnel at school headquarters, moreover, would assign too few bilingual teachers, and confusion would develop periodically about whether bilingual modes of teaching were to include the non-Hispanic students. Compounding the confusion, of course, was the fact that the bilingual department at headquarters lacked the means to screen and identify students accurately and with dispatch.

By the fall of 1977, however, these frustrations subsided and Hernandez began to become the exemplary model the masters had intended. Again, the leadership of Professor Maria Brisk made a significant contribution to this new stage of orderly development. Word of the success of Hernandez began to spread and in 1979 the Ford Foundation funded a proposal from Barry MacDonald of the University of East Anglia in England, one of England's most distinguished educational researchers, to study the social organization, curriculum, and instruction of the Rafael Hernandez School.

Critics of bilingual education tend to fall into two groups. One is represented by Dr. John Silber, the president of Boston University. He devoted part of a commencement address, and later part of a magazine article, to attacking bilingual education because it seemed to him to offer a double standard for lingual minorities: According to Dr. Silber, it excuses students for not being proficient in English and then victimizes them as adults because they cannot compete since they are tied to a monolingual standard of competence. In this view, the most dangerous feature of bilingual policies is the possibility that they may foster subcultural pluralism rather than hasten assimilation into the *de facto* dominance of the Anglo social system.[8] Holders of this view tolerate bilingual instruction strictly to the extent that it is brief, transitional, and aimed at instilling competency in English.

The second group of critics is skeptical of the pedagogy itself. Its members doubt that bilingual instruction can achieve optimal learning outcomes for students. A federally contracted evaluation conducted in 1978 by the American Institutes for Research (AIR) reported overall results of "no effects" from the bilingual pedagogy, and the AIR findings cheered on the critics who hold this view.[9]

Abt Associates Inc. and Development Associates are currently designing a new series of evaluations that will test the hypotheses about the impacts of bilingual programs once again; this time, however, it will be done in a much more complex and detailed fashion than was feasible for AIR. Bilingual advocates and the two kinds of critics are girding for a major national debate in 1983, when the enabling legislation of federal Title VII comes up for review.

It is questionable whether evaluation research will put the national debate to rest. If well designed and executed, however, it may show that, as with desegregation plans, research that deals exclusively with hypothesized learning outcomes falls far short of the great range of purposes served by bilingual policies.

Most of those policies must go through a cycle of social and educational maturation. They began with a quest for civil rights and as such they embodied the subcultural aspirations of roughly eighty different lingual minorities, all spearheaded by Puerto Rican, Cuban, Latino, and Chicano leaders who saw the possibility of achieving parity of status through programs over which they would have some substantial control.

In a second stage of the cycle, teachers had to be prepared. Dr. Celia Lascarides, a Greek-American social scientist, did a systematic field study of Boston kindergartens in 1976, comparing four monolingual classes with four bilingual classes.[10] The observable and then measurable differences between the two were negligible, with the amount of actual bilingual interaction depending almost completely upon the competencies of the teachers.

For the most part, all of the classes were conducted in accordance with long-standing assumptions held by early childhood teachers about the activity rituals of kindergartners, and the pedagogy was not yet capable of incorporating bilingual features of any significance into these rituals. Indeed, Dr. Lascarides found that some of the teachers had not yet developed rudimentary competencies in monolingual preschool approaches to instruction.

Substantial programs of teacher preparation did not get underway until 1973, and after the first few years, faculty realized their knowledge base was inadequate. A new stage of the cycle was entered where applied research was undertaken, together with programs of technical assistance to practitioners. Only now are educators coming to the demanding stage where exact knowledge about teaching strategies and consciously designed learning outcomes has begun to be pursued, with early contributions from researchers in Canada.[11]

It would be preposterous to have approached bilingual programs in Boston before 1980 with questions about effectiveness. One would have to contrast long-established conventional programs with new, tentative experiments in bilingual teaching. One would have to overlook the political fact that bilingual programs were imposed by the state board and then the court upon a reluctant and culturally insular school committee and administration. Managerial supports lagged each season far behind the attempts to get classroom programs launched. Funding alone will not make up for lack of experience and for the confounding conditions of bringing new pedagogies into being in settings riddled with tension, avoidance, and ignorance, as well as a system burdened mightily with dozens of imperatives for instantaneous transformation.

ADVANCED WORK CLASSES

Before the court intervened, most Boston elementary schools operated programs that constituted tracking arrangements for allegedly gifted students. These were called advanced work classes (see Table 7.7). They began in the fourth grade, sometimes extended through the eighth grade, and served as havens for students destined for the Latin schools and for others being prepped for futures as college students.

Neither we nor the masters were in sympathy with these classes. We received representations that they were usually segregated and that access was sometimes politically arranged or a matter of teacher favoritism. It seemed to us that advanced work classes were of a piece with the Boston Latin schools in functioning as a reinforcer of the essence of a dual, racially isolated system.

TABLE 7.7

Students in Special Programs
by Racial/Ethnic Group, 1980

Special Program	White	Black	Asian	Hispanic	Native American	Total
Bilingual (7 languages)	707	761	830	3,812	0	6,110
Vocational training	590	584	15	42	10	1,241
Extended-day kindergarten	586	693	33	303	16	1,631
Advanced work class	423	501	91	70	7	1,092
Special needs	3,456	5,891	92	1,257	49	10,745
Subtotal	5,762	8,430	1,061	5,484	82	20,819
All other students	18,255	21,653	1,803	2,879	211	44,801
Total	24,017	30,083	2,864	8,363	293	65,620
Percentage in special programs	24	28	37	66	28	32

When the court plan came out, it said nothing one way or the other about these classes. Within a few months, the school committee presented a proposal to start them up anew, but on a desegregated basis. We advised against approving the proposal, restating our earlier views and adding to them our belief that existence of these classes would work against the new heterogeneity of groupings in schools and regular classrooms and would come to be a source of contention among teachers and parents.

Judge Garrity found these arguments to be extraneous, for appeals had already been filed charging that his plan would make incursions into the curricular and organizational purview of the local committee. He did follow our advice on three controlling features, however. He kept the program very small, limiting the number of students to be enrolled in advanced work classes to no more than 4 percent of those in the fourth and fifth grades; he established a selection standard that would be impartial, defining eligible students as those who ranked above the 70th percentile on the annually administered reading portion of the Stanford Achievement Tests, with teachers recommending students from within this eligible group and parents consenting; and he directed the assignment unit to work out the locations with us. We chose schools that we thought might otherwise have trouble attracting or holding white students. The presence of these classes would thus attract white students and aid in school desegregation.

After the usual hitches involved in working out questions of who would go where, hitches again resulting from faulty student records and weak planning, the advanced work classes were launched. They proved to be as popular as administrators said they would be, and in 1977 the judge approved a motion to expand them to include sixth graders in middle schools; he would not, however, approve extension above that level.

In 1979 the Department of Implementation proposed expanding the size of the program from 4 to 6 percent of all students. In the hearing that followed, plaintiffs' attorney Larry Johnson challenged the whole program, asking whether the classes had a curricular aim, a set of instructional guidelines, and some evaluative analyses showing effects of the special treatment. He said expansion was not in order and continuation should depend upon a showing of purpose and value. Judge Garrity asked the Department of Implementation to report a year later on such questions.

No report was filed early in 1980, but in February both the court and school headquarters received a rash of parent complaints. According to reporter Richard Kindelberger's article in the *Boston Globe*, parents were resentful of a second round of tests that had been scheduled for private school students. The article stated that the parents of public school students believed that their children might lose out to these other students in the competition for admission to advanced work classes because they had taken the test earlier. They also felt that private school students should not be placed on an equal footing with those students already attending public schools. It became quite evident that advanced work classes were one of the few features of the public school system that had some magnetic attraction for parents with children in the parochial schools. To some in public school headquarters, the magnet was worth waving as vigorously as possible. Many parents were confused because some administrators and teachers were speculating openly that the court might move to discontinue advanced work classes in 1980.

Judge Garrity offered assurances from the bench that the court was not considering discontinuing the classes because, in fact, the court had no intentions of involving itself. But underneath the public controversy was the ancient principle of educational misplacement at work: The one programmatic feature of advanced work classes that causes controversy, just as it did in so many school programs for generations past and at every level, is student selectivity. "Giftedness in," other things remaining constant, will usually result in "giftedness out," and some parents, teachers, and students alike enjoy the magic of this substitute for pedagogical imagination.[12]

EXTENDED-DAY KINDERGARTENS

On the recommendation of the masters, kindergartners were virtually exempted from the coercive features of the court plan in 1975. The only thing the plan said was that

> most but not all elementary schools shall contain kindergartens. Kindergarten assignments shall be made by the School Department to appropriate facilities, and may include inter-district assignments. Kindergarten classes shall be desegregated wherever possible. If kindergarten students must be assigned to schools outside their home neighborhoods, the assignments shall be made in accordance with two principles: (1) the resulting student bodies shall be desegregated, and (2) the burdens of distance and transportation shall be distributed equitably across ethnic groups.

Kindergartners were exempt for two reasons. First, the Massachusetts Board of Education policies for the state do not require local districts to provide kindergarten programs; thus, the programs are correctly viewed as optional rather than state mandated. Second, the masters and others were convinced that walk-in facilities for the four- and five-year-olds would maintain one aspect of the neighborhood school concept and would ease parental anxiety about the alleged dangers of busing.

Eight out of every ten elementary facilities had the rooms and equipment required for what the system called K1 and K2 programs—K1 for four-year-olds and K2 for five-year-olds. School administrators committed every available room for use, but for the first two years they assigned students almost without exception on the basis of the nearest school. About one-fourth of the preschoolers needed transportation even under this principle, and for three years an inordinately expensive arrangement was maintained under which children were picked up by buses, vans, and taxis at their doorsteps.

In 1977 we reported to Judge Garrity that the kindergartens in eight out of the ten schools that had them were extremely segregated and, even worse, that minority children were greatly outnumbered by whites. In other words, the exemption of these grades enabled continuation of a *dual* system at this level and the dualism was working in a way that discouraged enrollment of black and other minority children who needed preschool education.

As court hearings on the issue were scheduled, Superintendent Marion Fahey rose to the occasion and acted affirmatively in a way that had not been risked on any issue by anyone in school headquarters before 1977. Miss Fahey called for the establishment of K1 and K2 classes that would operate for six rather than the customary three hours a day, in the belief that this would attract more parents, including many in need of day care services, and would combine an occasion for desegregating some kindergartens with improving educational services.

Her proposal was approved enthusiastically by the court. Under her leadership and with exceptionally effective administration from Jane Burgess, a campaign of publicity and invitation was mounted and extended-day programs were established in every district, all of them based in schools whose desegregative capacities needed reinforcing and all of them composed voluntarily of student groups reflecting city-wide racial/ethnic proportions.

Response was cautious at first. Some of the extended-day programs operated throughout the first year well under capacity. Nonetheless, most began to flourish in 1978 and the campaign had the encouraging side effect of drawing into this program and into regular kindergartens growing numbers of black and other minority children.

Marion Fahey also challenged the wisdom of continuing the costly provision of door-to-door transportation. The changeover to corner stops and pickups was accomplished, although complaints were intense and were amplified greatly by a series of planning botches within the transportation unit of the Department of Implementation. Nonetheless, all of the extended-day classes and a significantly higher proportion of the regular kindergartens are now desegregated and the numbers of children enrolling, numbers that declined from 1974 through 1977, have remained high and stable.

Neither the court plan nor the implementation of changes has reconciled kindergarten services with the first through fifth grade classes in elementary schools. Children often adjust happily to one school during K1 and K2 and then must be assigned to a different school for first grade. Many white families have made use of the kindergarten services and then switched their children to parochial school at first grade, a pattern that evolved long before desegregation. This destabilizes enrollments and undermines the social familiarity essential to early schooling for those who stay and for those who switch out of the public systems.

In our view, kindergartners should never have been exempted from the court plan. Their presence affects the annual establishment of racial/ethnic ratios in every district. Each school should plan its curriculum around students who will, in the main at least, tend to remain enrolled from K1 through fifth grade. This arrangement would enable parents to invest time and effort in making a particular elementary school worthwhile. The split between preschool and the other grades persists and undermines both social and educational stability at a juncture where it counts most. It may be that a future moderate school committee may be led by someone with the courage and vision Marion Fahey exhibited. If so, preschool education may be unified with elementary school education, for there is nothing in the court plan that prevents these initiatives.

CONCLUSIONS

Four among some ten special programs offered in the Boston public schools have been discussed in this chapter. The four were selected because they resulted from, or disclose in their development, the impacts of court plans and efforts to implement a remedy. Together, they also express the ways in which public school districts differ from one another in their attempts to provide special subgroups of students with individualized services.

Each of the programs provides strong evidence of the consequences of poor public education planning. Special needs services as well as bilingual and advanced work classes were all in place before the court intervened; only extended-day kindergartens were novel to Boston. Still, none was supported by an effective management information system or educational evaluations of a kind that would enable the programs to be revised to complement other programs or school sites, or to meet public needs. Court planning was hobbled by these deficiencies and the haste of its own initial planning contributed to the mass of difficulties that plagued the first few years of implementation.

Poor planning is seldom defeated by efficient implementation, and in the instances of special and bilingual education, poor planning had its negative effects multiplied by poor execution. A year after the court order, for example, Dentler visited the Jackson-Mann (magnet elementary) Community School and witnessed the temporary chaos that had been generated. This school was a new, magnificently designed facility that was meant to serve as a model for the mainstreaming of hearing and speech impaired students with regular students. It opened in September 1975, but seven months later it was shuddering internally with unanticipated problems.

Furnishings and equipment were still stacked in unopened boxes in the halls; some had arrived late but others were untouched because of insufficient custodial help, according to the principal. (In the nearby suburb of Melrose, Dentler had seen the superintendent, the principal, and some teachers join voluntarily in uncrating and installing such stuff in a new high school; but in Boston, volunteerism could produce new problems because the custodians are paid to do this work and they are part of the school committee's historic patronage system.) Leadership controversies erupted because the school had two connected buildings, each with its own administrator. Some classrooms were overcrowded while others were half empty. The principal's plan for the balanced integration of hearing-impaired students with regular students was sabotaged by the uncoordinated and unbalanced mix of students being assigned to the school by headquarters. The kindergartners who were enjoying the new school very much were destined to be assigned elsewhere the next year.

Some parent advisors who lived nearby, as well as some of the teachers, did not understand that Jackson-Mann was *not* a neighborhood school. The valiant principal, Ralph Mann, spent vital energies trying to smooth out relations between very discrepant constituencies. He faced, among others, neighborhood influentials, Chinese and Hispanic bilingual parents, and parents of severely handicapped children, all in search of "their" magnet. The school's most promising program was an infant care and stimulation program operating in the basement on an informal basis.

After many difficulties, Jackson-Mann emerged as a genuine magnet school with multiple services of high quality by 1978. A visitor today would have no sense of the chaos that engulfed the school for nearly three years. The positive differences between this school and a conventional elementary school are tremendous. Without the court's intervention, Jackson-Mann would have become two separate schools—a conventional neighborhood school and a school for the hearing and speech impaired. It is, instead, an extraordinary multicultural resource that may eventually become a regional center for language learning and communicative disorders.

Evaluation research might show that to date these special programs have had few tangible effects upon student achievement. We think that these positive effects will become evident in the 1980s, when special educators, bilingual teachers, teachers of the gifted, and early childhood educators have built up collective expertise and a network of mutual supports. The quality of teaching, not special programs, is what affects students most.

In the meantime, useful program evaluations will concentrate on the changing conditions that surround teacher performance in these special programs. The programs are no longer optional. They are mandated and regularly funded. Increasingly skilled staff have been hired. Racial isolation and the deprivations it produces have ended. Parent participation has extended enormously as a part of the change. The school committee has new, large, and vocal groups of constituents, and children have begun to receive effective advocacy from interest groups and volunteers.

At the same time, the changes have been problematic. Black students have been placed in special classes with relatively excessive frequency while white students who need the benefits of the new services have been transferred to very conventional nonpublic schools in excessive numbers. The chaos from poor planning and poorer implementation has lessened public confidence in the special programs at a time when increased confidence is needed. If that confidence finally becomes self-restoring, the conditions on balance are ones that could foster better learning for all children. Until then, on playgrounds and in a thousand classrooms, any visitor can witness the promise: Spanish, French Haitian, Portuguese, Chinese, Vietnamese, Greek, and Italian words and sentences fill the air. Children with handicaps are fully visible participants in the scene. Four- and five-year-olds have a full share in each school day.

NOTES

1. National Center for Education Statistics, *Digest of Education Statistics, 1979,* U.S. Government Printing Office, Washington, D.C., 1979.
2. John Gliedman and William Roth, *The Unexpected Minority: Handicapped Children in America,* for the Carnegie Council on Children, New York, Harcourt, Brace and Jovanovich, 1980.

3. This interpretation is partially supported by frequency data on classifications, with a slightly greater than chance lumping of blacks in the behavioral categories and whites in the organic and emotional. It is further supported by the comments made to us by school department officers on several occasions.

4. This view is based on our belief in the relative superiority of a system requiring *individualized* educational plans for exceptional children over the customary alternative of providing undifferentiated classroom groupings for all students.

5. *Morgan v. Kerrigan,* Civ. No. 72-911-G, Memorandum of May 10, 1975, pp. 64-66.

6. The application process could be used with great effectiveness as an annual educational audit. This example of expressed parental interest in second language instruction is one among many clues to public needs and interests that appeared on the applications. The process has never been used for this purpose in Boston, however, and the data were treated as a mistake.

7. Charles V. Willie, *The Sociology of Urban Education,* D.C. Heath, Lexington Books, Lexington, Mass., 1978, pp. 66-68.

8. For an excellent analysis, see Joshua A. Fishman, "Philosophy of Bilingual Education in a Societal Setting," in *Language Development in a Bilingual Setting,* National, Multilingual, Multicultural Material Development Center, Los Angeles, National Dissemination and Assessment Center, 1979.

9. American Institutes for Research, *Evaluation of the Impact of ESEA Title VII Spanish/English Bilingual Education Program: Overview of Study and Findings,* Palo Alto, Calif., 1978.

10. Celia Lascarides Vassiliku, *Describing Children's Experiences in Regular and Bilingual Kindergarten Classrooms,* Doctoral Thesis, Boston University, 1979.

11. O. Anthony and G. Colallo, editors, *French Language Instruction: Papers from the Ontario Institute for Studies in Education (OISE) Conference on French Language Instruction,* Toronto, OISE, 1979.

12. We make no brief against individualized instruction for gifted students. Special programs have often been devised to facilitate this exceptional subpopulation, and rightly so. These are not to be confused with simplistic approaches to sequestering high scorers on paper and pencil tests, however.

SOUTH BOSTON HIGH SCHOOL

8

EXAMINING A SCHOOL IN CONFLICT

MOST INTENSE POLITICAL CONFLICTS, PARTICULARLY THOSE intrinsic to a region or place, require a staging area in order to be waged effectively. This area is often a particular neighborhood and a facility within it where it is feasible to mobilize groups by word of mouth, to limit and focus communications economically, and to display the sides of the conflict to a much larger audience in a dramatic way.[1] South Boston High School became the principal staging area in the school desegregation case for the legion of those committed to preventing desegregation and, subsequently, for counterforces and those with at least a partial stake in the preservation of constitutional justice.

This chapter recounts a few aspects of the South Boston High School story. It does not presume to provide a complete history.[2] It may take years before anyone gets an opportunity to write a history.

170

In the summer of 1979, for instance, the National Institute of Education requested proposals from researchers who might want to compete to make a case history of the school. The request marshalled very little money for the task—up to $25,000—and it was announced in the simmering month of August, when few scholars are at their desks. When a bitter dispute erupted between a proposal writer interested in doing the study and South Boston High's headmaster, who refused to provide him with the required letter of cooperation, the institute withdrew its request.

Only one proposal was actually submitted, although the request was disseminated nationwide. It was prepared by Dr. Susan Greenblatt, a sociologist who had begun a study of the school earlier and who had earned the cooperation and respect of its administration and some teachers. Her proposal was mooted by the institute's withdrawal, although she continued to study the school at her own expense. The subject is still too controversial to allow for open inquiry, and the story is not yet complete.

ORIGINS OF THE CONFLICT

> *We have Biff Mahoneys,*
> *And Buff Maloneys,*
> *And clowns who know how to clown,*
> *So, if you want to stay healthy,*
> *Stay the hell out of Southie,*
> *'Cause Southie is my home town.*
>> From the neighborhood song
>> of South Boston

In the aftermath of World War I, the struggle of Irish-American groups and their political leaders to secure and then preserve hegemony over both city hall and the school committee, a struggle that had reached its pitch twenty-five years before the turn of the century, became concentrated in the two wards of South Boston. For example, Irish-American Mayor James Curley, although a resident of Jamaica Plain (a neighborhood outside of South Boston), aimed his patronage and most of his public works at South Boston.

South Boston includes Dorchester Heights, where heroic resistance against the British contributed to the War of Independence. But the area also extends downward from the Heights to what were once the seeping, smelly marshlands on the edge of the harbor, lands that became a cherished foothold for second and third generations of Irish immigrants in search of homes of their own. By the 1920s, South Boston residents had fashioned a little city unto themselves, an authentic and militant ethnic enclave that included some German-Americans and Lithuanians as well as other East Europeans, but a place culturally identified with the customs and mores of nineteenth century Ireland.

Louise Day Hicks, the leading figure in the politics of opposition to desegregation, did not gain her position accidentally. The daughter of a judge, she stood in a long and amazingly influential line of political leaders whose power base was the wards of South Boston, but whose elective positions extended from the school committee member to the governor, and from federal subcabinet officer to the Speaker of the House, Representative John McCormack. South Boston was the power base not only for the McCormacks but also for the Kennedy family, a still significant fact that was expressed in the tributes paid to South Boston on the day of ceremonies opening the John F. Kennedy Library. Located on the edge of South Boston, in Dorchester, the library is not far from the original home of Joseph Kennedy, Sr.

South Boston High School was erected in 1908 at the peak of one of the hills overlooking the harbor. Its architecture and the costly materials used to construct it make the school look like a cross between a fortress and a city hall. For sixty years, its custodians, administrators, and teachers (in that order of importance) labored to preserve the role of this bastion in the furtherance of the political and cultural hegemony of the enclave it served.

Louise Day Hicks was not only a lawyer, she was also a former teacher. This is expressive of the importance that the second-, third-, and then fourth-generation Irish-Americans who built South Boston placed on education.

Edward McCormack, a distinguished state attorney general and one of the masters in the schools case, was one of the four graduates in his class at South Boston High to go on to college. He could not do so directly after graduation from South Boston, however; the school's program of instruction had helped make him a brilliant ice hockey player but had left him semi-literate. This was a situation that was remedied by a year at prep school.[3]

If Louise Day Hicks had not led the vanguard of opposition to school desegregation, some other politician from South Boston would have headed the movement. In the 1960s black Bostonians were not making plans to buy or rent housing in South Boston; they were jammed together in the segregated public housing apartments on Columbia Point, less than a mile away, and thousands of black families were finding homes and apartments in Dorchester, just a few blocks from the ward boundaries of Southie (as the residents call their neighborhood). Yankee Brahmins and their aides, after all, had fostered the Columbia Point Housing Project for blacks. The state Racial Imbalance Act, passed by the "same" interests, was enough to convince many Southie residents that it was time to take a strong stand.

With their backs to the sea, but with their leaders well placed in every decision-making body in the commonwealth, Southie residents made resistance to desegregation *the* symbolic expression of efforts to preserve the enclave. Their actions were based on the baffling and dismaying realization that Southie could disappear. Better housing in West Roxbury and the suburbs and job security in the Sunbelt had been drawing off the area's young and the upwardly mobile in increasing numbers ever since the end of World War II.

In the months before Phase I began in September 1974, many South Boston politicians, led by Louise Day Hicks, consolidated most of the anti-busing groups of Boston into a single organization—ROAR, for Restore Our Alienated Rights. Many public officials supported ROAR and the coalition held several antibusing rallies through the months from July to September.

No desegregation design plan could have prevented a showdown in South Boston, but the Phase I plan contained a component that seems, in retrospect, to have been designed to feed the flames. That component paired all-white South Boston High and its three annexes with what had been Girls High School in Roxbury, under the name of the South Boston–Roxbury High School Complex. The complex was to contain 3,000 students, with 1,700 slated for cross-busing; ninth and tenth graders were to go to South Boston High, eleventh graders to Girls High in Roxbury, and twelfth graders to both.

Six different housing projects were included in the attendance zone, all of them occupied by very poor and segregated black and white households. The bus routes and pickup points for the students from these projects had not been well planned, nor had they been announced to parents as late as three days before the schools opened. In sum, the Phase I plan did not merely propose to desegregate South Boston High; it proposed to disestablish the school through long-distance pairing with a high school no Southie student had attended for a generation.

Three days before the schools opened, ROAR spearheaded a protest rally at Boston's Government Center in order to demonstrate mass opposition to the court order. Senator Edward Kennedy was among those who had been invited to speak to the crowd of about 8,000 white protesters. Senator Kennedy stated his support for busing to achieve school desegregation and refused to oppose Judge Garrity's order, but added an expression of respect for the attitudes of the protesters. As he spoke, hecklers began to shout, tomatoes and eggs were thrown at him, and the crowd pressed toward him menacingly as he moved toward city hall. As he entered and the doors closed behind him, some of the demonstrators shattered the glass panes. ROAR leaders pledged not to forget Edward Kennedy.[4]

On the opening day of school, September 12, 1974, Louise Day Hicks stood outside the gates of the fortress-like high school with about 500 demonstrators, most of them boycotting students and their kinfolk. On that first day only 56 black and 68 white students out of a projected 1,300 arrived to attend South Boston High. At Roxbury High only 235 out of 900 materialized, all but 30 of them black.

On that day the conflict was staged and the form it took—boycotts, the stoning of buses, and attacks on black students, precipitated by Southie residents hurling epithets, eggs, and rotten tomatoes—persisted for the next year and a half. The success of these activities was powerfully reinforced by the presence of rising waves of policemen—Boston's own, the Metropolitan District force, and state police—and by the convergence of streams of reporters, correspondents, and television and radio crews from all over the world on Boston in the months that followed.

On October 7, less than a month after the eventful school opening, Haitian-born maintenance man, Andrew Yvon Jean-Louis, driving into South Boston to pick up his working wife, was dragged from his car and beaten by a mob of Southie antibusing demonstrators and others who happened to be present. This tragedy enlarged the range of possible actions that could (and did) become a regularity in the staging of the struggle.

Finally, the effectiveness of the form was demonstrated two days after the attack on Jean-Louis, when President Gerald Ford told a reporter for the Associated Press:

> The court decision in that case, in my judgment, was not the best solution to quality education in Boston. I have consistently opposed forced busing to achieve racial balance as a solution to quality education. And, therefore, I respectfully disagree with the Judge's order. But having said that, I think it is of maximum importance that the citizens of Boston respect the law.[5]

On March 2, 1980, the Sunday *New York Times* published a report by Stevene V. Roberts headlined, "Many Dreams are Dying in Boston as Kennedys' Legend is Tarnished." Roberts reported:

> Boston reflects the way that so many urban areas have changed in 20 years, and why liberalism has got such a bad name. When John F. Kennedy first went to Washington, being liberal meant helping the Irish and Italian families who were still mired in the lower working class. Today those groups have grown more prosperous, liberalism means helping poor blacks and other racial minorities, and the doctrine is not so popular with Senator Kennedy's long-time constituents . . . . The deepest issue is racial. "Kennedy let this area down," came a typical comment from Jack Leeman, a house painter. "He was supposed to represent his constituents and he didn't represent us."

CONTINUING ELEMENTS OF THE CONFLICT

As a result of the violent confrontations at the gates of South Boston High, Mayor White was drawn further into the case than he ever planned. His efforts to place responsibility for public safety on the court failed, and Thomas Atkins, president of the Boston chapter of the NAACP, called for a black student boycott of South Boston High, denouncing the site as too dangerous to go near. Judge Garrity attached the mayor to the case as a defendant because of disputes surrounding the provision of police protection.

The boycott efforts of ROAR were so successful that system-wide attendance hovered at 50 percent daily during the school complex's first months and did not move toward 70 percent until November. Heavy police cordons around South Boston High and Hyde Park High and, later, lines of police within these buildings exacerbated the situation—not as a result of police inaction, but because the target of opportunity for provocation, taunting, and incitement to conflict was improved.

Assaults on students and teachers soared during September and October to four times the rate common in high schools the previous year. Later investigations disclosed that these fights were stimulated by promptings from the antibusing leaders. Most white students stayed at home or on the streets and among those who attended were many who took on the role of deliberate troublemakers.

On December 11, five days before the school committee was obligated to present the court with a permanent plan for desegregation, a white student named Michael Faith was stabbed during a general melee between white and black students at South Boston High. School superintendent Leary closed the school, along with four other South Boston facilities and Roxbury High, for two days, later extending the period to the first week of January.

The responses and counterresponses thus escalated. Judge Garrity greatly increased the number and intensity of the school security directives he issued. He also warned that if order were not restored, he might close the public schools of South Boston and reassign their students elsewhere. He then required the drafting of a reassignment plan by the school committee. Black leaders organized marches, teach-ins, and student boycotts, but none of the conflicts extended from Southie to Roxbury-based schools, demonstrating again the staged features and one-sidedness of the battle.

In meetings with school committee members, ROAR leaders were certain of support for their antidesegregation only from Paul Ellison, whose political beginnings were rooted in South Boston. After the stabbing of Michael Faith, however, the group's pressuring of the committee members intensified and held sway with John Kerrigan and John McDonough. The committee's 3-to-2 vote to reject the school department staff plan for Phase II desegregation encouraged the widening belief that public clamor might succeed in preventing establishment of a permanent desegregation order.

NOVEMBER AND DECEMBER OF 1975

The presence of hundreds of police officers in Southie, the promulgation of security orders by Judge Garrity in August, and investigative activities by the U.S. attorney and the agents of the FBI took the claws from the paws of ROAR in September of 1975. For a month in 1975 reporters filed stories about the demise of conflict and editors began to call them home for different assignments.

ROAR and its propaganda unit, the South Boston Information Center, headed by James Kelly (who also served as president of the South Boston High School Home and School Association), renewed activities in October. By November, conditions had once again become unbearable for the black students who risked their lives going and coming from the high school each day. Attorneys for plaintiffs moved that the court hold hearings on whether to close South Boston High School as unfit to conduct public instruction. In addition, they moved that one teacher, the football coach, and a white aide be removed from their jobs on the strength of testimony from black students about racist, hostile, and discriminatory actions.

Martin Walsh and his staff from the Community Relations Service, an arm of the U.S. Department of Justice, as well as school monitors from both the black and white neighborhoods, had been watching South Boston High School throughout September and October. We had been assigned elsewhere and had no previous direct involvement in the conflicts. In mid-November Judge Garrity asked us to visit the school and to appraise its internal situation from our perspective as educators. It seemed awkward to attempt this analysis since we did not know what other reports the judge had received, nor had we met with his other advisors, but that was characteristic of the degree of interaction that took place in that year, and we decided to do our best.

Metal detectors and police presence in every corridor and doorway were disturbing to see, but mostly we were overwhelmed by the educational void inside South Boston High School. Scott's comparison of the number of teachers actually present and the number of teachers whose names appeared on the sign-in roster revealed a significant discrepancy. That is, the head count he made as we toured every nook of the building, including the teachers' lounge, produced fewer teachers than did the roster. Teachers union officers were later indignant when we asked their impression of our inference that some teachers either had others sign in for them or signed in and then left the job. More importantly, classroom after classroom appeared empty or contained two or three students being instructed by a teacher who spoke as if the room was filled with students, using group methods suited for a student gathering of thirty.

After interviewing administrators about the curricular and extra-curricular programs, we left and reported in writing to the judge our observations and recommendations. South Boston High School, we told him, was an educational wasteland with a curriculum more suited to the 1940s, a program schedule designed to accommodate the overcrowded classrooms of the 1960s, and an extracurricular program that consisted of nothing more than varsity sports for boys. We also told him that the school should be kept open on principle; the plant, dilapidated and filthy as it was, could be made habitable and new educational leadership could revive the programs. Often, however, we wondered if revive was even an appropriate term, since improving facilities and programs would amount to the creation of a new school.

This report and others Judge Garrity received fused with strong, courageous testimony in court by several black students to convince the judge to visit the school himself, something Martin Walsh had urged earlier and that we seconded vigorously. We accompanied him on November 26, just a few days after he had toured Bridgewater State Hospital for the Criminally Insane in connection with a different suit brought by inmates.

Our visit included the L Street Bathhouse Annex, occupied by ninth graders, most of them black students, at the foot of the hill where the high school was located. Judge Garrity was profoundly affected by what he saw at both locations. He confided to us that he found the scenes more depressing than those at the state hospital.

Reflecting more closely on the hearings and on his first visit to a school since the case had begun, Judge Garrity decided to deepen his familiarity and to test his first impressions by making a second visit. We accompanied him again on December 2, 1975. In a memorandum issued on December 16 (the anniversary date of the school committee's defiance of his order to file a plan one year earlier), Judge Garrity wrote:

> The central impressions of the court as a result of its visit were that the services being afforded the students were primarily custodial and only incidentally educational and that the situation in the school was characterized less by racial tension, or indeed by any sort of tension, than by a pervasive lassitude and emptiness.

> At an evidentiary hearing on the afternoon of the court's first visit, the court described the small numbers of students in many of the main building's 29 standard classrooms and 27 other learning stations such as shops, gyms, and laboratories. On our second visit we counted 8 classrooms which were completely empty.... More than half the remaining classrooms appeared to contain 6 or fewer students....

> Generally speaking, except for the special needs and bilingual classes, the whole place was devoid of the youthful spontaneity that one associates with a high school. It was not just a matter of students of one race not speaking to or paying attention to students of another race, but of their seeming to pay little attention to fellow students of the same race. The students appeared to be calm compared to many of the non-uniformed personnel; nor did they seem inclined to exchange hostile glances or prone to take offense. They simply seemed to be the victims of constant cynical surveillance, unconcerned, uninvolved, and cowed.

His 24-page memorandum drew upon several sources of evidence besides his observations, but the power of firsthand witness shines through every page of the document:

> The school is surrounded by evidence of racial hostility. The word "Resist" is written in large lettering with white spray paint on the south doors of the main building, and the word "Never" is written with black paint in one- to two-foot lettering on one wall of the L Street Annex. The word "Nigger" is written in one-foot letters with white paint on a lamppost on the street adjacent to the school. Racial slurs are painted on the

pavement at most street intersections near the school. Virulent handouts have been distributed to white students en route to schools, e.g., "WAKE UP AND START FIGHTING FOR YOUR SCHOOL AND TOWN. ITS TIME YOU BECOME THE AGGRESSORS .... DON'T BE SCARED BY THE FEDERAL OFFENSE THREATS. A FIGHT IN A SCHOOL ISN'T A FEDERAL OFFENSE .... BE PROUD YOU ARE *WHITE* AND FROM SOUTHIE AND SHOW EVERYONE THAT THIS IS HOW YOU ARE GOING TO KEEP IT NO MATTER WHAT."

Judge Garrity's order of December 9 kept the school and its annex open but placed it in receivership of South Boston District Community Superintendent Joseph McDonough, the younger brother of school committee member John. The later memorandum gave his reasons for these actions and for his decision to remove the school's headmaster, Dr. William Reid, and his assistant headmasters, and called for an immediate process of appointing new leadership. He listed ways in which the programs of the school could be turned at once away from total preoccupation with repressive social controls and suspensions and toward effective teaching and learning.

PLACING THE SCHOOL IN RECEIVERSHIP

In ancient medicine, a receiver was a bladder or other vessel used to transfer body fluids or parts during surgery. In law and government, it was the office of the person who gathered and held taxes or other payments for the state. Always, though, it has meant something that is superimposed but can withstand force. In modern court procedures, receivers perform a variety of functions, but they are usually persons assigned to take over the authoritative functions of leadership or controllership, and thus the ancient implications persist.

The U.S. Civil Rights Commission had recommended that the entire Boston school system be placed in receivership, and both the plaintiffs and El Comite had seconded the proposal in September 1975. However, Judge Garrity narrowed the scope of the receivership to apply only to South Boston High School and its L Street annex. For the court, it was a way of demonstrating that the school would continue to function but under the direct authority of the court rather than the school committee.

On our recommendation, Judge Garrity ordered that the receiver be the community district superintendent because, in the chain of command built into the May 1975 plan, this officer was the next administrator in charge above the offices of principal and headmaster.

By order of the court and by the administrative action of the new receiver, then, headmaster Reid, the nonteaching assistant headmasters, and the football coach, Arthur Perdigao, were transferred from South Boston High on a vote taken by the school committee on December 29. On receiver McDonough's recommendation, assistant headmaster James Corscadden, formerly the head of mathematics at the school, was appointed interim headmaster and the search for a new headmaster began.

Superintendent McDonough retained the receivership through the winter, visiting occasionally with Judge Garrity and arranging and conducting the search for a new administrative staff. A biracial committee of parents participated in screening candidates, as did Judge Garrity. In the midst of a renewed campaign by ROAR to halt desegregation, Jerome Winegar, a white middle-aged school administrator from St. Paul, Minnesota, was appointed headmaster by vote of the school committee, although it was only a formality required by the court since the appointment was made under court order.

It was apparent within weeks after the receivership order that the strategy could work. McDonough asked to be relieved of the appointment after a brief period of service and Marion Fahey was appointed to replace him. What was not as apparent, however, was the extent to which the new leadership would affect the functioning of the school.

Winegar was new to Boston. He was suggested for the headmaster post by Mario Fantini, dean of education at the University of Massachusetts and a distinguished figure in urban educational policy planning. Fantini had a vision of what South Boston High might become. He imagined it could prove to be a demonstration model for other high schools in the system and in other big cities. Fantini, a mentor to both Fahey and Winegar, was retained as a consultant for planning by Fahey. In outlining a programmatic course of action for the school, Fantini expressed confidence that Winegar would be an ideal expeditor of this approach or something like it.

Winegar succeeded in hiring Geraldine Kozberg, a curriculum developer and arts educator from St. Paul, for a new position, that of program developer. He also brought in exceptionally vigorous talent in the person of Ronald Rosenbaum. These three and others who were added, including three black administrators, went to work to implement the court order and to invent a program of activities for the school. Under the receivership, Winegar had the authority, with approval from Fahey, to transfer teachers. While he retained many from the old faculty, including some who faced the wall each time Winegar tried to talk with them, the changes made were sufficient to begin the reconstruction of teaching and learning.

One strategy employed by Winegar and Kozberg was the multiplication and decentralization of study activity options for students. The school-wide, rigid schedule of course offerings was abolished and replaced by a variety of magnetic subprograms capable of generating student-centered learning activities under the direction of clusters of teachers. The school offered an art major, a School Within a School, and an expanded Flexible Campus series of offerings that took students beyond the confines of the building. Also established were programs of study in six occupational specialties, a reading support system, and something called the After-School Suspension Program, which later generated a during-school-hours program for students charged with violating the discipline code. Among other magnetic programs were the Transportation Learning Center built in an old facility in downtown Boston, a work-study program, a program in cooking and food services that came complete with a small restaurant and kitchen built into the old school, and a program of active work in mass communication.

All athletic programs were desegregated. Teams for girls were also added in basketball, swimming, and track. By 1977 the only competitive team sports that were still all-white were swimming, ice hockey, and cheerleading. The plant was renovated and repaired on direct orders from the court and later on recommendations from Winegar.

As the new programs took hold, the number of student altercations declined. Winegar eliminated the indiscriminate use of suspensions, which had once been the sole means of discipline. He converted one of the holding rooms, where students charged with offenses under headmaster Reid were placed to await transport or arrest, into a snack shop for student use. The rooms had once been two windowless, stuffy areas—one for whites and another just like it for blacks.

Security and communications monitors were hired, along with a security coordinator, four investigative counselors, and twenty-five security aides, and a plan of training was carried out for this force. The number of city and state police deployed about the building was reduced each term as the new civilians took over the task of social control.

A Racial/Ethnic Parents Council and a Racial/Ethnic Student Council were formed and began to meet frequently. Women who had first been seen among the demonstrators outside the building in 1974 and again in 1975 began to be hired (and to work as volunteers) to help in some of the programs. The restaurant and food program hosted and fed visitors, including, on many occasions, the elderly from a neighborhood public housing project.

The University of Massachusetts in Boston had been paired with South Boston High by the court. Efforts of faculty and staff there to plan supportive activities were rebuffed by the high school teachers in 1975. Under Winegar this pairing was revived somewhat, although the university never made significant investments in the plan after its initial discouragements. The other pairings were intensified profoundly, however. The Gillette Company Safety Razor Division, for instance, sponsored tours, career education, instruction in merchandising, and job hunting assistance. The Federal Reserve Bank of Boston, under the inventive leadership of Jeannet Hargroves and Edwin Gooding, helped with such job tasks as placement, work-study hiring, computer course development, student workshops, a student art exhibition, and tutoring.

In spite of extraordinary progress accomplished inside the high school and through programs that drew students beyond the neighborhoods and into the larger life of Boston, a menacing tension surrounded the fortress on the heights for two years. The L Street Annex was closed by mutual agreement between the school committee, the city, and plaintiffs. Its ninth graders were integrated into the mainstreams of life on the heights. Buses began to come and go with comparative safety, although frightening incidents continued to break out every month or two for three years.

Winegar and Kozberg, while supported by Fahey, were ignored and avoided by all but a few headquarters personnel. Superintendent McDonough proved a reliable source of support and never contributed to the opposition that plagued the new high school administrative team. Enough of the teachers took pride in the new programs, which they helped design and implement, to change organizational behavior inside the school. Still, no more than half of the teachers ever actively cooperated with the new leadership.

Rosenbaum and others who had joined the Winegar team withdrew in 1978, and by 1980 Winegar and Kozberg constituted an incredibly valiant and determined but lonely pair of educators. Winegar's family, residing in another part of Boston, was subjected to terrorism, vandalism, and ostracism that persisted for more than two years. In 1979, his wife and children moved back to St. Paul to try to resume their previous lives, while Winegar remained in Boston.

Heavy resources were poured into South Boston High. Many individuals and groups contributed precious time and effort toward reintegrating the school into the civilized life of Boston. But what truly changed the school was the injection of a fundamentally different approach to curriculum and instruction, an approach that seriously considered the needs and expressed interests of the students and their teachers.

THE RECEIVERSHIP ENDS

With prompting from the court in response to repeated queries from the school committee about when the receivership would be lifted, the parties began arduous negotiations late in 1977 toward designing a universally acceptable consent decree. Judge Garrity had received regular written and oral reports on progress and problems at the school. As an added test, he dispatched us to visit South Boston High again and to report to him on whether one part of his December 1975 order had been achieved: "The development of innovative programs to remedy the educational void and attendant marked decline in attendance at South Boston High School."

We made our visit and reported to him our enthusiasm and respect for the progress that had been made. We sat in the new little school restaurant with Winegar and Kozberg, eating cookies and hot chocolate made and served by the students. We listened and recorded their concerns about what ought to be included in the consent decree. We toured classes where students were dissecting a shark and cooperating with one another across racial lines as if working in a biology laboratory was the best way to spend one's life. Students greeted one another and us in the halls as if they were pleased to be there and as if the place were theirs. The little library was filled with students who were reading books and magazines.[6] A genuine set of vocational shop classes was underway, with black and white students working shoulder to shoulder there.

We sat in Winegar's office and observed him handle a complaint from a student and his mother, who were accompanied by a representative of the South Boston Information Center who had arranged the meeting. What was stunning about the brief incident was that the student's complaint concerned being *excluded* from the media program. The representative alleged that this was because there were "no white slots open." Winegar countered that it was because the student's attendance record was too poor (he had not attended classes for four weeks) to make him eligible, adding that the boy would be welcomed when he showed he had really begun to go to school. The meeting ended with the mother taking the youth to task as they left for misrepresenting where he had been for a month and with the youth pledging that he was "signing back in for regular school right away."

The school's suspension rates were among the very lowest in the city for all middle and high schools. The highest percentage of college-bound students in the history of South Boston High before 1975 was 8 percent for one year The rate doubled in 1978. Student dress, grooming, posture, and bearing were all visibly improved. Teacher involvements became much more direct and intense. The uses of the old plant had changed markedly as well, with the cavernous rooms and wings that had once seemed interchangeable and impersonal now modified to reinforce the curriculum design of separate but cooperating centers of instructional activity.

Some things have not changed, however, including an external milieu of awkward and sometimes menacing hostility. South Boston High School has in fact been "taken away" from the people of its neighborhood. It is now the property of a much enlarged geographical area that includes parts of Roxbury and Dorchester as well as all of historic South Boston. Its programs extend beyond the district into other parts of the city and they no longer reinforce the *status quo* of the self-enclosed enclave in which most of South Boston's adults reside. The programs teach that there is life beyond the enclave and that the larger life can be worthwhile rather than a betrayal of one's heritage. It teaches that respect is due all humans and cannot be parcelled out according to ethnicity, class, or residence.

Several key politicians who strongly supported the antibusing movement have changed in one important way, too.

Raymond Flynn, an alumnus of South Boston High whose brilliance at basketball gave him the opportunity to go to college, has been a tireless opponent of desegregation. As a state representative and then as a city councillor, he has vocally opposed the court orders. Since the receivership, however, Councillor Flynn has also been a tirelessly faithful supporter of efforts to upgrade South Boston High School, and he has never mobilized his followers against the new efforts of Winegar and Kozberg.

State Senator William Bulger, who became president of the Senate in 1978, has opposed the court with violent rhetoric and flaming oratorical indignation for six years, but he has refrained from including the transformed high school among the targets of his outrage. Not being a target of Bulger's anger is as great an accomplishment as having Flynn for a friend in the marketplace of state and city politics.

South Boston High is still not as completely renovated, repaired, and clean as the court and the new school administration have struggled to make it. Some of the custodians from the old era survived the transformation and maintain the plant in the manner to which they had become accustomed. But, late in 1977, the most apt symbol of the change from 1975 seemed to us to be the great stack of cockroaches that were shoveled away following an extermination and cleanup campaign initiated by Winegar.

Winegar's winning strategy from 1976 to 1980 has included more than a reconstruction of the curriculum and approaches to instruction. It includes hospitality toward those in the immediate neighborhood, even those conspiring to threaten the security of the school. It includes avoidance of rhetoric about racial integration and offers repeated assertions of optimism about improvements in opportunities for teaching and learning.

Any strategy followed during a high-pitched conflict carries costs. One incurred by Winegar was a withholding of support from some black leaders, parents, and students. For example, here is an excerpt from a memorandum dated May 17, 1977, sent to the Freedom House Coalition, a black leadership group, by black educator Ron Edmonds, a member of the Harvard University faculty at the time:

> Judge Garrity is profoundly in error about the nature of schooling for black children at South Boston High School. Jerome Winegar, Bob Wood, and Marty Walsh for many months have been regaling the Judge with stories of the progress in the quality of teaching, learning, and race relations at South Boston High School. I believe that our recent breakfast meeting with Bob Wood caused him to mitigate the aggressiveness of the stories he tells in admiration of South Boston High School. However, since then, Jerome Winnegar [sic] and Marty Walsh have continued to deluge the Judge with daily anecdotal descriptions of the great strides they are making in assuring black children equal educational opportunity in South Boston. Without repeating our long and laborious analysis of this morning, let me say, as aggressively as I can, that I do not think we have any hope for progress in South Boston unless we can counter the kinds of stories being fabricated for Garrity by Winnegar [sic] and Walsh . . . .
>
> I adopt this tone of urgency because I do not believe we fully appreciated how close Garrity has come to ending receivership at South Boston. Neither do I think we fully appreciate his determination to leave black children to the tender mercies of the Boston School Committee unless we can do something to interrupt him.

The memorandum from Edmonds followed a group action by black students at South Boston High on the morning of May 11, just six days before. They discussed a number of concerns with Winegar and presented a series of demands. These included demands for black literature studies, more black teachers, fewer suspensions, more black guidance counselors, and a black aide with a white aide on each security team. The group's chief demand, however, was that the school be closed and its students moved to a neutral site.

It is not at all likely that the students or Edmonds actually expected the school to be closed once the court took its stand. But Winegar's strategy had not considered the needs of black students, although it had entailed presenting the court with positive progress reports which announced improving safety conditions for all students.

What many black students and then some black leaders were concerned about in May of 1977 were the approaching termination of the receivership, the hostility of the white neighborhood, and the indifference of the school committee. The possibility that conditions at the school could revert to their 1974 and 1975 levels was terrifying to anticipate. Too much optimism about the changes in the school threatened to sap the ability of attorneys for the plaintiffs to argue successfully against the consent decree, which would end the receivership, during negotiations.

Although the court did approve the consent decree in 1978, its clauses reflect with painstaking evenhandedness the interests of the plaintiffs and of Winegar's administration. Special powers to select staff, to reject student assignments and to modify programs were continued. Special resources were pledged for continuation of the school's programs, and security provisions that would safeguard minority students were maintained. Above all, of course, the governance of the school was returned to the school committee— but under conditions that drew them into explicit obligations to be accountable for continuation of the new rather than reversion to the old design of the school. Politically, the decree signified a deep change in the conduct of the school committee. For the first time, the committee was consorting with attorneys for the plaintiffs, negotiating on terms elicited by the court, and disengaging its power base from the base held by ROAR.

CONCLUSIONS

By 1980 South Boston High was hosting 897 students, the average daily attendance rate had soared from 60 percent in 1974 to 78 percent. The school's student population was 45 percent white, 46 percent black, and 8 percent Hispanic, within a community district with a student population that was 48 percent white, 35 percent black, and 17 percent Hispanic. It was a viable, enterprising environment for both teaching and learning surrounded by a neighborhood whose adults still managed to muster 300 marchers, down from 3,000 in 1974, in protests against desegregation.

Attorney and certified school teacher Louise Day Hicks, chairperson of the Boston School Committee, member of the U.S. House of Representatives, and Boston city council-woman, spearheaded the drive to resist desegregation.   Boston Globe Photo

This fine old municipal structure was renovated for use as the new Boston Public Schools Administration Building at 26 Court Street in 1976. The new headquarters, two blocks from the U.S. Courthouse, was relocated from the ancient and incredibly dilapidated location on Beacon Hill.

Courtesy of the Boston School Department

Pro-desegregation rally attended by Mrs. Coretta Scott King and her three children marches down Park Street in Boston on November 30, 1974. Thomas Atkins, head of the Boston NAACP, is at far right.
Boston Globe Photo

Children with signs march down Broadway in South Boston, led by Southie marshalls, to protest desegregation on October 24, 1976.
Herald-American Photo

An aerial view of South Boston High School shows its central, fortress-like location on the hill above the residential enclave and depicts the relation of Southie to downtown Boston.

U.S. District Court Judge W. Arthur Garrity, Jr. leaves South Boston High School surrounded by U.S. marshalls, Boston police, court expert Marvin Scott, and others after a surprise visit in November 1975 to talk with staff and students.

South Boston High School Headmaster Jerome Winegar addresses the Convocation of the Covenant of Brotherhood, a city-wide interfaith group that is attempting to mobilize racial harmony, at Boston's Trinity Church on March 30, 1980.

Boston Globe Photo

What is important about the story for those attempting to understand the process of school desegregation, we believe, is that the opposition that crystallizes around a particular school will be intense and a grave danger to the public safety, and that it must be met head on by the court or others who initiate desegregation.

In Boston as in other cities from Pontiac, Michigan, to Los Angeles, the desegregators underestimated the scope and intensity of the conflict that would be waged and they failed to concentrate their forces on South Boston High, just as the Massachusetts Board of Education failed to anticipate what would come of inventing a clustered pairing of high school facilities that would link such a neighborhood as South Boston with one such as Roxbury. It was not that the leadership of ROAR kept its intentions secret; it was that no one appears to have believed that the group would be able to stage a struggle so violent or so protracted. When the realization began to dawn, however belatedly, the determination of Judge Garrity to take a stand was unshakeable, a point the ROAR leaders, in turn, underestimated for two years.

What is important about the story for education is that the provision of responsive programs and of fair-minded discipline can, in combination, reverse the conflict and convert it into cooperation. This conclusion is not at all obvious. Most of us do not expect that schooling, as the tail on the dog of society, can ever wag the dog, and while the transformation of South Boston High comes close to doing just this, there are ample political and economic circumstances remaining under which renewed conflict could overwhelm the progress made by the school.

In the same sense, as Gerry Kozberg has reminded us, most of the students at the transformed school continue to read and to compute at levels well below national norms. The programs have not reversed the effects of poverty, deprivation, discrimination, and neglect that impair the learning of black and white students alike.

What we mean, then, is that the programs and the fairness of the new administration have generated a climate of hope that extends beyond the confines of the building and they have done this under conditions that appeared to be hopeless. What is more, if the positive climate persists and expands, it *will* modify levels of learning, expectations in the elementary and middle schools that feed it, and will change behavior toward the next generation among adults in South Boston itself.

NOTES:

1. Robert A. Dentler, "Brownsville: Community or Staging Area?" *The Center Forum*, Vol. 3, November 13, 1968, pp. 11–14.
2. Although some of his facts are in historical error, Jon Hillson's *The Battle of Boston*, Pathfinder Press, New York, 1977, presents the most vivid and socially detailed report to date on conflicts in South Boston from 1974 to 1977. Alan Lupo, *Liberty's Chosen Home*,

Little, Brown, Boston, 1977, provides a fuller depiction of the politics of Boston and their ramifications in South Boston ethnic history. The play, *The Last White Class*, by Marge Piercy and Ira Wood, gives a meaningful portrayal of a black family in a white neighborhood on the edge of South Boston during 1974–1975. The Crossing Press, Trumansburg, N.Y.

3. Later, McCormack graduated with honors from Annapolis and was editor of *The Boston University Law Review*. Somehow, American society is structured so that serious miseducation in high school does not prohibit later intellectual growth and the achievement of professional distinction—at least not for some late adolescents.

4. In 1976, the group tried to rally support for George Wallace, with some modest success, and in 1979, they tried to gain primary campaign support for Phillip Crain.

5. *Boston Globe*, October 10, 1974, p. 1.

6. Edward McCormack told us in 1975 that as a student at South Boston High he had never set foot in the school library and that "no red-blooded guy in my class ever did." Raymond Flynn, who graduated about fifteen years later and won a college basketball scholarship, told us that while in high school, he borrowed one book, *The Life of Babe Ruth*, which he recommended to us as an unforgettable story.

TEACHERS AND PARENTS 9

BOSTON'S TEACHERS

IN THE VINTAGE YEARS FOR PUBLIC INSTRUCTION IN BOSTON, those from 1890 to 1925, classroom teachers were normal school graduates. In the colonial era, teaching had become a "substitute occupation" for surplus and often second-rate ordained Puritan ministers, so Harvard may be said to be the first North American supplier of teachers.

The training at Harvard was off the mark, however, and in 1789 the first article calling for teacher training appeared in the *Massachusetts Magazine*.[1] The call was to "prepare young gentlemen for college and school keeping," so they might teach the subjects (then termed branches) they chose "with ease and propriety."

The call was not answered, though it echoed across each decade, until the Reverend Samuel Hall opened the first teachers school in Concord, Vermont, in 1823. Seven years later he opened a second one in Andover, Massachusetts. The first State Normal School was opened by the new State

Board of Education in Lexington in 1839. After delays and failures due mainly to the Civil War, formal teacher training began to become universal in New England forty years later.

By the time of World War I, nearly all Boston public school teachers were licensed graduates of Boston State Normal School, known for a period as Boston Teachers College and then, much later, as Boston State College. Boston University established the first full-scale baccalaureate School of Education in 1918, and many students were Normal School alumna who taught all day and went to the university for further part-time study.

The Boston public school system had its own examination and licensing system by the 1920s, and by World War II, the symbiosis of the city system and what became Boston State developed until it was 90 percent complete in its hegemony. Boston College, then run by the Jesuit Order, provided an elite cadre of Latin school teachers and many system administrators, but other colleges and universities supplied systems outside of Boston.

The hegemony was consistent with the domination Harvard had exercised for 200 years. Indeed, Harvard later renewed its sovereign role by founding its Graduate School of Education and emphasizing the preparation of men for top policy positions for many decades. The Boston State College arrangement, however, substituted women and catered more and more exclusively to Irish-Americans, just as Harvard had catered to male WASPs. The less visible but most critical difference between the two institutions lay in their faculty, however.

Harvard used its burgeoning wealth to draw upon accomplished scholars and widely known men from "public affairs" to teach in its professional schools. Boston State used its poverty to recruit Boston public teachers into higher education and to provide a few slots for local, and later state, politicians. When we entered the case in 1975, for example, John Kerrigan, chairman of the school committee and a local attorney, was a lecturer at Boston State. From 1930 to 1970, the fulfillment of a dream of teacher preparation had also created a way station on the road to political patronage.

As a result, with all of the usual exceptions generated by an imperfect system, the Boston teacher force—like that of many other cities such as Washington, D.C., Buffalo, Jersey City, and Chicago—had achieved a level of educational mediocrity that was only slightly superior to that of remote rural districts in South Carolina and Texas. The system was profoundly inbred; it seeded and then harvested its own local crop of beginning teachers imbued solely with the Boston Way, until it opened a bit to outsiders in the cultural watershed years after 1967. The inbreeding produced side effects; the force was, until 1967, 94 percent white and overwhelmingly composed of native Boston Irish-Americans, 80 percent of them women.

THE TEACHER FORCE CHANGES

The first great revolution in Boston teaching came from the advent of militant unionization. After decades of incomplete, only sporadically successful union organizing, with much wrangling over representation, the methods of militant trade unionism used by Albert Shanker in New York City were exported to Boston, and the American Federation of Teachers (AFT) achieved stunning victories in mobilizing teachers and negoiating favorable contracts.

Shanker's approach within the Boston Teachers Union (BTU) Chapter of the AFT was fully consolidated by 1972. And although the school committee could still risk violating clauses in the contract, and lines of political patronage still ran like little cowpaths across the face of Boston, salaries, benefits, seniority rights, and influence over working conditions had been improved. By 1974, salaries for tenured but still very young elementary teachers had outstripped salaries for junior faculty at Boston State College.

This revolution built great strength into the organized ranks of teachers, but it had few consequences for racial justice or educational reforms. The BTU opposed moving toward compliance with the State Racial Imbalance Act and, as an intervenor in the federal court case in 1974 and 1975, worked diligently to forestall desegregation. The union voice was always temperate on racial policies, however, at least in the courtroom and the press. Its approach merely supported all facets of the *status quo*, save those involving improved teacher wages and working conditions.

When, as we stated earlier, Scott, at the invitation of union officers, represented the masters and experts at a meeting of about 300 building representatives of the BTU, his description of the masters plan in March 1975 stirred the audience into a snarling, cursing mob of furious teachers. They hated and feared the changes he outlined, just as they had hated the Phase I desegregation plan.

In September of 1975, moreover, the BTU went on strike for a brief time, forcing the passage of a new contract and proving to everyone that the union could make or break the system, regardless of federal court orders. Had the school committee ever realized the potentialities inherent in coalescing with the BTU, desegregation could have been blocked permanently. The BTU had been so shabbily treated for a decade, however, that the union's alienation from the committee and its headquarters was the condition that helped Shanker's original strategy succeed.

During the 1975–1976 school year, this alienation and the realization that nothing in the court plan need impede contract negotiations produced a pervasive change in BTU tactics. The union leadership did not resist or defy implementation of the plan. Participation in court hearings was limited to efforts to safeguard labor contracts and to defend the teachers charged with discrimination at South Boston High School. BTU leaders preached stoic patience. They depicted teachers as the courageous and neutral "soldiers" standing watch over the massive changes, and they absorbed the extreme shocks of readjustment. In response, Judge Garrity bent over backward to avoid intruding even indirectly upon the sanctities of the labor contracts.

What accounts for this change? The single most important explanation is that the revolution of unionization was working. Salaries and benefits improved dramatically between 1970 and 1975, seniority rights were holding up, and jobs were secure even if building assignments were changing. And although all-white student groupings disappeared everywhere except in East Boston, and teaching tasks seemed more demanding at first within multiethnic classrooms, sharp enrollment declines eased daily burdens everywhere; teacher/student ratio plunged from 1/26 in 1973 toward 1/13 in 1977. Those relocated to other buildings included hundreds of teachers liberated from substandard, dungeonlike facilities and assigned to new or renovated classrooms. As teacher aides were introduced by the hundreds under court orders and through state funding, teachers found them helpful and organizable as fellow unionists. The common enemy, the committee, was weaker in all respects than it had been in three decades.

In addition, the desegregation plan did not affect teaching itself. Just as contracts were left alone, so pedagogy could continue on its "normal" course. Teachers who gave their allegiance to ROAR could do so on their off time. Those who were apolitical felt no heavy pressure to take a stand. Human relations training was fended off. A policy of racial neutrality seemed to offer students and parents a substitute for affirmative action. The *content* of instruction was left unaffected except in schools where faculty senates or committees elected to make efforts to change it.

TEACHER DESEGREGATION

The court ordered that teacher desegregation would occur through several means. Recruiters would seek out and hire black teachers. All hiring of regulars would occur on a one-to-one basis, one black to one white, until at least 20 percent of the permanent teacher force was black. And, every building would contain a proportionate share of black teachers.

If teacher retrenchment had kept pace with enrollment declines, the BTU would have broken its truce. Marion Fahey lacked control over money and personnel, however, as William Leary had before her, and Associate Superintendent for Personnel Paul Kennedy was the answer to the BTU's prayer. Over a five-year period, when enrollments sank from 80,000 to 62,000, he reduced the teacher force very little—from 5,443 to 5,064.

From 1975 through 1978, the school department increased the overall number of black teachers from 620, half of whom were added in 1973 and 1974, to 649. The court rule of one-to-one hiring was evaded through the hiring of white provisional and temporary teachers. Minority recruitment activities languished and the personnel department gave its attention to the complex challenges of staffing assignment changes and the appointment of special and bilingual educators. The number of special education teachers rose from 400 in 1974 to 983 in 1979 and many regular white teachers got acting positions and checked into Boston State to pick up new certificates on the side.

In 1978, on initiatives from black plaintiffs and El Comite, the court deemed teacher desegregation a failure and issued a new and more definite order. This took place after many hearings in which BTU concern was restricted carefully to safeguarding labor agreements. By then, after all, the BTU had absorbed and helped to organize the new black and Hispanic teachers. The new court order required an overall increase in black teachers of at least 1.5 percent a year over the 1977 baseline.

Kennedy was left with no loopholes and with a new superintendent —Robert Wood. Proof of Kennedy's flexibility came out when Wood continued him as a senior officer in his reorganized department, even though Kennedy had been the chief contender to replace Marion Fahey. Under Clarence Cooper, a skilled black administrator recruited from Harvard, the new order was implemented vigorously. He not only met but exceeded the court standard. Within the court, incidentally, our lesson learned was that court orders that are very simple yet very concrete or exact are the ones most likely to be implemented in equity cases, especially when the methods are left to the local authorities.

Another court order in teacher desegregation deserves mention in connection with this point. In January 1975, Judge Garrity wrote that

> one aspect of that segregation was the racial composition and distribution of faculty. . . . The court found the low percentage of black teachers to be the result of unconstitutionally discriminatory use of a cut-off score on the National Teachers Examination (NTE), inadequate minority recruitment efforts, and the reputation of Boston as an anti-black, segregated school system.[2]

The NTE had just begun to replace Boston's homemade teacher tests, administered by a school committee-appointed board of examiners, when Judge Garrity rejected it. The Boston test had been used to exclude blacks and other outsiders for many years and the NTE sounded better, since it was produced by the Educational Testing Service (ETS) but served the same purpose.

According to the ETS, the NTE was not constructed for use as a selection instrument. The test's producers had explained repeatedly that it was devised as a measure of knowledge *about* education within a major subject field and was meant to serve as an indicator of that knowledge level for college faculties and teacher supervisors. Still, the NTE has been used for licensing and hiring by whole states and by many school districts since 1965, and it has subsequently been rejected by courts because it does not predict performance. Indeed, some evaluation studies have shown negative as well as zero correlations between NTE scores and measures of teaching performance on the job.[3]

The court goal of 20 percent black teachers, with an added phrase naming 25 percent as a long-term aim, came out of estimates of the city's black population of 19 percent in the 1970 U.S. census. This goal did not reflect an educational policy, which would have taken the multiethnic mix of parents and students into consideration. Had that policy been formulated, a goal of 50 percent black and other minority teachers would have been reasonable.[4] Both the 1974 and the 1978 orders of the court based the goal upon overall residential population figures, a criterion that is also used widely in industry and government Equal Employment Opportunity cases. With the help of the court, the number of black teachers in the Boston system has grown from 373 in 1973, before court intervention, to 872 in 1980 (see Table 9.1).

TABLE 9.1

Boston Public School Teachers by Racial/Ethnic Group, 1975–79

Group	1975		1976		1977		1978		1979	
	N	%	N	%	N	%	N	%	N	%
White	4,697	86	4,473	85	4,283	83	4,121	79	3,908	77
Black	620	12	630	12	649	13	808	16	872	17
Other Minority	126	2	182	3	201	4	258	5	283	6
	5,443	100	5,285	100	5,133	100	5,187	100	5,063	100

SOURCE: Personnel Department, Boston Public Schools.

Recruitment has become a perfected routine and with job shortages in public schools rising nation-wide, black candidates have become abundant. Thus, in 1981, we expect the number will reach 1,000 with ease (see Table 9.2). We also expect it will remain at that level, as pressures to reduce the teacher force will become very intense. Because of the court orders, black teachers, although mostly recent hires, will not be the first to be fired. It will be a major test of BTU reasonableness, however, to remain silent while tenured whites are terminated and newcoming blacks are retained. This will be the crossroad where the two revolutions—unionism and desegregative racial justice—will meet or collide.

Who are the black teachers? A 1980 survey conducted by the school system's personnel department showed that black and other minority teachers have been drawn mainly from Massachusetts. While only 30 percent

TABLE 9.2

Boston Public School Teachers by Racial/Ethnic Group and Program Type, 1975 and 1979

Group	1975			1979		
	Regular	Special	Bilingual	Regular	Special	Bilingual
White	3,964	619	114	3,089	703	116
Black	534	73	13	609	238	25
Other Minority	33	9	84	83	42	158
Total	4,531	701	211	3,781	983	299
Percentage	83	13	4	75	19	6
			5,443			5,063
			100			100

SOURCE: Personnel Department, Boston Public Schools.

were born in the state (24 percent in Boston), 70 percent were educated there. About 24 percent were born in the South, but only 7 percent graduated from southern colleges. The other minority teachers, nearly all of them Hispanic and Asian-American, account for most of the foreign-born and foreign-educated teachers in the system. Of the 283 other minority (OM) teachers in the schools in 1980, only 29 percent are regular rather than bilingual or bilingual special educators.

While the minority recruiters reached out to Deep South and border states, then, the historic role of Massachusetts as an alternative site for college-bound, upwardly and "outwardly" mobile minorities had already generated an ample local supply of candidates. This previously untapped pool has merely needed supplementing from outside the state. This condition has changed substantially since 1975. Boston University's black enrollments have shrunk as it pursues a course of becoming an expensive elite institution, and blacks who go north to college now go there for degree programs in fields other than education. Meanwhile, southern colleges have begun to host and retain black students in growing numbers and employment opportunities in the Sunbelt region make Massachusetts look unpromising except in a few professions. Since we expect minority recruitment to grind to a halt when the 1,000 mark is reached in 1981, the changes will make very little difference.

What is important educationally is that the minority teachers come equipped to offer real alternatives to the normal-school tradition. They are not, with a tiny handful of exceptions, products of Boston State College or the other state colleges, which have remained overwhelmingly white. The in-state graduates have graduated from Northeastern University and the University of Massachusetts in Amherst. A few are from Boston University, Simmons College, and Boston College. The important point is that they are carriers of alternative approaches to instruction. They owe nothing to patrons at school headquarters, to Boston State, or to the BTU—except to the extent the BTU gives them a share in its leadership.

OTHER MINORITIES

OMs were left out of the 1974 and 1975 orders for teacher desegregation. When the issue was rejoined in 1978, El Comite pressed hard for a policy that would include Hispanics in the revised order. We advised Judge Garrity of the educational merits of lawyer Carolyn Playter's motion. In our view, the faculty's multiethnicity should be congruent with the students', and the only growth sector in enrollments for the next decade will be Hispanic and Asian.

Judge Garrity expressed regard for this view from the bench, but limited his order to blacks. Two considerations were at work. First, he had accepted the argument for a simple, concrete order, and that argument rested on the logic of limited aims. Second, data on city population proportions of OMs were outdated and unreliable. He thought their novel inclusion might make the revision subject to appeal, especially since attorney Marshall Simonds opposed including them. Simonds pointed to a rise from 126 to 240 OMs from 1975 to early 1978, noting a rapid and "uncoerced" increase. In his remarks, however, the fact that OMs were absent from regular rather than bilingual classrooms was obscured. No one, ourselves included, had data on the outside availability of OM regular teachers, although Playter tried to obtain some evidence.

One long-term effect of limiting the court order, then, will be that in 1990 the student composition will be over 30 percent OMs, while the faculty will be 8 percent OMs at most. Nevertheless, among large central cities in the United States, Boston, with a roughly 70 percent white public teacher population, will be more fully multiethnic than nearly all others.

THE SCHOOL PSYCHOLOGISTS

As we said in our chapter on special programs, there are two "sorcerer's apprentices" at work in the Boston schools. One gathers in students with special needs and the other gathers in bilingual learners. The vast and rapid growth of special needs classes, unlike the bilingual classes which, except those for French Haitians and Cape Verdians, became a province for OM teachers, had consequences for black teachers.

The role of the school psychologist in diagnosing and classifying students, and in helping to devise educational plans for exceptional students is pivotal under state law. The school psychologist is, in many ways, the high priest of public school systems. Required to meet especially demanding standards of course work and supervised clinical training in order to be certified, he or she is to be a professional psychologist and an experienced teacher. Highly qualified school psychologists have many options and thus tend to gravitate toward schools whose boards, administrators, and teachers will facilitate their arcane and difficult work.

When Boston began the race to comply with State Law 766, it was short on its supply of school psychologists. The school department sanctioned full speed in efforts to evaluate students, but it temporized in recruiting school psychologists. Still working from its own traditions, Personnel made a cadre of veteran teachers acting school psychologists and hired consultants from among licensed professional psychologists outside the system but in local private practice.

In 1979, attorney Larry Johnson moved the court to remedy the segregative effects. By that time, Boston had built up an in-house staff of thirty-five white school psychologists, most of them in acting status. The superintendent proposed to add eight black and OM members to the staff. Because few black school psychologists exist, Johnson moved to open the ranks to include licensed professionals who lacked school credentials. Superintendent Wood proposed having these uncertified staffers enroll at Boston State College for part-time study to gain the state certificate. Without referring to a particular college, Judge Garrity heard the arguments and approved Wood's plan with very minor changes.

Again, the legal minds in the case did not connect desegregation with educational effects. We believe, from sampling evaluation files during student assignment reviews, that racial/ethnic prejudice and amateurism are both at work in the diagnostic thinking of the acting school psychologists. Two examples should suffice: "Johnny needs more structure," was the sole conclusion that appeared in one file. "Joe is a nice black boy and the parent who accompanied him to the test is not educated," read another. These were among hundreds of casually handwritten reports. Some of the typewritten reports were riddled with typographic errors and misspellings.

State law provides superb due process and appeal protections as part of 766. What is more, several very diligent child advocacy groups have worked to guard against misevaluation and discrimination. With all of this, and with a vigilant, well-intentioned State Department, there is reason to hope that psychological assessments will be conducted in a more professional and ethnically sensitive manner over time. Meanwhile, in 1980, 17 out of every 100 black students and 14 out of every 100 OM students had been assessed by white psychologists, some of whom were unlicensed and others of whom were untrained in public education. Ironically, 24 percent of the system's special educators were black. In the coming years, these students will be tested by certified alumnae of Boston State College.

THE GAVIN SCHOOL FIVE

In September 1978 we received a carbon of a letter sent to Superintendent Wood by five minority teachers on the Patrick F. Gavin Middle School faculty in South Boston. It was so noteworthy that we quote it in full, without the signatures.

> For the past five years we, the black faculty members of the P. F. Gavin Middle School, have had to work under extremely adverse conditions which have made it more than difficult for us to utilize our full potential in the performance of our duties.
>
> Because of possible and probable confrontations from a community that has demonstrated hostility toward minorities upon numerous occasions in past years, we are subjected to the daily humiliation and inconvenience of having to ride a van to and from school. When circumstances are such that we are forced to drive in to work, we find ourselves battling feelings of anxiety due to fears of bodily injury and/or destruction of our property (i.e., automobiles)... fears that are substantiated by very real incidents in the past.
>
> Once in the school building we must function in an environment permeated with animosity and resentment from other faculty and staff members thereby creating an atmosphere of undue stress for each of us. When family emergencies necessitate our immediate departure from the

school we cannot do so promptly, but must wait to make the necessary transportation arrangements.

There are those of us who are close to experiencing nervous breakdowns. It is indeed small wonder that we have survived thus far. We are concerned. We are concerned about our physical well-being, our mental stability, and our students. It is obvious, or should be, that we cannot possibly service our students to the best of our capabilities under such immense tension and stress.

We understand that the court order demands a racial balance among the faculty members of various schools. We fully support this decision. However, we also consider our present assignments to be "hardship duty" and after five arduous years feel the only equitable solution would be the rotation of such assignments among the newly appointed minority employees of the Boston Public Schools System.

Through John Coakley we arranged to meet with the teachers, the Gavin principal, and others. Our letter summarizing the meeting is also quoted in full.

Thanks to your good office and that of Dr. Ellison, we held a very informative meeting with five minority teachers from the Gavin School, District Superintendent McDonough, Gavin School Principal Glennon, a Teachers Union headquarters representative, and others pertinent to the issue of the burden described in the September 26, 1978, letter from the five black teachers at the Gavin to Superintendent Wood. This letter summarizes our tentative findings and our even more tentative remedies. We look forward to receiving your comments and those of colleagues in Personnel or other units of the School Department. When we have them in writing, we hope to confer with you and associates in the Department of Implementation prior to advising Judge Garrity.

1. The problem in question is that of freezing black and other minority teachers into positions in schools in the name of "racial balance," with the result that minority teachers in some schools come to bear the heavy burdens of ethnic isolation, intergroup hostility and endangerment, transportation difficulties, and job performance determinants harmful to the education of their students.

Our first question was whether this problem exists with the Gavin Middle School. The answer from *all* present at the meeting is an emphatic yes. No one challenged the gravity of the problem for the five teachers who wrote Dr. Wood, four of whom have been serving at the Gavin for four years or more.

Our second question was whether this problem exists in other school facilities throughout the system. We found this question could not be answered by those present at our meeting, although no one disputed the hypothesis that there are probably a series of facilities—of an unknown number, to be sure, where the problem exists.

2. One aspect of the problem, we learned during the meeting, derives from a departmental personnel policy concerning the distribution of minority teachers throughout the schools in the system. Everyone agreed that the policy prescribes a quota of black teachers (black hires) for each facility, though no one present was familiar with the details of the prescription. In addition to a quota, the policy apparently defines black teachers as "protected" in their positions, with that term translating to mean "stuck" or "held" in their positions in order to guarantee a modicum of racial balance. The policy extends, apparently with Teachers Union participation, to the definition of "black vacancies" and "black slots" in the teacher personnel deployment negotiations and practices. This policy, moreover, is represented consistently at all levels as the result of "court orders." The Teachers Union representative expressed the belief that the policy and the practices stemmed from adherence to court orders, as did others who were present.

3. A second aspect of the problem consists of the unavailability of desirable or workable remedies under current policies and practices. Here are some of the features of current arrangements:

a. Teacher transfers take place on the basis of a clause in the teachers contract. Transfer rights may be exercised on the basis of seniority, apparently, after the excess policy has been implemented each year. Black teachers with seniority have been unable to exercise their rights because there is no way for "black vacancies" to open up when both Union chief officers and system administrators conform to the policy cited in paragraph 2 above and believe it to be an expression of the will of the court. The Union has taken no initiatives in the direction of affirmative action to relieve this dilemma.

b. Black teachers may submit a medical statement indicating that, for health reasons, a transfer from school X is necessary. This is tacitly undesirable because it obligates a black teacher to seek a diagnosis from a physician that is entered in his or her permanent record and that detracts from future career opportunities. It is also a point of pride for some black teachers to emphasize that their burden may be gigantic, yet it is not one that will undermine them psychiatrically or physically. Some black teachers who might seek a transfer, fear they will be placed in a situation more tenuous than they are presently in.

c. A teacher may apply to be placed in the "excess pool," and at least two of the black teachers at the Gavin School have made such applications. None considers this desirable, however, for what seem to us to be self-evident reasons.

4. A third aspect of the problem concerns the nature of the isolative and threatening experience itself. Here were some aspects of the experience that were expressed at the meeting;

a. No black teacher has been a member of the Faculty Senate of the Gavin School for the past five years; thus, the group is neither represented nor included in the leadership cadre of the school's faculty.

b. Some white teachers are openly antagonistic toward black teachers. Others are cold and avoidant. Black teachers use the teachers lounges only on those occasions when they have reason to believe the hostile and the avoidant teachers are not present. Some white teachers have refused to cooperate with black teachers, and others have openly disapproved of the existence of a Spanish bilingual program in the school and of the use of Spanish as a language in "their classroom."

c. Black teachers cannot leave the building to eat lunch, or to conduct other business or personal errands. Conditions are too unsafe outside and around the Gavin to permit this, with the result, in the words of one of the veteran black teachers at the meeting, that "it feels after a while as if I'm in prison."

d. The black teachers have never been included in the meetings of the Racial/Ethnic Parents Council, nor in their view has the Council had any concern with their situation.

e. Many students and nearby white residents are hostile and verbally abusive, so that black teachers are subjected month by month over the years to racial slurs and threats, inside the school and outside.

5. A fourth aspect of the problem is that the ability of the black teachers to teach and advise students effectively is impaired in at least these ways:

a. Black teachers must come by special van and cannot use their own cars. The trip itself is harrying and anxiety-inducing. It also means that their day is limited to the length of the student day, so that planning and conferencing is not possible for them. The van prevents their bringing materials and equipment for displays and teaching presentations, as the white teachers do.

b. Last year, the van did not operate for two months. When black teachers brought their own cars on a few occasions, the cars were vandalized and damaged seriously and racial epithets were scrawled on some of their vehicles.

c. Tension, anxiety, and the agoraphobic feelings of being imprisoned indefinitely within the Gavin reduce the ability of the teachers to teach well.

d. White teachers turn over from year to year, while black teachers are perceived as "stuck" there and thus as less mobile and prospective in the eyes of some white teachers and students.

6. None of these four dimensions of the problem has been worked on by the School Department, the Union, or the parent councils to date. Mr. McDonough announced his intention to work remedially in cooperation with 26 Court Street and the principal and teachers at Gavin, and stated that he would undertake his work promptly.

a. Prepare a teacher and staff personnel minority distribution policy proposal that explicitly discards the fiction that the court has ordered a quota method or some other form of racial balance and that replaces standing policy with a desegregative approach that is at the same time flexible, de-isolative, and responsive to the needs of all teachers.

b. Identify the school facilities in which minority teachers at present experience a combination of isolation and intergroup hostility. Then, develop a plan for giving direct organizational development assistance to the administrators and faculties—as well as staffs—of those facilities, with the help of the top echelons of the entire School Department and the Union.

c. Develop a plan that includes as part of the personnel supervision and evaluation system sanctioned ratings of personnel—white, black, and other minority—on the quality of their contributions to the imperative for affirmative action toward one another and toward students.

d. Above all, develop a plan that enables currently isolated and deeply burdened black teachers with explicit and immediate opportunities for transfer or other rotation into inclusive, welcoming, and encouraging settings, with key consideration going to those teachers who have been giving service in difficult settings since 1974 and 1975.

Thank you for your attention to this matter. We look forward to hearing from you and to discussing your comments and ideas prior to any action on our part that would involve advising the court.

The 1975 court order did indeed require desegregative distribution of black teachers across schools, as we noted earlier. Until Gavin teachers complained and included us in their complaint, however, no one connected with the judge had known how that order had been construed and implemented.

We withheld taking the matter to court, although we discussed it informally with Judge Garrity, in the hope that remedies would be attempted by the school department. District Superintendent Joe McDonough made several earnest forays and succeeded in negotiating transfer offers for several of the teachers with Paul Kennedy. They were not offered with a view to redressing the injuries, however, and two of the teachers rejected them as "worse deals" than Gavin offered. One of the five was planning a resignation anyway.

The more complex remedies we listed were never developed and we therefore reported on the matter as a serious, persisting problem deserving of treatment by the court. In the judge's view, the complaint needed initiation by one of the parties. We had already tried the BTU and found them to be unreceptive. We also communicated with the attorney for the black plaintiffs with no result.

We bring this problem up here to illustrate how redistributive justice can harden into callous confinement for minority members if implementation is left to local authorities. We hope that in other cities where desegregation is taking place close monitoring of *all* facets of teacher desegregation plans and orders will be built into operations from the outset. In Boston, all but superficial aspects of both administrative and teacher desegregation have gone unsupervised since 1974. Under that arrangement, black teacher withdrawal will generate its own stimuli over time and Boston will again be known as an "antiblack city," as Judge Garrity termed it in 1975.

PARENT INVOLVEMENT

Before the court intervened, parent involvement was limited to two kinds. There was the Home and School Association (HSA), financed by the school committee, with a voluntary membership in each school unit and city-wide officers. And there were schools such as George Bancroft in the South End, Dennis C. Haley in West Roxbury, and a few others where parents spent much time contributing ideas, advice, and free service in close cooperation with principals and teachers. The HSA was *almost* exclusively white until 1973 and it was regarded as a vest pocket trinket of the school committee by many city dwellers. The informed parent groups tended to form only in naturally unsegregated neighborhoods and only among middle- and upper-middle-class parents.

Above all, the historic role accorded parents by the Boston system was miniscule in scope and subordinate in status. Where themes of parent participation did take hold in Boston from 1965 to 1973, they tended to be expressed through separation from the system.[5] The changes introduced by the court in 1974 and again in 1975 were therefore in extreme contrast with long-standing tradition. In Phase I, the court created Racial/Ethnic Parent Councils (REPCs) for all schools and a Citywide Parents' Advisory Council (CPAC). The key aim was to rely on parents to help resolve interracial problems and to signal the court when the law was being violated. In Phase II, the court added Community District Advisory Councils (CDACs) and a court-appointed Citywide Coordinating Council (CCC), strengthened the role of REPCs, and retained the CPAC. In addition, federal and state programs of several kinds required active advisory councils for special programs and for project funding. As funds were pumped into Boston again early in 1975, these groups sprang into being and amplified the volume if not the harmonics of parent participation.

We have, in our work for the court, had very limited association with the various parent organizations. Therefore, we have not presumed to portray their work in any detail. We have concentrated on the things we have learned from our infrequent contacts, however, and recommend examination of the massive study done by the Institute of Responsive Education for further information.[6]

The Racial/Ethnic Parent Councils were very hard to launch. Elections for them were threatened by ROAR and other protest groups, and turnouts in 1975 were very small. Meetings for 1974 and even 1976 were dangerous to attend because of the vandalism and harassment practiced by hate groups and crackpots. Other schools did not get full-size REPCs off the ground until 1977. Even meetings of the blue-ribbon Citywide Coordinating Council were subjected to disruption and fear tactics. The reactions told us of the importance ascribed to parent groups by opponents—an importance that has grown each year.

The Community District Advisory Councils were designed to represent the parents at the district level. Each contained elected REPC members plus some teachers, college and business pairing agents, police or social agency members, and the district superintendent. These councils were to make recommendations on race relations and educational policies, help make an annual plan for filing with the court, and communicate directly in writing with the court on desegregation activities. The Citywide Parents' Advisory Council, in turn, was the umbrella group. Composed of multiethnic representatives from each district, the CPAC was funded by the city, which allowed it to have a downtown office and staff.

The CCC proved to be superfluous. It was created on recommendation of the masters, who envisioned a twelve-person commission empowered to oversee desegregation implementation and to speak for the public interest. Judge Garrity designed a much larger body and appointed some leaders who were opposed to desegregation, as well as some who opposed the court orders. In our view, his sincere attempt to build a diverse group that would eventually reach consensus failed politically and operationally. Some members were hostile, others were preoccupied with their own leadership aspirations, and others seldom attended. Staff efforts were often thwarted by wrangling within the council and staff plans to mount real monitoring operations were deflected by cross-pressures. In addition, the school committee helped to diminish the strength of the CCC by refusing to consistently or sincerely interact with its members. Of equal importance in rendering the CCC superfluous was a gap that existed between it and the court that could not be closed as long as court hearings, the attorneys, and the judge remained the center of the case, with the CCC left at the periphery. In

1978, Judge Garrity negotiated with CCC leaders to plan the dissolution of the court's role.

By that time, the third basic revolution in the Boston schools had come into being. With indirect help from the CCC and with vigorous leadership from CPAC, a coalition of parents and teachers took shape around the aim of electing a moderate school committee in the November 1977 elections. The unifying slogans stressed the quest for quality education and the swift adoption of compliance with court orders so that the quest could gain momentum. This revolutionary movement was an outcome of unionization and desegregation linked with parent council formation. The coalition succeeded. The new committee appointed Robert Wood, then chairman of the CCC, as its superintendent, and the new power bases of teachers and parents were welded solidly together. No development in the entire case compares with this one in significance.

AFTER THE PARENT REVOLUTION

The CDACs and CPAC found that they could build power if they wanted it. The BTU had organizational skill and a shared objective: They wanted a friendly committee and parent votes could get it for them. The parent councils threw a much wider net than the HSA. They included thousands of otherwise uninvolved or excluded minority parents. The slate of candidates thus changed dramatically to include John O'Bryant, a black educator from Roxbury.

The import of every local revolution can only be discerned in its aftermath, however. The fusion of teachers and parents was of a kind that generated only a few changes in the direction of educational reform. The new regime did speed up compliance and changed the internal dynamics of court hearings away from protracted conflicts and toward consent decrees and moderation. The new committee attorney Simonds emerged more as a manager of short-term controversies rather than as a champion of opposition. And the Wood regime tried to clean house at headquarters and to emphasize district-level autonomy of operations.

What was missing from the political transformation, however, was a parent-generated agenda for educational reform. CPAC became instead a major advocate for continuation of the *status quo* in protecting against transfers of principals, reductions in the teacher force, and school closings. A few efforts were begun to upgrade instruction but the ways to accomplish this tended to be defined by the same teachers who created the existing programs.

In order to illustrate the import of the new coalition, take the instance of parent monitoring of classrooms. Monitoring of buses and hallways was routine from 1974 to 1978, but monitoring of classrooms, although mandated, did not surface as a CPAC issue until 1979. At that time, CPAC announced its monitoring plans and discovered their partners, the teachers, were outraged. There were threats of a September strike.

John Coakley and Mary Ellen Smith (founder of the City-Wide Education Coalition and then a senior officer under Wood for Community Relations) intervened and began to negotiate a monitoring plan acceptable to parents, teachers, and the administration. Their first version was filed with the court and Dentler sent the judge the following appraisal of it:

> The comments below arise from study of the request from Marshall Simonds filed with the court on June 24, that an attached memo from John Coakley and Mary Ellen Smith become the basis for court orders in the future.

> **1.** The memorandum's definition of monitoring falls far short of the repeatedly expressed instructions of this court. It defines monitoring this way: ". . . The alerting or warning to concerned parties of the possible evidence of noncompliance or ineffectual compliance concerning [sic] the Court's desegregation orders."

> In 1663, a monitor was defined as a defender of the King or a defender of the faith. In the history of education, a monitor is one authorized and charged with keeping order and enforcing rules. It was also the name for an iron collar placed around the necks of disobedient pupils. In Australia, it is the name of a lizard who gives advance warning of the dangerous presence of crocodiles. For three centuries, it has referred to one who admonishes and who gives advice on proper conduct. Surely, this suggests a more active, comprehensive, and authoritative role than is suggested by the pale language of Coakley and Smith!

> In view of the common usage of the term as well as the court's frequent use of it in prescribing wide-ranging activities of many kinds, let me suggest this definition: To monitor as intended by the court means to observe, investigate, appraise, advise, and admonish the Boston public school committee, administration, faculty, and staff on all aspects of compliance with court orders and related processes, including committee policies, staffing practices, delivery of services, curriculum and instruction, discipline, police-school relations and security, budgeting and resource allocation, student transfers, and intergroup relations.

> **2.** The memorandum also distorts the meaning of *evaluation*, which they try to distinguish from monitoring. (See page 4 of memorandum.) Contrary to their formulation, part of monitoring entails evaluation, which means simply to assess the worth or effectiveness of a program, operations, or performances.

If a CDAC sought to determine whether affirmative action prescription of this court were being implemented in a district, for example, they would monitor selected policies and their implementation. In the course of this, their work would be evaluative by necessity. A district superintendent might of course seek a separate, independent evaluation. But, I believe the aim of the Coakley-Smith memo is to downgrade monitoring to a minor, preliminary, and impressionistic activity, and to countervail it with "official" evaluations.

3. The memorandum is inappropriately unilateral. It presumes to tell CPAC, the CDACs, and their REPCs what the court intended them to do and it asks the court to sanction its views. The correct procedure would be to *co-develop* definitions, activities, division of labor, and channels of communications. The memorandum has the earmarks of a report from the home office of the British colonial administration. On page 6, for instance, it admonishes parents to unite with the Department around the "common goal of improvement of instruction." In fact, this is but one concern among many and its content may be very differently defined by different interest groups.

4. Pages 7 and 8 set up permission-giving procedures that protect the interests of teachers and administrators, at the expense of giving access to parent monitors. On page 7, we read, "Parents are welcome to visit classrooms...by appointment." On page 9, we read that "Classroom visitations are not part of the monitoring process." The content and tenor are contradictory and insulting to the intelligence of duly elected parent members of councils!

A year later, a mutually acceptable parent monitoring plan was filed with the court, with but two tiny disputes left for resolution. The concept of monitoring remains timid, parental approaches toward classrooms are hedged in with a thicket of advance notices and permissions, and any semblance of evaluation is rejected. The hegemony of classroom teachers is preserved and the school department has no recorded obligation to do *anything* in particular with the results. A safe, polite, and ultimately inconsequential monitoring procedure has been devised six years after Phase I began. Coming as it did, as an anticlimax, Judge Garrity simply ruled on the tiny disputes and approved the plan.

COOPTATIVE CONSENSUS

In 1980, the parent-teacher, or CPAC-BTU, coalition was expanded under the heat of facility planning (see Chapter Four) to include these parties: black plaintiffs, El Comite, the Boston Association of School Administrators (BASAS), and even, for some purposes, the Home and School Association. The new coalition termed itself The Joint Plaintiffs in opposing school closings and revised geocoding of student assignments.

From January through April, the court sought to mediate between the joint planners (school department, state board, and city hall) and the new joint defendants. It did so with a widening realization that the differences between the two were minute and that the court itself was in danger of being isolated.

In the final rounds of facility planning, then, Wood and Simonds moved to co-opt Larry Johnson, attorney for the black plaintiffs, by pledging mutual cooperation in the quest for facility equalization. When Simonds appealed the court's orders to close schools and revise geocodes late in April 1980, Johnson and Playter for El Comite joined him in calling for a stay. CPAC, the BTU, HSA, BASAS, and the school committee had congealed into a solid mass opposed to changes in facilities or assignments. Only the Massachusetts Board of Education stood apart from this mass, more isolated in its noble integrity than it had been in 1972.

CONCLUSION

In a booklet disseminated in 1976, CPAC gave this answer to the question, "Why Parent Involvement?"

> When Phase I of Judge Garrity's court order was implemented in September of 1974, parents in this city reacted in a variety of ways. Some moved out of the city, some enrolled their children in private schools, and many kept their children at home and boycotted. The majority of parents, however, complied with the court order. Prior to the opening of schools, open house was held in all Boston Public Schools and, although filled with fear and apprehension, parents visited schools to which their children had been assigned. In many cases they found the school facilities in poor condition and were angry. They met with school principals, district superintendents and school department personnel to discuss building repairs, Chapter 766, transportation, and a host of other issues. Parents joined Racial-Ethnic Parent Councils, the Citywide Parents' Advisory Council, and, later, Community District Advisory Councils. They became actively involved in the educational process of their children's schools.

> Through their efforts, building repairs were made, special programs were initiated, and for the first time, parent involvement meant more than sponsoring social functions at individual schools.

> Why did parents get involved? Not because they favored Phase 1 and 2 of the court order—compliance does not mean acceptance. They became involved initially out of fear for their children's safety and education. Soon, however, as parents became more and more involved in their children's schools, that fear changed to anger and then to action.

People ask, "Why parent involvement?" The answer, put quite simply, is their children. The Boston School System can become the standard of excellence in education—through strong parent participation.

The BTU, its new black coalition of 872 teachers, and the thousands of newly involved parents together have realigned the power structure of the Boston public schools. This coalition can move in any of several directions in the future. It can sit in the vest pocket of the school committee in common pursuit of shared goals. It can carry the school department in its vest pocket if it decides to go somewhere of its own devising. It can unify in support of the continuation of poor services, poorly delivered, or it can invent an agenda for reform. Each year, the choices will renew themselves.

The early years suggest that the parent-teacher coalition has a growing storehouse of power, but that this will be put into the service of narrow union objectives. Teachers and administrators have learned to include parent leaders, but the leaders depend on them to set agenda and directions. To this extent, the court made substantial structural changes that redistributed justice and power, but it could not change *cultural* trends. Boston's parents have new roles but they appear for now to be subordinating their performances out of deference to the professional bureaucracy. Minority teachers, too, are absorbed in this pattern at present.

It is possible this will change, one school at a time, as new forms of collective effort are channeled toward improvement. How parents and a new, small minority of minority teachers can accelerate this slow process when the larger system is encompassed in the "normal school way" we described is too uncertain to predict. Perhaps it will be the demographics of declining enrollments, combined with the advent of new electronic technologies, that will trigger movement toward reforms of teaching. If these forces are dramatic enough in their impact, the new coalition will help to channel them into service in the public interest.

NOTES

1. "Rise and Growth of the Normal School Idea," Bureau of Education, Washington, D.C., Circular No. 8, 1891. Also see Thomas W. Bicknell, *A History of the Rhode Island Normal School*, 1911, Providence, R.I., no publisher named.
2. *Morgan v. Kerrigan*, Memorandum and Order on Teacher Desegregation, January 1975.
3. Robert J. Menges, "Assessing Readiness for Professional Practice," *Review of Educational Research Journal*, Vol. 45, 1975, pp. 173–207.

4. For an illuminating treatment of the educational importance of racial/ethnic congruence between faculty and students, see Robert E. Herriott and Nancy Hoyt St. John, *Social Class and the Urban School*, John Wiley and Sons, New York, 1966, pp. 75–83.

5. Jonathan Kozol, *Free Schools*, Houghton Mifflin, Boston, Mass., 1972.

6. Marilyn Gittell, with Bruce Hoffocker, Eleanor Rollins, and Samuel Foster, *Citizen Organizations: Citizen Participation in Educational Decision-Making*, final research report, Boston, The Institute for Responsive Education, NIE Contract 400–76–0115, July 1979.

OUTCOMES 10

INTRODUCTION

A FORMIDABLE ARRAY OF LAWYERS AND SOCIAL SCIENTISTS has expended great energy for twenty-five years in perfecting the policy arguments *against* school desegregation. University of Texas law professor Lino A. Graglia has done the nation a service in summarizing, as if in preparation for an ultimate re-litigating of *Brown*, the best of all of these arguments.[1] We have used his inventory in organizing this concluding chapter, or at least parts of it, because those who in the future will be engaged in resolving segregation conflicts in our cities will want to know how the Boston case confirms, controverts, or changes the recurrent policy arguments. It has been our experience that the arguments are revived every time there is a school desegregation issue. In his work in the 1960s, Dentler heard some of the arguments raised so often that he wrote an article to codify them.[2]

We both think that educational policy analysis in America could be enhanced by the creation of an Educational Questions and Answers Archive within the new U.S. Department of Education. The archive would be linked to the Educational Research Information Center (ERIC), which provides research abstracts by computer printout, and would not presume to provide *knowledge*. It would precode all questions about educational policies and pedagogical approaches and then inventory all possible answers in a pro, con, and neutral fashion so that the opportunities for regenerating rhetoric would be reduced. The archive would help everyone distinguish between research-based evidence that may illuminate policy analysis and the process of debate through which public sector decisions are reached, tested, or rationalized. Most of the literature on school desegregation, perhaps 3,600 items among the 4,000 that comprise it, would go to the archive and the remainder would go to ERIC.

RACE AS A PERMISSIBLE

Students of constitutional law from the late Alexander Bickel of Yale to Raoul Berger of Harvard have helped to shape Graglia's major objection to *Brown* and the handful of Supreme Court decisions that have followed its principles. As Graglia sums it up:

> The most unfortunate result of the Court's integration requirement may well prove, if it has not already proved, to be simply that it has, in this multiracial and multiethnic society, reintroduced race as a permissible, and made it for the first time a sometimes constitutionally required basis of government action.[3]

A high school studies teacher in Boston, led by this paradox, wrote us a series of letters. These were published in 1977, with Dentler's replies, in *The Philadelphia Inquirer* and *The Washington Post*. The teacher's mind was boggled by the paradox of taking a daily *racial* census of his homeroom students, under federal court order, as part of a method of remedy for racial segregation. For him, as for many students of the law, the U.S. Constitution is color blind.

And, indeed, thousands of Boston teachers believed they were delivering racially neutral public instruction before and after the court intervened in their classrooms. They not only believed this, they tried diligently to make it happen. For this reason, public school teachers shunned the topics of race, ethnicity, and racial/ethnic problems (and their resolution) in their lesson plans and in their communications with one another.

There were still ethnic festivals and celebrations, of course. In 1977, three years after the Phase I intervention, Scott visited an elementary school that was 70 percent black. When he asked about multicultural instruction, the principal showed him, with visible pride, a hall display celebrating St. Patrick's Day and the coming of the Irish to Boston. In 1976, Kathleen Sullivan Alioto, president of the school committee and a former teacher, proposed the creation of a series of ethnic "Heritage Schools" as magnets. Apart from the days given over to celebrating Puritan Thanksgiving and cheering for the United Nations and Christopher Columbus and a few other luminaries, the norm of racial/ethnic neutrality was preserved as sacred. When Dentler recommended to the corresponding teacher that he use the stuff of the court case as a major unit of instruction, the proposal was rejected as morally outrageous. When the Community Relations Service of the Justice Department proposed race relations training, administrators and teachers rejected it with equal intensity.

Indeed, in one sense, it was the norm of racial neutrality that triggered the conflict and later the court case in Boston. In 1963 Louise Day Hicks, in prematurely adjourning a school committee public hearing for black parents to express their views, was enforcing color blindness. When she heard the offending term *de facto* segregation spoken and responded by ending the hearing, she could not have known how popular her reaction would prove to be. Racial awareness and its political manipulation by white leaders were latencies made manifest by the advent of the civil rights mobilization. The latency was shared by the black parents who later brought suit—ten years later, to be exact. As one of them, Ruth Batson, noted, their attention was first heightened by the realization that their children's school work was given A's in some schools and, when they moved to other neighborhoods, F's in others. Connecting this with a deep-seated policy of segregation came much later.

The entire line of the argument is, in our view, rhetorical. As Richard Kluger has shown in *Simple Justice: The History of Brown vs. Board of Education*, the U.S. Constitution was framed on the premise of color.[4] According to Kluger, the premise that the Afro-American was subhuman was maintained for seventy-eight years, until passage of the Thirteenth Amendment in 1865. The rhetorical nature of the argument is disclosed, too, in the fact that resistance to school desegregation was intense before as well as after *Brown*. The fact that the Massachusetts Legislature banned racially segregated public schooling in 1855 attests to the active presence in the law of color tests for more than a century.

Has the Boston case affected this argument? The answer is yes, most profoundly, for good and for ill. For the public good, Bostonians have now discovered their increasingly multiethnic diversity. The black population grew from about 50,000 in 1950 to an estimated 170,000 in 1980. The Hispanic population increased from about 5,000 in 1950 to an estimated 70,000 in 1980. With desegregation these substantial minorities have gained new visibility, as have such subgroups as French Haitians, Cape Verdians, Laotians, and others. What is more, in the past, racial neutrality, as formulated by the Yankees, had been predicated upon the processes of *deracination* of the first generation, followed by coercive cultural assimilation of the second and third. Contrary to these processes, desegregation has meant the advent of at least *bicultural* socialization for newcomers and their children.

For the public ill, the argument against racial/ethnic heightening possesses a significant grain of truth. In 1974 and 1975 intergroup hostilities, white against black and Hispanic avoidance of black, were intensified. When the rock of customary neutrality was lifted, more than a new tolerance was generated. Sociopathic forces were unleashed in every neighborhood, resulting for a time in increased violence, fear, and psychic tension. Graglia is correct in warning that *Brown* and its corollary in Boston, *Morgan v. Hennigan*, forced convulsive changes in the social *status quo*. He stands in the tradition of Madison, Jefferson, and Lincoln in wishing for a less dramatic upheaval. It is a tradition that has been overwhelmed by events in every era, and it is the tradition invoked in the early 1960s by Bostonians like James Breeden, who found it scorned by the city's white leadership. In short, voluntary school integration was highly feasible in 1965. It was rejected intentionally by city leaders.

ABANDONMENT OF NEIGHBORHOOD SCHOOLS

In 1972 Nathan Glazer wrote that, "In busing to distant schools, white children were in effect being conscripted to create an environment which, it had been decided, was required to provide equality of opportunity for black children."[5]

Glazer contributed to the Boston case by offering this argument to a colleague who analyzed student distributions for the Home and School Association. The idea is that court-imposed school desegregation presumes to surmount residential segregation and, in doing so, forces unnatural burdens of travel and dislocation upon *innocent* white children. Glazer's argument is indisputably correct as far as it goes, but as with many policy arguments, it goes only part of the way.

As Judge Garrity noted in his May 10, 1975, memorandum on Phase II:

> Nor is a simple rule of attendance at the nearest school adequate, when that rule is imposed on a pattern of segregated housing attributable in part to the segregative practices of school authorities. Such a "neutral" geographic attendance arrangement in Boston would sanction a freezing-in of the effects of past discrimination. Long-continued efforts by the school authorities to keep the races apart are reflected in both residential patterns and school locations and capacities. . . . This is not to say that ethnic and racial housing patterns result entirely from school segregation, but that past school policies would render discriminatory any simple nearest-school policy.[6]

Later in the same memorandum, Judge Garrity added this observation:

> The court does not favor forced busing. Nor, for that matter, have the plaintiffs advocated forced busing. What the plaintiffs seek, and what the law of the land as interpreted by the Supreme Court of the United States commands, is that plaintiffs' right to attend desegregated schools be

realized. That right cannot lawfully be limited to walk-in schools. If there were a way to accomplish desegregation in Boston without transporting students to schools beyond walking distance, the court and all parties would much prefer that alternative.[7]

Not one of the nation's thirty largest urban school districts comes closer to fulfilling Glazer's dream that students not be bused long distances than Boston. Most of these districts cover larger land areas and require much more long-distance busing than Boston—with or without desegregation. Sociologist Phillip Hauser made an analysis of Chicago in 1966 that showed how much desegregation would be achieved by introducing a nearest-school policy, for example. The effects were very great, and it was apparent that busing was being used to maintain segregation. By 1975, however, after a decade of inaction, the residential ecology of Chicago would have little effect.

If Boston schools had been located by this policy principle, the kind of "conscription" Glazer abhors would not have been required. Instead, the Boston Housing Authority built segregated public housing, the Boston Redevelopment Authority fostered "human removal" in the name of urban renewal, and the school committee planned sites, old and new, with city hall, that reinforced the practice of student relocation.

Boston is one of the few cities in North America to have the benefits of what planners call "human scale." It takes only an hour *at most* to travel across the city. Housing is interwoven with commerce and other land uses. When school construction and renovation was resumed in the 1950s, however, after a lapse of twenty-five years, it served *some* interests—financial, real estate, white parent groups—at the expense of others. Undergirding the policy of reconstruction was a policy of racial and ethnic dominance. The chance to utilize the human scale was sacrificed irretrievably between 1960 and 1973.

In May 1980, the U. S. Department of Justice announced plans to sue for metropolitan desegregation of the Greater Houston public schools. In turn, Houston's Mayor James McConn (one of the real estate developers of that city) announced that he would press to have the proposal withdrawn because it would threaten the source of Houston's genius for growth, its no-zoning policy. According to Mayor McConn, metropolitan school desegregation will hamper business growth in Houston; he is probably correct. What Houston's leaders have avoided is what Boston's leaders avoided as they struggled to rebuild their city in the 1955–1973 period, namely, "a flywheel governor" whose inertia would oppose, or at least moderate, economic growth. As the flywheel has cut cruelly into the life chances of black Americans, the *Brown* decision and other countervailing policies that it led to have been the main recourse available to minorities.

The Boston experience does not contradict Glazer's argument. It merely shows that much, much more is at stake in school desegregation than the forced busing of "white children." That children are subjected to the remedy when the wrongs that led to it are the wrongs of adults older than their parents is indeed unfair. But, Glazer's proposition that this is done *in order to* create majority-white environments for black children is false. It is done in order to redress a host of wrongs, one of them being school environments that are otherwise isolated and educationally inferior.

ALSOP'S FABLE

In 1969, nationally syndicated columnist Joseph Alsop visited some segregated public schools in New York City and came away convinced that what black students needed was massive compensatory education, not desegregation. Because he pitted the two policies against one another as if they were mutually exclusive, and because he judged the quality of teaching in the schools he visited for two hours effective in spite of being given evidence to the contrary, some of us called this argument Alsop's Fable.[8]

That fable has been re-enacted in wide-screen production for four years in Los Angeles. There, under the patient but politically strained aegis of State Judge Paul Egly (who was elected, not appointed), the plaintiffs are facing the fable in its most fulsomely developed form. The Los Angeles Board of Education has begun to desegregate some schools on a majority-white basis. It has next listed about 200 schools as "Racially Isolated Minority Schools" (RIMS) and has begun to devise policies intended to make these schools educationally more effective. In 1980 teachers working in many of these schools received a service bonus. The board has elicited improvement proposals from RIMS administrators, and a court expert, UCLA law professor Munroe Price, has worked extensively with school headquarters in reviewing elaborate plans for instructional enrichments. Some of the parties and their experts believe that a legal remedy can be worked out using these two components—desegregation of schools where majority-white student bodies are convenient and compensatory aid for RIMS.

Other parties, including the NAACP, the ACLU, the Los Angeles Center for Law and Justice, and the Integration Project, have challenged that view and pressed for a system-wide, multiethnic approach. Experts such as Robert Crain, Gary Orfield, Dan Dodson, Thomas Pettigrew, and Christine Rossell, among others, have urged a full-desegregation, or at least triethnic, plan. John Caughey, Professor Emeritus of History at UCLA, filed a detailed plan through the project intervenor in April 1980 that showed how every school could be desegregated by using the following definition:

> The multiethnic desegregated school is one in which students of all racial and ethnic backgrounds may be included. It may have more minority students than white, but a critical limitation is established—no single minority may be larger than the white enrollment.[9]

What is particularly illuminating about this case is that all kinds of options and issues closed by now to federal court consideration have been examined exhaustively for seventeen years. Among these is the acceptance of a proposal from the defendant to implement a completely voluntary plan (in order to avoid "white flight") that would leave hundreds of thousands of students segregated. Alsop's vision, shared by millions of Americans who do not think desegregation *itself* has merit, may well be tried on a vast scale.

Judge Egly issued his plan on May 19, 1980. He took some features from the Boston plan, such as subdistricting the city into eleven areas with no busing between areas. He allowed city-wide magnet schools, but only on a 40-percent-white basis. He kept the 11 percent salary bonus in place for RIMS, involving 6,000 teachers in 102 facilities. In short, Judge Egly tried hard to find a middle ground between the plaintiffs and the Los Angeles School Board. While many students will receive mandatory reassignments beginning in September 1980, four of eleven areas will be left racially isolated. Implementation of his plan will deserve careful study as an example of an amalgam of court-ordered desegregation and separate-but-compensated education. His plan was upheld by the California Court of Appeals in August, but that body deleted the multiethnic remedies.

In our estimation there are three deep flaws in Alsop's Fable. If we are correct, adoption of the Los Angeles School Board plan will allow everyone to see these flaws magnified.

First, compensatory education does not alter intergroup *power* relations. Whites still control the public system. They decide what RIMS will get and in the long term this system will merely sustain and enhance the order of deprivation that whites have historically controlled. Second, the learning content itself will be monocultural, yet aimed at multiethnic minority learners. Under this condition, the compensatory aim is very likely to be misdirected. And third, Alsop's compensatory education plan is *not* a policy alternative; it is different language for the separate-but-equal argument framed by Massachusetts Justice Shaw in *Sarah Roberts v. Boston* in 1849, and made the law of the land in *Plessy v. Ferguson* in 1896.

In going beyond equalization of buildings, curricula, and teacher qualifications and salaries, Chief Justice Warren in *Brown* said the Court could not compare "merely tangible factors." He wrote, "We must look instead to the effect of segregation itself on public education." And in assessing this issue in *Brown*, Justice Warren stated that, "Segregation with the sanction of law . . . has a tendency to retard the educational and mental development of Negro children." *Keyes* and other later decisions extended this to include other racial/ethnic minorities.

Alsop and Los Angeles would have us move from "separate but equal," to "separate and permanently isolated but compensated." The difference is not great enough to comprise an authentic policy alternative. The change is based on tacit acceptance of 1896 separatism.

IS CONSTITUTIONAL DEMOCRACY TOO COSTLY?

Mayor Kevin White borrowed the theme of costliness from others. The complaint was voiced before Boston in Nashville, Kalamazoo, and Tampa, and it has been replayed since in Dallas. The lyrics avoid direct opposition to school desegregation and point instead to its allegedly high costs.

Three-fourths of the extra costs incurred to enforce school desegregation in Boston from 1974 until June 1976 resulted from *double time* wages paid the police for security services. In many cities, including Boston, other heavy expenses have been the result of busing itself, although the state reimburses cities nearly in full, and of salary additions stemming from administration and faculty desegregation. Boston teetered on the verge of bankruptcy in 1976, Cleveland fell in during 1979, and Chicago is threatening to follow. However, New York City, Yonkers, and Newark, among other cities, went broke *without* desegregating their schools.

There is certainly a fiscal issue at the base of school desegregation, but the issue must be separated from litigation and court intervention and examined in cost-analytic terms. When the Harrisburg, Pennsylvania, Board of Education voted to desegregate in 1970, it also pledged to make reforms while remaining within the confines of its operating budget (which was low and tight) and its standing capital facilities. A plan based on this premise was developed slowly and with great regard for citizen participation. Disciplined by fiscal prudence, the political will of informed elected leaders can bring about educational change. It is avoidance, ineptitude, confusion, and then conflict, that give rise to the costliness of desegregation in some cities. It is not busing that is *pro forma* so expensive; it is poor planning and poor management of bus and taxi leasing arrangements that made costs skyrocket in Boston.

Some time late in 1980, Boston will open its forty-million-dollar, 400,000-square-foot Occupational Resource Center (ORC) (see Figure 10.1). The school department withheld its plans for this center from the court for a year. When they were revealed in May 1980, it was at once obvious that the newly named Hubert H. Humphrey ORC might open half empty and black segregated. When asked about his, John Coakley acknowledged that possibility and volunteered, "But that is because whites won't want to go to Roxbury or to use Dudley (subway) Station." That thousands of whites have for years attended Madison Park High at the same site and Boston Technical High only a mile away has not changed school committee thinking or planning. If the worst had happened, as Coakley feared, the ORC would be labeled a wasteful expense incurred because of desegregation. But in fact, within a few weeks enough whites applied to enable it to open fully desegregated on a voluntary basis. Thus, desegregation generated a vitally needed resource and its

FIGURE 10.1

Occupational Resource Center Application Form

STUDENT APPLICATION

HUBERT HUMPHREY OCCUPATIONAL RESOURCE CENTER
SKILL TRAINING HALF DAY (ENTRY AT GRADES 10, 11 and 12 ONLY)

Name of Student_____
                    Last   First   Middle Initial
Date of Birth Mo._____ Day_____ Yr._____

IN ADDITION TO MAKING ONE, TWO OR THREE CHOICES FOR DISTRICT OR MAGNET HIGH
SCHOOLS ON THE REVERSE SIDE OF THIS APPLICATION, YOU MAY CHOOSE TO PARTICIPATE
IN A SKILL TRAINING PROGRAM AT THE HUMPHREY CENTER. YOU WILL ATTEND ONE HALF
DAY AT YOUR ASSIGNED HIGH SCHOOL AND ONE HALF DAY AT THE HUMPHREY CENTER.

DIRECTIONS: You may make as many or as few choices as you prefer from the
              twenty-three programs listed below. (HA through HW) Use
              numbers 1, 2, 3, etc. to indicate the order of your choices.
              You may make one, two, or three choices, or you may make
              several choices.

HA____ BUSINESS (Office Machines, Records Management, Advanced Office
                                                    Procedures)
HB____ CONSTRUCTION (Basic Carpentry, Bench and Mill Carpentry, Framing
                        and Roofing, Basic Plumbing, Residential and
                        Commercial Plumbing, Building Maintenance and
                        Repair)
HC____ DATA PROCESSING (Introductory Data Processing)
HD____ POWER MECHANICS (Automotive/Truck Mechanics, Small Engine Chassis,
                        Suspension and Steering Systems, Fuel Electrical
HE____ HEALTH-HEALTH AIDE   System and Accessories Lab)
HF____ HEALTH-MEDICAL OFFICE ASSISTANT
HG____ HEALTH-NURSING ASSISTANT
HH____ METALS/FABRICATION/MANUFACTURING (Welding Laboratory, Sheet Metal
                                        Laboratory, Auto Body Repair
                                        Laboratory)
HI____ BASIC ELECTRICITY
HJ____ BASIC ELECTRONICS
HK____ COMMERCIAL MALL-BANKING
HL____ COMMERCIAL MALL-CHILD CARE
HM____ COMMERCIAL MALL-COSMETOLOGY
HN____ COMMERCIAL MALL-FASHION/INTERIOR DESIGN
HO____ COMMERCIAL MALL-FOOD SERVICE
HP____ COMMERCIAL MALL-HOTEL/HOSPITALITY
HQ____ COMMERCIAL MALL-RETAILING, MARKETING AND MANAGEMENT
HR____ GRAPHICS MEDIA-PRINTING
HS____ GRAPHICS MEDIA-COMMERCIAL DESIGN
HT____ GRAPHICS MEDIA-PHOTOGRAPHIC TECHNOLOGY
HU____ GRAPHICS MEDIA-MACHINE DRAFTING
HV____ GRAPHICS MEDIA-FASHION ILLUSTRATION
HW____ GRAPHICS MEDIA-TELEVISION PRODUCTION

IF YOU DO NOT WANT TO MAKE CHOICES FROM THE PROGRAMS LISTED ABOVE, CHECK BELOW:

              _____ No, I do not want to participate in the half-day Skill-
                    Training programs offered at the Humphrey Center

Signature of Parent/Guardian_____

Date_____

deliberately integrative site will not detract from its full (and fully desegregated) utilization.

Court-ordered student *and* teacher desegregation also give the school committee an excuse for featherbedding teachers. Student makeup seems volatile, hence teacher reserves are rationalized each August. Teacher desegregation requires hiring minorities at a rapid rate, but does not *mandate* white teacher cutbacks. Some 30 percent fewer students were enrolled in 1980 than in 1974, but the full-time teacher force declined by only 8 percent. This was partly due to the advent of bilingual and special needs classes, to be sure, but our analyses found an overall teacher-student ratio of 1 to 13 in 1979.

As educators ourselves, we see the Boston teachers as buffeted victims of their employers often unwise decisions, reassigned on a moment's notice, unable to rely upon committee compliance with more than twenty different clauses in the union contract, and cut off from co-planning educational improvements with a remote set of headquarters bureaucrats. Even when Robert Wood radically reorganized headquarters in 1978, ostensibly to decentralize authority, his design intensified his *own* control over the legion of classroom teachers.

That Boston teachers would struggle to avoid massive layoffs in the late 1970s when other jobs in education were nonexistent seems to us natural. What is not credible is a pronouncement that school desegregation is the cause of extreme overruns in the annual school system budget. Missing from all of it is a plan for retrenchment fitted to the inexorable realities of severe declines in enrollments.

ACADEMIC ACHIEVEMENT?

The outcomes in Boston add to the already substantial evidence that racial/ethnic desegregation is in itself *not* a contributor to increased academic achievement. As Richard Light and Paul Smith concluded from their effort at a "meta-analysis" of the data, "The contradictions among the studies are more striking than the similarities."[10]

There is evidence from Boston to show that minority students in some grade levels, especially grades 2–5, have made gains and that white achievement test scores have not declined (see Table 10.1). We do not view these partial improvements as direct or even intended outcomes of court-ordered desegregation, however. Instead, the massive challenges of multiple readjustments imposed on classroom teachers have stimulated many of them—especially those with less than 15 years on the job—to reach out for new and superior pedagogies.

Indeed, we are not at all confident that the achievement test scores we have seen have any validity. Several principals and headmasters have told us that the tests are very indifferently administered; that middle and high school students know when they are scheduled to take the tests and elect to stay out on those days; that they are not administered on one day, which leads to much

TABLE 10.1

Reading Achievement Test Score Means of Boston Public School Students, 1976-79

Student Group	Third Grade Percentiles				Sixth Grade Percentiles				Ninth Grade Percentiles			
	1976	1977	1978	1979	1976	1977	1978	1979	1976	1977	1978	1979
White	60	60	60	50	46	50	42	54	50	57	56	56
Black	36	36	40	36	20	22	22	36	10	25	23	26
Hispanic	24	28	28	22	16	18	18	24	20	23	23	11
Asian	60	64	58	52	58	62	58	60	39	59	60	62
Native American	60	40	36	40	36	36	36	42	20	49	38	42
Total System	46	46	46	40	32	34	32	40	30	39	36	38
Number Tested	—	—	3893	3800	—	—	4256	4052	—	—	4081	4059
Tested as % of Enrollment	—	—	79%	82%	—	—	75%	77%	—	—	66%	60%

a Tests are the Metropolitan Achievement Test (MAT), 1970 edition for grades 1–8, Iowa Silent Reading Test (ISRT) for grades 9–11. Source of Data: Boston School Department of Management Information Services.

NOTE: Percentiles are based on nationally normed scores, so that the national mean for any grade level is 50.

confusion over who has and has not taken the tests already; and that some teachers emphasize their importance, others play them down, and still others express indifference. School headquarters has lacked a research staff and a testing unit since the 1960s, save for a few persons charged with these duties who lack psychometric expertise.

We had expected the college and university pairings we developed to contribute to improvements in teaching and learning and to generate evaluation research literature that would inform this issue. The Massachusetts Education Department requires independent evaluation of the pairing projects it supports. Over a five-year period, more than 150 of these evaluation reports have been issued. The most startling feature of these evaluations is that only half a dozen treat the question of project effects on student achievement.[11] This is not a defect in the evaluations. It is due to the fact that very, very few college faculties have had a chance to work on this aspect of public instruction.

In the main, colleges have been asked to provide in-service assistance to teachers, to supply "enrichments," and to give support to the program activities desired by Boston teachers and parents. Boston University, for instance, has had no impact upon Brighton High School, its only high school pairing, because the headmaster and faculty have avoided coparticipation. Hyde Park High is paired with Stonehill College. When the faculty coordinator of the pairing, George McGarry, tried to press for meaningful exchanges with teaching staff and for collaborative planning between the college and school administrations in 1979, Hyde Park administrators complained and he was asked to resign by the college at midyear.

This is not to conclude that, in general, the pairings have failed. Some have achieved considerable distinction in helping to design better school programs. These include pairings led by Stanley Russell for MIT and Wentworth, by Gregory Coffin for Northeastern University, and by Miriam Clasby for Boston University, to mention a few. Maria Brisk, the coordinator of pairings for Hispanic bilingual classes, has also achieved considerable success. However the *achievement effects* of their efforts are not known. Other pairings have resulted in tutoring services, help with music and theater from such universities as Brandeis, and assistance from businesses with work-study options and college planning.

We have no reason to doubt that, as a direct result of implementation of the court orders, teaching in Boston's public schools is significantly better than it was before 1974. Many young teachers, mainly black, Hispanic, and Asian-American, have been recruited, bringing with them new and more cosmopolitan pedagogies. Hundreds of other able teachers who once were limited in their outreach to one ethnic and one ability group stratum now teach diversified groups of students. What may be most crucial is that the little islands of teacher isolation have been formed into new groupings that are increasingly district-wide. The age-old system of teacher patronage (with lines extending upward to some committee member or associate superintendent) has deteriorated under the massive force of redeployment, school closings, parent monitoring, decentralization, and, above all, dissolution of hegemony over small constituencies of learners.

The effects of these changes on achievement cannot be measured, however, for the court orders did not penetrate the veil of local authority over instruction and its effects. Those who oppose court intervention most vigorously tend to be those who criticize court-ordered school desegregation for its uncertain, contradictory effects on academic achievement. There seems to be a mental gap yawning here that cannot be bridged by reasoning. Academic achievement will be enhanced when educators who know *how* to enhance it are mobilized to plan for educational change.[12]

A school board whose members are pitting their every resource against the implementation of school desegregation is extremely unlikely to appoint competent planners to improve the quality of instruction. In spite of these deterrents, though, forces determined to reform the structure have made gains. But just as frequently, there have been no effects on school learning simply because there have been no new inputs. And sometimes, as sociologist Richard Boardman found, there are negative effects as a result of bad planning and poor execution.[13]

What, then, could the justification for school desegregation be? Black plaintiffs, made aware of the fact that they are being denied what whites are getting, sue for equal protection. When they get it, they often discover that "it" did not include educative stimuli, except in some of the many once-inaccessible white schools. This is the beginning, not the end, of the process, however, and when power relations have been altered and shared interests realized, a new force that presses for educational improvement may be generated. The Boston case is filled with demonstrations of this process in the rise of a moderate interracial coalition of parents and teachers in particular.

There are powerful possibilities set in motion that could result in greatly enhanced learning, then, but if these possibilities are not built in by the local authorities early on, they will take years to reach fruition and more years than that before the authorities learn to test for their emergence. If student achievement effects were to change substantially, then, the time frame should be ten to fifteen years.

Even these structurally induced possibilities depend for their realization upon the availability of appropriate curricular and instructional designs. We saw how some of these came into play at South Boston High School when court control led to the appointment of Jerome Winegar, Geraldine Kozberg, and their associates. By and large, however, with the exception of models supplied by the State Education Department and a few of the college faculties, local teachers and parents have little to pool but their earlier ignorance *and* what they learn through radically altered local interaction patterns.

The part of the pool of ignorance that is drained away most dramatically by desegregation is that which conditioned thousands of adults to believe that mental abilities were distributed along some sort of grid that was biogenetic

221

and corresponded magically with ethnicity and with the ecology of residential locations. When that belief system is shattered, new approaches have a chance to emerge. Eventually moreover, failures in learning outcomes cannot be explained away by reference to race and household.

IMPROVEMENTS IN RACE RELATIONS?

While at Harvard, Rand sociologist David Armor reviewed what he called "The Evidence on Busing," and concluded that

> one of the central hypotheses in the integration policy model is that integration should reduce racial stereotypes, increase tolerance, and generally improve race relations . . . . We discovered that, in fact, the converse appears to be true. The data suggest that, under the circumstances obtaining in these studies, integration heightens racial identity and consciousness, enhances ideologies that promote racial segregation, and reduces opportunities for actual contact between the races.[14]

There is plenty of evidence to the contrary that was not acknowledged by Armor,[15] but our point is that most people *do* think, as he asserts, that school integration will increase the quality of intergroup relations. Like Armor, they tend to overlook certain conceptual and empirical considerations. For instance, they confuse integration with mandatory desegregation. Others are like James Coleman who, at least in 1966, lumped naturally unsegregated settings with desegregated ones. As Dentler and Elkins found in 1967, students attending "racial frontier" schools—those serving biracial neighborhoods—express much more racial antagonism than do affluent whites living in white enclaves along the fringes of a city.[16]

Much is compressed into Armor's phrase, "Under the circumstances obtaining in these studies." What this means is that in most desegregating districts, including Boston, no efforts on any scale worthy of note are made to prepare students for interracial encounters or to help them after desegregation to build mutualism. These matters are ordinarily left to local authorities, whose own knowledge and tolerance may rise no higher than the standards set in Boston by Louise Day Hicks, John Kerrigan, and Paul Ellison. One cannot expect improved academic performance or race relations from learners placed in environments that were not *designed* to affect these dimensions of growth. Without a design and with old prejudices intact among teachers and parents, the new encounters are bound to induce antagonisms.

We have visited many Boston schools where real improvements have taken place. They are places where administrators, teachers, parents, and student leaders have willed a change in their intergroup relations. Political scientist Harold Isaacs of MIT, moreover, did what David Armor, Nathan Glazer, and Lino Graglia have never done: In 1976, Isaacs spent weeks observing intergroup conduct at a newly desegregated middle school in Boston and interviewing the actors. His findings, while impressionistic, were positive and showed the process through which social respect and esteem was developing, albeit slowly.[17]

In the schools where tolerance and social affection across previously separated ethnic groups were directly observable, we have noted several common conditions. First, the building administrator is a person who displays respect and social understanding. Second, there is a small yet critical mass of teachers who share these skills and attitudes. Third, the school's curricular and extracurricular activities are well enough designed and executed to maintain a learning environment that warrants extensive student involvement, such that ethnic relations are not incidental and awkward.

Journalists Pamela Bullard and Judith Stoia are among the few attentive and systematic observers of the Boston schools case who have reported on the life histories of children and youth in the city. As they noted, "We've heard from the psychologists, the politicians, the educators. But the students who daily lived through desegregation have been silent. And it is perhaps their simple stories that are the most important lessons of all."[18] Their chapters amplify our observations: Living through this period has been turbulent, stressful, and instructive for some, miseducative for others.

The Los Angeles School Board is spending millions on multicultural education reforms. In Cleveland, the court mandated human relations training. In Minneapolis, the school board spent two years and its own resources improving race relations as a preliminary to desegregation. In Boston, the events of desegregation rolled on without these aids. Under the Boston circumstance, therefore, what can one expect?

There are vast structural changes inherent in the Boston plan that have, over the first six years, induced powerful improvements in race relations. Most of the elementary schools are genuinely multiethnic now. In these, the children are developing associations that are apt to outlive all of the distortions that adults can heap upon them. In the majority of these schools, most of the teachers are genuinely child centered, rather than subject oriented. While many teachers glide along on their pathway of self-imposed racial neutrality, this behavior does not prevent positive interpersonal development. Any visitor to a first or a fourth grade class can observe the richness of spontaneous intergroup interdependence, and it may be observed on the bus rides as well. By the time these first graders are in middle school, David Armor's finding will be reversed, we believe.

This prediction is based upon the fact that the court-ordered parent councils are operational and, as such, multiethnic. In the first three years, the Racial/Ethnic Parent Councils (REPCs), Community District Advisory Councils (CDACs), and Citywide Parents Advisory Committee (CPAC) tended to avoid the issue of race relations, although there were many exceptions to this rule. Since early 1978, intergroup respect and social ease has grown at a rapid rate. At the same time, faculties have become multiethnic, with new possibilities for teacher-parent reinforcement in reducing stereotypes resulting from the work of shared agendas.

There is no question but that desegregation has increased race consciousness in Boston. Contrary to Armor's view, however, we are not convinced that this effect is antithetical to improved race relations in the long term. The structural changes imposed by the court begin with this social fact. *All* actors in the public school scene are classified and even labelled. Then the interaction begins. Under the prior condition, however, low consciousness was synonomous with invisibility, subordination, and perceived inferiority for minorities. Now there is a solid minority presence—in the black principal's office, in the classroom, on the bus, and in the many-language information booklets. As everyone copes with these new social facts, the old mode, the one that helped shape a granitic form of racism, will give way to the new.

In the meanwhile, race relations are in transition. School desegregation in Miami's Dade County did not prevent massive violence and racial protests in the Liberty City section of that city. The black and Hispanic residents of Boston could explode under similar circumstances, according to some informed observers. To date, however, violence has, with just a few memorable exceptions, been the weapon of poor and isolated *whites* in Boston. More importantly, that violence has subsided. It has given way to a new, church-organized Covenant of Brotherhood, and there exist intergroup infrastructures that were absent in 1974. Race consciousness in transition toward more equalized power relations is likely to stimulate improved race relations. But if the transition is toward intensified race conflict, it will not be the result of school desegregation but of macroeconomic and political trends.

WHITE FLIGHT

The last refuge of skeptics and adversaries alike in most desegregation cases is that of white flight. Since at least 1950 urban commentators have fretted over the exodus of whites from America's central cities. By 1965, suburbanization had become so extensive and was so overwhelmingly a white movement as to give rise to the metaphor of "the white noose" around the neck of nearly every big city. James Coleman and Christine Rossell have specialized in exploring the implications of court-ordered school desegregation for white flight.[19] In the case of Los Angeles, the flight was measured with all of the technology social scientists could muster, and was found to be omnipresent. Some 27 percent of white households withdrew their children from the city's schools in the first areas desegregated in 1978.

What about Boston (see Table 10.2)? White flight there began in 1973 and reached a high velocity in 1975. Enrollments went from about 55 percent white in 1973 to 36 percent in 1980. Our efforts to account for this change lead us to think that roughly half of it was associated, however directly or indirectly, with desegregation. We concur with Rossell's analyses and interpretations of how this flight occurs. She found that flight occurs when some whites react negatively to assignment of their children to schools with very high proportions of black students. She also found such flight to be exaggerated in its

TABLE 10.2

Withdrawals from Boston Public School System by Racial/Ethnic Group, 1977–80

Year	White	Black	Other Minority	Total	Total System Enrollment
1977–78	57,213	4,556	2,142	13,911	70,192
1978–79	7,404	5,587	2,500	15,491	66,557
1979–80	6,622	5,409	2,807	14,838	65,620

extent. In a research note shared with us in August 1980, Rossell presented evidence supporting three substantive findings about Boston: (1) The actual proportion of whites in Boston in 1979 was about seven percent below what she found from projecting enrollment trends from 1969 to 1973 and assuming no school desegregation; (2) the degree of racial imbalance in public schools has declined dramatically since 1973; and (3) despite significant white flight, the "level of absolute interracial contact . . . is twice as great as it would have been without desegregation." She found that "the proportion white in the average black child's school is twice as high as it would have been without desegregation."

We also concur with Judge Garrity's opinion when he wrote that white flight is *not* a practicality that "can be weighed against the rights of the plaintiffs." According to the judge:

> Another ground for refusing to limit a remedy for fear of "white flight" is that a court would be presumptuous to try to predict the effect upon long-term trends in population movement of its adoption of a particular element, otherwise constitutionally required, in a desegregation plan.[20]

White flight is not only a poor reason for denying justice; it is also a partial outcome of a prophetic fallacy. From 1973 through 1975, white flight was *the* talk of Boston. Hicks, Kerrigan, Ellison, and later Kathleen Sullivan Alioto, continually prophesied its coming. These and other school committee members, including John McDonough and "Pixie" Palladino, amassed votes by warning of its tidal wave character, long before the movement actually began. Leaving the public schools became defined as the informed action to undertake (see Table 10.3). Thousands withdrew, in fact, *before* the liability opinion was issued in June 1974.

There is no question as to whether white flight is occurring, although early in 1975 we were not able to foresee its scale and were tempted to downplay its importance in our public statements. At that time, the Catholic Archdiocese had pledged support of the court's desegregation orders and had moved to block waves of transfer applications. We did not know for certain until 1976 that the parish schools in and around Boston had ignored the

TABLE 10.3

**Reasons Given for Withdrawal from Boston
Public School System by Racial/Ethnic Group, 1978**

Reason	Black	White	Others	Total
Attending an out-of-state public school	503	1.082	221	1,806
Attending an out-of-state school	715	429	514	1,658
Attending parochial school in Boston	210	1,180	125	1,515
Attending parochial school outside Boston	423	577	152	1,152
Attending private school in Boston	205	652	80	937
Attending private school in Mass., not Boston	82	244	20	346
Attending Boston evening high school	32	25	1	58
Over 16, dropped out	346	390	193	929
No forwarding address	222	140	179	541
Gone to work	71	204	38	313
Registered for school but did not report	230	185	105	520
Stayed or kept at home	35	43	8	86
Entered military service	11	22	5	38
Married	3	5	9	17
Deceased	7	5	2	14
Parents desired withdrawal	6	12	4	22
Error in classification	27	4	7	38
None given	125	49	67	241
Total	3,253	5,248	1,730	10,231
Percent by race	32	52	16	100
Total school enrollment	32,029	28,311	11,514	71,854
Withdrawals ÷ Total enrollment	10%	19%	15%	14%

SOURCE: Department of Implementation

cardinal's directive. Our study for the masters showed no transfer volume into 20 surrounding suburban districts. We did not anticipate the relocation of thousands of households to places far removed from the Greater Boston metropolitan area.

Heavy white flight took place and it damaged not only school desegregation but also the income mix of students and the tax base of Boston. Public leaders capable of conserving the city's human resources were missing. Had they been present, court intervention itself would not have become necessary. In their place were leaders who failed to build a broad commercial base for Boston in years when the high technology industry was beginning to grow up around the city's beltway, Route 128. These are the leaders who have been inattentive to neighborhood needs and interests while attempting to renew Boston. And, these were the leaders who specialized in patronage, small graft, and narrow constituency building, excluding the emerging minorities from their deals. Among the many whites who left Boston were many who had never secured patronage and others who had a set of small advantages but saw their hold on them as precarious.

SUSPENSIONS AND NON-PROMOTIONS

While whites were flying away, black and Hispanic students were being *pushed* away from school. The fact that black students were being suspended more than twice as frequently as whites was proved conclusively in 1976 when attorney Marion Wright Edelman from the Children's Defense Fund appeared before Judge Garrity. We have been encouraged greatly by the evidence that shows suspensions in general, and black suspensions in particular, have declined significantly since 1976. (The entire history of student discipline and suspension in Boston has been published by Russell J. Dever, *Equity in Discipline: Boston*, doctoral dissertation, Boston University, 1981. Dever did analytical work for the court on this aspect of the case.)

A subtler form of discrimination is embedded in the annual Boston practice of handing out what the schools call non-promotions, that is, of failing thousands of students at the end of each school year (see Table 10.4). This practice first came to our attention in June 1976, when Albert Tutella pointed out the operational difficulties inherent in assigning those students who were being failed. When he gave us the data, we were stunned to find that teachers were failing hundreds of first and second graders and that rates for black and Hispanic students were much higher than for whites at all grade levels. As with the suspension issue, we learned gradually that little or nothing would be done with the issue by the lawyers in the case or by the judge. These were, in their view, *educational* concerns of the school committee.

Judge Garrity did discuss our several reports on non-promotions with us and he encouraged independent research. Boston University sociologist J. Michael Ross took up the matter in his graduate research seminar, using data provided by us. For two months, five students conducted an in-depth analysis that included field interviews with principals and some teachers. Under the leadership of Claire Paradiso, the group authored a report on "Non-Promotion in the Boston Public Schools: A Study of Racial Neutrality."[21] It was issued just one month too late to affect policy changes in the annual court orders and revisions, but its conclusions continue to have urgent significance.

Non-promotion rates are quite constant from year to year. In 1977, 14 percent of all blacks, 13 percent of all Hispanics, and 9 percent of all whites were failed. In ninth grade, failure rates peaked at 30 percent for blacks, 26 percent for Hispanics, and 24 percent for whites. Even in first grade, 1.8 times as many blacks as whites and 2.5 times as many Hispanics as whites are failed (see Tables 10.5 and 10.6).

The students also found that the chances of a black student moving from grade 1 to 12 without failing once is 15 out of 100; for Hispanics, 18 out of 100;

TABLE 10.4

Reported Suspensions of Boston Public School Students, 1973–80

Year	White		Black		Other Minority		Total	
	Suspended	Enrolled	Suspended	Enrolled	Suspended	Enrolled	Suspended	Enrolled
1973–74	2,401	53,593	2,215	31,963	222	8,091	4,827	93,647
1974–75	3,848	44,957	5,898	31,737	406	9,152	10,152	85,846
1975–76	2,533	36,244	3,532	31,092	260	9,125	6,325	76,461
1976–77	2,291	32,393	3,228	31,053	280	9,560	5,799	73,006
1977–78	1,454	29,211	3,083	30,863	354	10,118	4,891	70,192
1978–79	1,605	25,956	4,014	30,073	425	10,528	6,044	66,557
1979–80	411	24,017	829	30,083	98	11,520	1,388	65,620

NOTE: Suspensions of students are often repeats, hence direct proportions of enrollment are only partially valid. Also, enrollments are for all grade levels while suspensions cluster heavily in grades 7–12. Still, cross-race comparisons are valid. For 1973–74, as percentage of enrollment they are: 4 percent of whites, 7 percent of blacks, 3 percent of other minorities. For 1979–80, they are 2 percent of whites, 3 percent of blacks, and 1 percent of other minorities.

TABLE 10.5

Non-Promotion Proportion by Race and Grade, 1977

| | Black | | White | | Hispanic | |
Grade	R	N	R	N	R	N
1	.1761	2612	.0979	2054	.2423	809
2	.0670	2357	.0315	2063	.1080	667
3	.0560	2358	.0257	2063	.0742	687
4	.0249	2450	.0137	2122	.0447	582
5	.0178	2585	.0112	2228	.0431	626
6	.1831	2551	.1084	2204	.1011	564
7	.1951	2666	.1131	2635	.1409	582
8	.1323	2480	.1155	2580	.1177	476
9	.3030	2624	.2367	2438	.2682	522
10	.2858	2180	.1854	2087	.1804	327
11	.1971	1720	.1140	2114	.1946	257
12	.0434	1382	.0166	2234	.0481	187
Total	(.1426)	27965	(.0913)	26822	(.1313)	6285

TABLE 10.6

Black-White and Hispanic-White Ratios Based on Non-Promotion Proportions, 1977

Grade	Black:White	Hispanic:White
1	1.799	2.475
2	2.127	3.425
3	2.179	2.891
4	1.818	3.263
5	1.589	3.848
6	1.689	.933
7	1.724	1.246
8	1.146	1.018
9	1.280	1.133
10	1.542	.973
11	1.729	1.707
12	2.615	2.898

and for whites, 32 out of 100. As the signal of failure peaks in grade nine, moreover, many students decide to become dropouts.

In its field interviews, the research team found that, for Boston school administrators, high failure rates signify "a school that is trying harder." Among those interviewed, *only* Kim Marshall, the curriculum coordinator of the Martin Luther King Middle School, was expressly appalled by the data. Like many others, he did not know the figures, but unlike them, he viewed a 25 percent failure rate of all black students at the King, a magnet school, as an index of instructional failure. Most principals viewed the data as irrelevant because so many students "do makeup work during summer school."

Many students are defined as ineligible for summer study as the result of a system-wide point system, and are thus forced to repeat the year. The policy is one that *prevents* students with the lowest grade point averages from making up work and thus dooms them to repeat the year. One principal noted that *before* desegregation, teachers in the "black schools" passed almost every student, but that now blacks must face point competition from blacks *and* whites. While there are universal criteria for failing students, they are applied in isolation by every individual classroom teacher and faculties do not confer or otherwise devise mutual reviews. This evaluative act is regarded as every teacher's professional prerogative.

We are not concerned here with the alleged merits of making a student repeat a school year. We should note, though, that according to the Boston University study, no plans for changing the teacher customs have ever been made in Boston. Nor are we concerned with the policy issue of minimal competency testing, although the study warns that it can be used in Boston to extend racial discrimination. *Our concern centers on how an expressed belief in racial neutrality and a laissez-faire approach to blaming the learner can parade as pedagogy.*

A good school is being defined by many as a school that *fails* to teach the largest number of its students each year. The practice is racially neutral in that it is carried out without group or policy definitions that contain racial bias. That the burden of this definition falls heaviest on minority children is a statistical outcome of the exercise of teacher expectations, attitudes, and abilities.

Someone might inquire, Could it be that relatively more minority students are *poor* students? Could the failure rates be the product of this disparity? The answer to the first question is, yes. Black and Hispanic students have suffered from isolation and the ravaging effects of discrimination. That is part of what desegregation is intended to redress. On the second question, however, the answer must be that failure rates are the product *if* teachers do little more than classify and appraise the September inputs as June outputs. If this passes for effective instruction, then schooling is as negligible an experience in relation to socioeconomic and family determinants as some social scientists would have us believe. The Boston University research team found in their interviews that the second question and its import for the education profession had not been raised by Boston principals, at least not by May of 1978.

Improvements in suspension rates suggest to us that educational changes are in the making. And while fairly high non-promotion rates still persist overall, and remain disparately high for blacks and Hispanics, we have found Boston schools where this index of instructional failure is improving; the rate has come down in three schools, including the King, and has been lowered at several high schools, including English High, where it reached a high of 33 percent in 1976. The reductions are correlated with observable improvements in the design, organization, and management of programs of instruction. If the U.S. Court of Appeals does not stay the closing of the system's smallest, oldest and, to the eye, coziest elementary school in Boston, the Oak Square, the highest black failure rate for first graders will be eliminated. We believe that the structural forces introduced by court action will, of their own speed and direction, induce a change in the practice of blaming the student victim, a practice enshrined as a Puritan heritage.

SUCCESSES AND FAILURES: SUMMING UP BOSTON

In 1979, Cleveland's court expert and monitor, Leonard Stevens, designed and disseminated a "Status Report" that schematizes nineteen generic areas in which a desegregating school system should make basic changes and provides a log for charting dates and evidence of task completion. It can be used anywhere with only minor modifications.[22] We have used it in assessing the successes and failures of the Boston case. In this final section, we offer that summative assessment, recognizing that changes are continuing and that the system deserves reassessment in 1985.

Boston public school students are nondiscriminatorily assigned to their schools each year. Roughly one-fifth of the schools are not in *full* compliance with court guidelines, but the departures are not great and most of them are the result of declining white enrollments combined with failures to revise geocode attendance units as residential populations shift. The schools these students attend, moreover, have fairly uniform grade structures (K–5, 6–8, 9–12) and operate as part of a decentralized, responsive subdistrict. None of this was the case before 1974. All of these successes are the result of a computerized, reliable, and valid student record system built into school headquarters as a result of court initiatives.

School facilities have been improved very substantially, although much remains to be done. The fire-unsafe, structurally unsound schoolhouses have been closed (save for ten still in use) and others have been renovated or repaired. Many fine new schools have been erected and, after incredibly costly repairs and corrections of faults built into them, put to good use. The capstone of court initiatives will be the completion of the forty-million-dollar Hubert Humphrey Occupational Resource Center in 1980.

The magnet schools ordered into being by the court have taken root and are flourishing. Their pairings (and the pairings of many other schools) with colleges, universities, businesses, and cultural agencies have proved effective in some instances and harmful or detractive in none. The greatest future task, though, will be to prevent magnet schools from undermining progress in the community districts by "stealing" students.

Thanks to the court, a sound system for maintaining safety and security has also been installed. School interiors are now peaceful and a reformed code of student discipline is in place. These accomplishments will not prevent outbursts of conflict in the neighborhood streets, but the public schools are safe places to attend today.

An efficient transportation system is in the making, although it will be another five years before busing itself has become a source of local satisfaction due to the snarls caused by leasing from private vendors that have yet to be untied. But there has been continued progress since 1978, and parents can and do rely on student bus services.

Special education and bilingual instruction both have a long way to go before they fulfill the objectives mandated by state law and reiterated by the court, but since 1974 the levels of their adequacy have risen from 0 to 6 on a scale of 10. Hundreds of certified teachers have been recruited from outside Boston, services are abundantly available in every district, and both program reforms have extended the principle of individualized instruction far beyond the point attained before desegregation.

The public service system itself has been significantly reorganized. District decentralization has made the subsystems responsive to parent needs and interests. An evaluation of parent group influence from 1977 to 1979 sponsored by the National Institute of Education gave the system some poor marks, but the gains made since 1973 are positively striking nonetheless.[23] Patronage-related corruption has dwindled and administrators have been appointed as a result of a community-based, merit screening procedure.

The teacher force has been desegregated. Black educators are well organized and have become a source of strong influence within the Boston Teachers Union. System reorganization has helped to improve the teacher hiring, promotion, and assignment operations. It has also led to reforms in financial management, although the superintendent's control over finances remains incomplete.

Improvements in community relations continue to elude the Boston School Committee and its departments. In 1974 and 1975 its Information Office was controlled by angry antibusing advocates. The Public Liaison Unit of the Department of Implementation has suffered from high turnover, neglect by other units in headquarters, and budget starvation. In 1978, Robert Wood created a new Office of Community Relations and appointed Mary Ellen Smith, the widely known executive director of the City-Wide Educational Coalition, to head it. She quit less than two years later after making only slight progress. The court-ordered annual orientation booklets in seven languages are a success, as are some school open houses and public hearings. Generally, outreach to the public is weak, amateurish, and fractured by intramural power struggles among the senior officers.

Far and away the gravest failures in the Boston story concern the continuation of generally poor instruction. The number of students denied promotions is still significant, and it reveals a sorry state of affairs. Academic achievement has been improved in a few schools but such is not the case in most. In-service training support for teachers was weak before the court intervened and it has remained weak, except in some schools where progress has been made by exceptionally able principals and with assistance from paired institutions. Student counseling remains severely underfunded. School psychology has been understaffed and teachers have served without special training.

Parent-teacher-principal coalitions have formed in growing numbers since 1977, with improvements in teaching and learning as their central aim. It may well be that this aim will gain increasingly fruitful attention over the coming decade, if it is not deflected by the demoralizing politics of retrenchment in a time when both dollars and children begin to disappear. Desegregation has been achieved in Boston. *Quality* integrated education will take longer.

CLOSING COMMENTS

In the twenty-six years since *Brown*, the arguments for and against school desegregation have been honed to such a fine edge as to cut through whole transcripts of a court proceeding. Only one Supreme Court majority opinion since *Brown*—*Milliken v. Bradley* (1974), which found that a metropolitan school desegregation plan for Detroit was not justified—has offered a serious setback to completion of the task. And Louisville, Wilmington, Delaware, and perhaps Houston, have shown that setback to be surmountable. In the same quarter of a century, the methods for researching, planning, and implementing school desegregation have been highly refined.

The Boston case proves Roscoe Pound's dictum that "Law makes habits, it does not wait for them to grow," but it also demonstrates the side effects of the dictum in action. Boston's habit of segregation was so ingrained that its replacement under law by equal protection made good planning and reliable implementation almost impossible to accomplish. Resistance and defiance generated a climate in the city that made affirmative compliance with court orders a cause for loss of employment. The same climate enabled incompetence in administration, discrimination in teaching, and graft in construction work to be rationalized.

The Boston plan could be made into a metropolitan system with technical ease. Indeed, we had that intention in mind when we helped to design it. Politically, however, the 97 percent white suburban districts that surround · Boston appear to be impregnable to desegregation. Not even an extreme energy crisis is likely to return many whites to the Boston public schools: From late 1976 through early 1980 about 3,600 white students a year were added to the Boston rolls as newcomers, but equal or larger numbers moved out of New England entirely each year. Nearly four in every five workers in suburban offices and plants, moreover, now also live in suburbia, not Boston. By 1990, Boston's public schools will be truly multiethnic—about one-third white, one-third black, and one-third Hispanic and other minorities. The region's pattern of human ecology would have led to *roughly* this same mix without court intervention, we believe, although it would have been closer to two-fifths white.

With the disengagement of the court, a process forced by the stay granted in May 1980, we will have a final test of Pound's dictum. Will reforms be effective, or will the old habits snap back into place? Will the attorneys for the plaintiffs make compromises about eliminating racial segregation in favor of promises of facility equalization? Will school committee members continue to run for office by avoiding the necessary realities of school closings, teacher layoffs, and fiscal retrenchment? New habits have been inculcated, but the forces working to reactivate the old are at least as formidable as the new forces of moderation and reform.

Our questions will most likely be answered through an examination of the *national* political economy of the 1980s. In *The Zero-Sum Society*, economist Lester Thurow notes that the national economy of the 1980s will not yield significant increases in real income.[24] Therefore, he argues, any important benefit for any considerable group will require an equivalent sacrifice somewhere else. He also notes that because of the power resources of the affluent, these sacrifices are most apt to come from reductions in public expenditures on behalf of the poor.

Boston has the ingenuity to avoid this disastrous future. More than one observer has noted that it could become *the* high-technology city of North America if it tried. But it also has the venality and the fatigue of age that make possible a repetition of its fateful decline in the Great Depression.

Alexander V. d'Arbeloff, president of Teradyne, Inc., a Boston-based high-technology manufacturer, told the Boston Private Industry Council in February 1980 that engineers and technicians will commute to Boston as readily as do bankers, lawyers, and insurance executives.[25] What they need is a centrally located site, room to expand, and municipal help with plant financing. His firm opened a plant in Roxbury later in the same year.

What they will also need, as *Boston Globe* columnist Kirk Scharfenberg noted, is a public school system capable of educating the next generation to the level required for work in this industry (and others). Reliance upon national trends, then, will push Boston backward in time to the era when methods of exploiting or neglecting the poorest of the poor were perfected. Reliance on Boston's own extraordinary reserves of ingenuity and scientific and educational capital, however, could lead to the development of an excitingly modern and humanized city. Public educational policies and practices are now equipped to serve *either* of these developments. As it did in 1930 and again in 1975, the choice will lie with locally elected leaders, the mayor and the Boston School Committee in particular.

POSTSCRIPT

Two weeks before schools opened in September 1980, and two months after the manuscript for this book was completed, a series of events began to take place that threaten to destroy public education in Boston. We record and interpret them here, however superficially, in order to close on a note consistent with the import of these events.

Robert Wood was fired by the school committee on a 3–2 vote. He was dismissed because of an alleged failure to bring spending under control and for refusing to name alternative candidates in the course of nominating a director of vocational education for the Occupational Resource Center. Beneath the surface of his termination, however, was loss of support from John McDonough, president of the committee, because of Wood's treatment of his brother, Joseph McDonough, acting deputy superintendent for the summer and because of Wood's aloofness in dealing with committee members. Paul Kennedy, a veteran administrator long in charge of all system personnel affairs, was made interim superintendent.

Simultaneously, Mayor Kevin White refused to accept the school budget, calling for a reduction from the proposed $236 million to $195 million, an amount that did not include the newly completed teachers union agreement that entailed a $15 million increase for salaries. Mayor White began to maneuver to avoid taking responsibility for a city tax rate increase. The teachers union threatened to strike and initiated state court litigation.

A few weeks later, school committee member Gerald O'Leary was arrested by the FBI for allegedly devising kickbacks from the major busing company, ARA, in the amount of $650,000. An attorney, formerly president of the Boston and Maine Railroad, and a school attendance officer who was a close relative of a former school committee member were arrested in connection with the same charge. O'Leary and the attorney pleaded guilty. The attendance officer was convicted. Witnesses implicated two other committee members in the felony.

Early in October student troublemakers at South Boston High, including two youths who had been kept out of that school in 1978 and 1979, fomented a brawl inside the corridors and classrooms. During the brawl, a panicky black youth picked up a peanut butter knife from a teacher's desk and brandished it.

The South Boston Information Center then organized the white students in a boycott, stating that metal detectors must be reinstalled before they would return. Headmaster Winegar and most of the teachers opposed this strenuously, noting that the school had achieved a good safety record before this outbreak and noting the demand was aimed at blaming black students for the new lack of safety.

Black students, meanwhile, could not journey to South Boston High School because the bus drivers went out on strike. They charged the ARA Company with failure to provide time for safety checks and for failing to supply bus monitors to ride the routes with drivers. Boston police were in deep turmoil over efforts to reorganize the force at this time, and they and other city employees suffered a "payless payday" as the mayor and the Boston City Council became embroiled in fights over budgets, emergency loans, and the policy reorganization issue. Public safety concerns became critically intense as a result, while the *Boston Globe* published a series of articles depicting the city as plagued with the nation's highest crime rate and the poorest record of crime control. At the peak of the dispute, Mayor White announced that in his opinion, "Boston is a racist city."

Back at school headquarters, Kennedy was busy reorganizing his deputies as well. Several key black administrators appointed by Wood resigned. White administrators were sent to the field, to be replaced by veteran managers with close ties to Kennedy and John McDonough.

Judge Garrity did not intervene, at least not during September and October, nor did the attorneys for any of the parties file motions to involve the federal court. The conditions leading to critical disorganization were building up, however, and the state courts were laboring with them while another federal judge jailed nine of the bus drivers' leaders for violating orders to cease striking.

The school committee spent money during these months at a rate in excess of the $236 million budget, setting up the possibility for a closing of schools by March 1981. The contract negotiated with teachers by the Wood administration did not reduce the size of the work force and guaranteed two years of security, with raises, before reductions would begin. The preliminary count from the Bureau of the Census indicated that Boston's population had shrunk substantially between 1970 and 1980, forecasting a reduced tax base and cutbacks in federal and state aid. These data were rejected by elected officials as the faulty results of a massive "undercount."

Seeds of hope for restabilization sprouted during the same period of mounting despair, however. O'Leary's successor to the school committee, a twenty-six-year-old newcomer to politics, Kevin McClusky, will make a return to a three-out-of-five member coalition of moderates a possibility once again. A state judge, Thomas Morse, appointed Alex Rodriquez, chairman of the Massachusetts Commission Against Discrimination, to serve as a special monitor in Boston for compliance with State Law 766. The publicity surrounding the events of October, moreover, gave new credence to the fact that the school system is extremely overstaffed and overbuilt.

Whatever the outcomes may be, it appears to us that the politics of desegregation have been supplanted, after fifteen years of turmoil, by the politics of city finance and that the new politics will include black and other minority constituents as full participants.

NOTES

1. Lino A. Graglia, *Disaster by Decree: The Supreme Court Decisions on Race and the Schools*, Cornell University Press, Ithaca, N.Y., 1976.
2. Robert A. Dentler, "A Devil's Advocate Catechism on the Suburban-Urban Pupil Transfer Issue," *The Center Forum*, Center for Urban Education, Vol. 3, December 23, 1968, pp. 15–16.
3. Graglia, *op. cit.*, p. 260.
4. Richard Kluger, *Simple Justice*, Alfred A. Knopf, New York, 1976.
5. Nathan Glazer, "Is Busing Necessary?", *Commentary*, Vol. 53, March 1972, p. 45.
6. *Morgan v. Kerrigan*, Civ. No. 72–911–G, May 10, 1975, Part 1, p. 31.
7. *Ibid.*, p. 57.
8. Joseph Krevisky, "Alsop's Fable," *The Center Forum*, Center for Urban Education, Vol. 2, July 5, 1967, p. 10.
9. *Crawford v. Board of Education of Los Angeles*, Superior Court of California for County of Los Angeles, No. C–822–854, "Brief Amicus Re: The Case for Multiethnic Desegregation," John Caughey, April 15, 1980, p. 3.
10. Richard Light and Paul Smith, "Accumulating Evidence: Procedures for Resolving Contradictions Among Different Research Studies," *Harvard Educational Review*, Vol. 41, 1971, pp. 429 and 443.
11. The Lincoln Filene Center for Public Affairs of Tufts University, Medford, Massachusetts, serves as the clearinghouse for university pairings. The Boston College Library hosts the records of the Citywide Coordinating Committee. Evaluations of pairing projects are on file in the Massachusetts Education Department.
12. Robert E. Herriott and Neal Gross, eds., *The Dynamics of Planned Educational Change*, McCutcheon, Berkeley, California, 1979.
13. Richard P. Boardman, *A Comparison of the Academic Performance and Achievement of Fifth and Sixth Grade Pupils in a Program of Pupil Transfer*, Columbia University, Teachers College doctoral thesis, 1971.
14. David Armor, "The Evidence on Busing," *Public Interest*, Vol. 28, Summer 1972, pp. 90–96.
15. See Meyer Weinberg, *Desegregation Research: An Appraisal*, 2nd ed., Phi Delta Kappa, Bloomington, Ind., 1970. For reviews since 1975, contact the Desegregation Studies Group, National Institute of Education, U.S. Department of Education, Washington, D.C.
16. Robert A. Dentler and Constance Elkins, "Intergroup Attitudes, Academic Performance, and Racial Composition," in R. Dentler et al., eds. *The Urban R's*, Frederick A. Praeger, New York, 1967, pp. 61–77.
17. Harold R. Issacs, *"Deseg": Change Comes to a Boston School. A Report of an Inquiry Made for the Citywide Coordinating Council*, Boston, March 10, 1977.
18. Pamela Bullard and Judith Stoia, *The Hardest Lesson*, Little, Brown, Boston, 1980, p. 17.
19. *Harvard Educational Review*, Vol. 46, February 1976, pp. 1–51, and Vol. 46, May 1976, pp. 217–233.

20. *Morgan v. Kerrigan, op. cit.,* p. 38, memo.
21. Claire Paradiso, Arthur Di'Mauro, Ruth Clarke, "Non-Promotion in the Boston Public Schools: A Study of Racial Neutrality," research manuscript, The Center for Applied Social Science, Boston University, July 1978.
22. Leonard Stevens, *Status Report* form, 1979 Office on School Monitoring and Community Relations, 1343 Terminal Tower, Cleveland, Ohio, 44113.
23. Marilyn Gittell et al., *Citizen Organizations: Citizen Participation in Educational Decision-Making,* final research report, The Institute for Responsive Education, Boston, NIE Contract No. 400–76–0115, July 1979.
24. Lester C. Thurow, *The Zero-Sum Society: Distribution and the Possibilities for Economic Change,* Basic Books, New York, 1980.
25. Kirk Scharfenberg, "A Boom by Any Name," *The Boston Globe,* March 1, 1980, p. 11.

INDEX